FESTIVALS EUROPE

By ROBERT MEYER, Jr.

IVES WASHBURN, INC.

New York

To

Maria Elena Casella

A section of illustrations will be found following page 52.

CONTENTS

INTRODUCTION

FESTIVALS are flourishing in the western world, particularly in the U.S.A. and in the twenty-one countries of Europe that began teaming up in 1949 to form the European Travel Commission, and thus promote tourism throughout the year from Iceland, the Hebrides, and Norway in the north, to Turkey, Sicily, and the Iberian Peninsula in the south.

That means more fun for everyone who wants to frolic with our friends abroad when they are in their most festive moods, or they can frolic with us if they are so inclined. Taking part in American as well as European festivals, and gathering and disseminating information about them, has been my chief occupation since January, 1946, and *Festivals Europe* is an attempt to bring many of these foreign festivals into focus.

Most of the European celebrations that I explored have roots deep in the past. It was amusing to trace them, because I uncovered many interesting anecdotes along the way. Yet the journeys into the past were made solely to find out how it could serve as a guide to the future, for I am interested only in those events that are current and give promise of continuing indefinitely.

Wherever it was possible to do so I tried to establish these points: when the festival was inaugurated; where and approximately when it is held; why it is held; and what one can expect to see and hear if he attends.

There are many reasons why a book like *Festivals Europe* can fill a need now and in the years ahead. Chief among them is the fact that more Americans than ever are taking advantage of improved, economical transportation and longer vacations with pay to go abroad and satisfy their curiosity about how other people live. Many who have gone to Europe since the end of World War II have come home and told researchers and survey-takers that their main interest there was people. As everyone knows, just about the best time to see the most people in any region is at a festival. That is also a fine time to learn what interests or amuses them, because a festival invariably reflects the character of the region in which it takes place, and dramatizes the economic and recreational attractions, as well as the spiritual and aesthetic aims of the people.

Fortunately, the true flavor of every one of the twenty-one E.T.C. countries is to be found in great quantity at their myriad festivals, and that *Festivals Europe* will point the way to them. As always, my definition of "festival" is very broad, because to me a festival is almost any activity planned to provide fun.

I hope that *Festivals Europe* will be a useful guide to the millions of Americans who will go abroad during the next few years, as well as to Europeans bent on exploring their own side of the Atlantic Ocean. Beyond that, I hope it will help writers and photographers of all nationalities who are increasingly aware of the growing importance of festivals in the field of travel, as well as those who devote their time and energy to the development of regional literature and photography.

Still further, I trust that the book will acquaint many Americans with the customs and traditions of the lands of their ancestors, and that reading about the Lord Mayor's Show in London, the thousand-year-old *Althing,* or parliament in Iceland, and the communal assemblies in Switzerland will make it clear that we Americans are not the only people enjoying democratic processes, nor did we invent them.

I began to concentrate on the festivals of Europe in January, 1948, when an important client of my Festival Information Service, to which editors and executives who must plan ahead subscribe, persuaded me to prepare a list of events scheduled for Europe that year. It contained 135 events in thirteen countries, and while working it up, I had difficulty convincing some of the representatives of the European countries that American tourists would be interested in such things. The 1953 list of European spring and summer events, prepared for the same client, filled two tabloid-size newspaper pages. In five years the problem had changed from what to include to what to leave out, because the number of events had increased from a reluctant trickle to a mighty flood. What is more, the high-water mark probably has not yet been reached, because new festivals are being added to the list almost every year.

There are twenty-one chapters in this book, one for each of the twenty-one E.T.C. countries. At least six hundred festivals are described in detail, and at the end of each chapter there is a chronological list of noteworthy events that normally take place regularly. The lists also contain the United States and Canadian addresses of the tourist and travel offices of the twenty-one countries, as well as national bank holidays. Since it is feasible to give only approximate dates of the festivals in this book, Americans and Canadians who plan to attend the celebrations should ask the countries' representatives for the correct dates shortly before they expect to go abroad.

Now all aboard for "Festivals Europe."

ROBERT MEYER, JR.

New York, New York

FESTIVALS
EUROPE

AUSTRIA

A LONG TIME ago the astute Austrians learned how to make the most of several wonderful assets to attract and entertain visitors at different times of the year. They taught the world to turn to Vienna for ballroom gaiety, to the Alps for exciting winter sports, and to Salzburg for the music of Mozart. Now the well-organized State Tourist Department entices visitors with a variety of pious religious observances, carnivals, traditional folk festivals, trade fairs, and exhibitions of precision and grace by the riders and beautiful white horses of the world-renowned Spanish Riding School.

Cultural Events

Every summer since 1922, except during war years, Salzburg has staged some sort of festival to remind the world that Wolfgang Amadeus Mozart was born there on January 27, 1756. Although the emphasis is definitely on Mozart's music at the annual Salzburg Festival which usually takes place from about July 25 to August 31, one notable nonmusical attraction is

Hugo von Hofmannsthal's *Everyman*. In fact, the current series of Salzburg Festivals, which now attracts approximately 85,000 visitors every year, grew out of a plan to stage *Everyman* regularly. Max Reinhardt managed the first presentation of it on the Domplatz in 1920. It was repeated in 1921, and in 1922 a program of music was added. The performances in the Municipal Theater included the operas *Abduction, Cosi Fan Tutte, Don Juan,* and *The Marriage of Figaro.* Richard Strauss and Franz Schalk conducted. In 1953 the program included, in addition to the Mozart operas, Strauss's *Rosenkavalier,* Gottfried Einem's *Prozess* ("The Trial"), Shakespeare's *Julius Caesar,* Hofmannsthal's *Everyman,* several orchestral concerts by the Vienna Philharmonic, two recitals, five concerts of chamber music, and six Cathedral concerts. Conductors were Karl Boehm, Guido Cantelli, Wilhelm Furtwängler, Clemens Krauss, and Bruno Walter. That season was the most successful in seven years. When the last notes had been played, and the final bows had been taken, the inevitable summing up showed that *Everyman* was still among the prime favorites at Salzburg. It ranked with *Cosi Fan Tutte, Don Giovanni,* and *Rosenkavalier* as the most popular productions of 1953. That year, too, publications and news services throughout the world devoted more space to the Salzburg Festival than ever before. Five hundred and one correspondents, representing 555 publications in 29 countries, covered the event. The largest contingents of newspapermen and music critics came from Germany, Austria, the United States, and Switzerland, in that order. The performances were attended by approximately 85,000 persons.

The Vienna Festival, first staged in 1930, usually takes place from the last week in May until about June 20. It features festival performances of the Viennese theater, orchestras, and the Vienna Choirboys, as well as exhibitions and international congresses. Open-air performances take place in the Schönbrunn Palace Park. In 1953 noteworthy events included an international music competition, a new drama *Lieber Augustin* based on the story of the Vienna minstrel of the plague era who either inspired or composed the world-famous song *"Ach, du lieber Augustin,"* and an outdoor drama in the Gothic arcades of the handsome Vienna City Hall.

The annual Bruckner Festival at Linz and St. Florian customarily takes place during the first two weeks of June. Typical programs include three Bruckner concerts by the Vienna Symphony Orchestra in Linz, a choir concert in the Chapel of St. Florian, which contains the famous Bruckner organ, and a concert in the Marble Hall of the Abbey. Anton Bruckner was organist there for many years, and is buried in the crypt with the Roman decurion-martyr Florian, for whom the baroque abbey is named. Sometimes the festival is embellished with a pageant to which all provinces of Austria send delegations of young men and women dressed in the brilliant costumes of their regions.

Among the up-and-coming postwar cultural conclaves in Austria is the festival at Bregenz. First staged in 1948, this mélange of ballet, concerts, and modern plays usually takes place from about the last week in July to mid-August. Of special interest are the operettas performed on a floating stage on Lake Constance. In 1953 the entertainment included *Boccaccio,* several performances by the State Opera, ballets, and *The Conspiracy of Fiesco,* a drama by Schiller.

The people of Graz launched a program of classical and modern plays in 1946, and since then have repeated the festival every year. The programs, designed to appeal to a wide variety of tastes, might include open-air performances of a classic like Shakespeare's *A Mid-Summer Night's Dream,* a modern play like *Andreas Baumkircher,* and Beethoven's *Fidelio in Schlosshof.*

In Vienna toward the end of April there is usually an International Religious Film Festival. Inaugurated in 1951, the celebration opens with a special mass at St. Stephen's Cathedral, and features the Vienna Choirboys, other Viennese artists, and a program of literary and musical works prior to the presentation of the films.

From about the last week in June to mid-July the city of Friesach in Austrian Carinthia, which is famous for its medieval walls and old-world aspect, stages in its local castle a festival that features such period pieces as *The Rise and Fall of King Ottocar,* a drama dealing with important events during the town's age of greatness, Schiller's *William Tell,* and *Goetz von Berlichingen,* Goethe's tale of high adventure in the days of chivalry and knighthood.

Winter Sports

The Alps are beyond a doubt Austria's most prolific earners of tourist dollars the year round. In summer they play host to mountain climbers, and in winter they entertain skiers from all parts of the world. Austrians also believe that the opportunity to survey the beauty of their spectacular countryside from the vantage point of an eagle floating lazily on high should be available even to those who do not care to endure the exertions and perils of mountain climbing, so they have tried to crisscross their mountains with more cable railways than any other country in Europe. In fact, Austria claims that she leads the world in the number, safety, and novel features of mountain cable railways, some of which are used to transport skiers and other sight-seers in winter, and just sight-seers in the summer.

Austria also lays claim to having the world's largest ice-skating rink in Vienna. The Eislaufverein Rink is at least nine thousand square meters in size and includes figure-skating rinks, an ice race track, and hockey rinks. Eight hockey teams can play on the rinks simultaneously. Also, to keep the musicians warm, their chairs are electrically heated.

The Alpine skiing season in Austria customarily starts at Christmas. The International Western Pokal Ski Races are at Lech am Arlberg early in January. The International Hannes Schneider Pokal Race takes place at St. Anton am Arlberg annually during the third week in January, except when the Arlberg-Kandahar Races are conducted at St. Anton. The Arlberg-Kandahar, now one of the solid traditions among winter sports festivals, was founded in March, 1928, and takes place every four years. The most recent was in 1953.

The height of the winter sports season at Bad Gastein, Bad Hofgastein, and Zell am See is late in January until mid-February, so the Salzburg International Winter Sports Weeks, featuring skiing, sledding, and ice sports, are celebrated then.

Also in January or February are the Tyrolean International Winter Sports Weeks at Innsbruck, Kitzbühel, and Seefeld. The main events at those places include the Hahnenkamm Race and contests for the Gold Ring and Silver Cup of Seefeld. Novelties include torch *slaloms* and jumps at night, and ice bicycling, accomplished by placing a skate where the front wheel should be, and skidproof chains on the rear tire.

In March the high season for skiing competitions is highlighted by the Kulm Jump near Klachau-Tauplitz, currently the largest ski jump in Europe. The longest jump to date measured 434 feet and was made in 1953 by the Austrian skier Sepp Bradl.

The crowds move on to Zuers am Arlberg in April where a giant *slalom* takes place, and in May the official closing competition of the Salzburg ski season is marked by the International Zehnerkar Giant *Slalom,* usually at Radstaeder Tauern Pass.

The largest glacier ski race in Europe takes place on the highest mountain in Austria. It is the International Grossglockner Glacier Ski Race at Franz-Josef Haus, Heiligenblut, in Carinthia during the first half of June, and invariably marks the official closing competition of the Austrian ski season.

Other Sports

Although skiing is Austria's main attraction for sports lovers, there are other activities that have their own claims to fame. Foremost among them, no doubt, are the world-renowned Spanish Riding School demonstrations. When the expertly trained handsome white horses are not on tour, or appearing as the stars of festivals, their exhibitions of the art of classical riding at its best may be witnessed by visitors to the school, which is now located in Wels, near Linz. What is more, the school is generally open to riders and trainers, and school horses are available for qualified instruction.

The school was started in Vienna in the sixteenth century and was called the Spanish Riding School around 1572 because in those days mainly Spanish horses were used for classical riding because of their suitability. Even today the Spanish Riding School follows the "High School" exclusively, and uses only Lipizzan stallions, the last descendants, still surviving, of the once proud race of Spanish horses. Cultivating the art of horsemanship in its highest form and breeding Lipizzan stallions of the very best quality is the object of the school. In the closing days of World War II the United States Army played an important part in saving the school and its animals for Austria. At the request of the director of the school, U.S. Secretary of War Patterson and General George S. Patton placed the school under the immediate care of the U.S. Army and had the Lipizzan stud, which had been transferred to Czechoslovakia by the Germans in 1942, brought back to Austria under military escort. Austrians insist that this act saved the Spanish Riding School from extinction inasmuch as the school and the stud farm are inseparable entities, and one cannot exist without the other. Another important horse event in Vienna is the Austrian Trotting Derby near the end of May. It is the main event of the spring trotting season from March to June. The fall trotting season runs from September through late autumn.

The principal attraction of the Austrian motor-sports world is the International Austrian Alpine Race for cars and motorcycles, which roar through the western provinces in mid-June. Many foreign entries participate, and the course traverses one of the most beautiful sections of the Austrian Alps.

The largest international rowing event in Austria is the Grand International held annually around the end of June on the Danube at Vienna. Kayak events are a special attraction.

Whole flotillas of kayak enthusiasts from many countries usually converge on Austria during the last half of July to take part in international championship races, because the mountain streams and rivers that pour down from the snow-capped peaks and melting glaciers provide a magnificent network of waterways that seem made to order for paddlers. For example, one year a typical group left Salzburg on what was probably the most romantic of all folding-boat trips. It led via the Salzach and the inn at Passau into the Danube past ancient castles to Linz. Side cruises on the Salzach for "wild-water" riders were also arranged.

Perhaps the most varied athletic event in Austria is the International Sport Festival in the towns of Klagenfurt, Pörtschach, and Velden on the Wörthersee, usually in mid-July. The program includes championship contests in ballroom dancing, boxing, cycling, football, golf, rowing, sailing, swimming, and tennis.

The largest annual Austrian cycling event is the six-day bicycle race across Austria around the end of July. In 1952 it began and ended in Vienna, the course winding through Graz,

Klagenfurt, Lienz, Grossglockner–Zell am See, Innsbruck, Salzburg, and Linz. The following year, in order to send all contestants over an unfamiliar route, the racers went from Vienna to Eisenstadt, Graz, Klagenfurt, Grossglockner and Zell am See to Saalbach. After a day's rest they continued to Salzburg, Salzkammergut, Bad Aussee, Windischgarsten, Linz, and Vienna.

Austria's number-one golf match, the International Golf Championship of Austria, usually takes place early in August on the links at Dellach in Carinthia, Pertisau, or Vienna.

Traditional Events

Dancing is synonymous with Vienna, so even in the dreary postwar years the Viennese attempted to recapture the gaiety of the "good old days" by staging their traditional *Gschnasfest,* three great fancy-dress balls, which are a prime attraction of *Fasching,* the pre-Lenten carnival, held usually in February. Typical themes of the three great balls recently were "The Ball of the Ancients," "The Good Old Days," and "The Nylon Age." Hundreds of other mask and costume dances, to which visitors are invited, take place during the week immediately before Ash Wednesday puts an end to such frivolity.

No doubt the weirdest of all Shrove Tuesday celebrations in Austria is the *Schemenlaufen,* or Dance of the Phantoms, staged every third year in the Tyrolean town of Imst. The most recent was held in 1952. This picturesque celebration, which usually takes place in February, symbolizes the ever recurring battle between winter and spring, and spring always wins. It dates back to primitive times when people believed that one could frighten away demons by wearing an unsightly mask. Nowadays at least eighty thousand spectators join in the fun, which includes the familiar dancing in the street and typical carnival amusements. However, the thing that sets the festival apart is the procession of men in masks that grimace or leer. Most of the masks are heirlooms highly prized by the families that own them. But all is not ugly. A touch of beauty is seen in the extravagantly decorated headpieces; their flower-trimmed cowls, mirrors, plumes, and colored silk are the bright spot of the festival. The maskers make much noise, jangle bells, sing, and shout because evil spirits flee from noise. Similar festivities are staged every few years in Nassereith and Telfs.

Christianity and the holidays of the Christian church play important parts in the lives of Austrians. There are at least two presentations of the Passion play in Austria each year, one at Fulpmes and the other at Thiersee.

Redemption, by Rudolph Henz, is the religious drama staged by hundreds of local residents at Fulpmes on Sundays and holidays during the summer, while *Christus* is the title of the medieval Passion play put on by villagers at Thiersee on Sundays from July to September. This centuries-old re-enactment of the gospel story is staged with simplicity, with all the actors being trained by the local priests and the choirmaster.

Corpus Christi, sixty days after Easter, is an important feast day to the Austrians. Ordinarily they stage their most impressive celebrations at Hallstatt in the Salzkammergut and in Traunkirchen-Traunsee. As a rule the priest leads the procession down to the shore of the lake where he and the party board a flower-laden barge that conveys them to the center of the lake for the simple religious ceremony. After the service the flowers are strewn on the water, and the worshipers, dressed in their richest costumes and headdresses, return to a carnival atmosphere in the town.

At the summer solstice, June 21–23, bonfires are lit on the hilltops and in the fields, especially in the Wachau, where one may enjoy the contrast of fires burning brightly on the top of

the hills while the Danube glistens as it flows through the
valley below. One superstition says that a farmer's hemp will
grow as high as he can jump over the fire. Many jump. Meanwhile, boys dance around the fires carrying torches of flaming
pitch, and girls toss flowers into the blaze.

The patron saint of lower Austria and Vienna is St. Leopold, so on *Leopoldstag,* November 15, there are wine festivals.
That occasion, and also St. Martin's Day on November 11, is
called *Gaensetag,* or goose day, because the traditional evening meal of goose inaugurates the new wine season. One
hilarious aspect of the whole party is the slide of the great
cask performed by those who take part in the pilgrimage to
St. Leopold's shrine at Klosterneuburg, a twelfth-century abbey. Men, women, and children take part, climbing the narrow stairs to rafters atop the cask. One by one they slide down
the smooth sides of the barrel, which was built in 1704 by a
Viennese wood carver and holds some 12,000 gallons of wine.
When the sliding is finished, everyone goes to a picnic where
new wine and sausage top the menu.

St. Nicholas, the kindly bishop whose generosity in early
Christian times started the custom of giving gifts at Christmas,
and from whom the Christmas character St. Nick got his name,
pays a visit to Austrian towns on the eve of his day, December
6. His traditional uniform is a bishop's regalia and a long
white beard. As he walks the streets on St. Nicholas eve he is
accompanied by the devil, who chases children who have been
bad.

Christmas fairs usually begin on the first Sunday of Advent
in November or December, and many of them last until the
singing of "Silent Night" on Christmas Eve, in the tiny onion-
spired churches of the high Alpine villages and the cathedrals
of Graz, Innsbruck, Salzburg, and Vienna. "Silent Night" has
particular significance for Austrians because it was written
and composed by two friends, a priest, Father Joseph Mohr,

and a teacher, Franz Gruber, and sung for the first time on Christmas Eve in 1818 at a midnight mass in Oberndorf, province of Salzburg. Nowadays it is usually heard on a broadcast originating in St. Stephen's Cathedral, Vienna. It is played on the great organ of that church, and often sung by the famous Vienna Choirboys.

Fairs

There are about half a dozen first-rate fairs in Austria every year. They are the spring and autumn fairs in both Vienna and Graz, and the International Export and Sample Fairs at Dornbirn late in July and early in August, and at Innsbruck in June.

The semiannual fairs in Vienna began in 1921. Of course, they were discontinued during World War II, but since then they have begun the climb back to their prewar place among important international exhibitions. Displays at the Fair Palace and Fair Grounds now accommodate about 28,000 exhibits and half a million visitors. Textiles, fashions, handicrafts, furniture, leather goods, and toys are shown at the Fair Palace. Machines, technical equipment, radios, agricultural machinery, food, and wines are to be found at the Fair Grounds. The spring fair usually begins early in March; the fall fair early in September.

The spring fair in Graz starts late in April, and the fall fair late in September. Since it takes place in southeast Austria there are many fine exhibits from Italy and Yugoslavia. All told about 1,200 exhibitors participate, and their wares are inspected by some 200,000 visitors.

Innsbruck's Export and Sample Fair, usually staged in mid-June, began in 1926 with nineteen fair events. Now this annual show, which is of special interest to merchants in Italy and West Germany, attracts as many as a thousand exhibitors and 150,000 visitors. This is a special fair for tourism and the travel business. The International Export and Sample Fair inaugurated in 1948 at Dornbirn is staged regularly late in July and early in August. It has become one of the top textile fairs in Europe, drawing about 1,000 exhibitors and 300,000 visitors.

The exact dates on which festivals will take place in Austria, as well as the latest travel information pertaining to that country, may be obtained by writing to the Austrian State Tourist Department, 48 East 48th Street, New York 17, New York.

Bank holidays in Austria: January 1; Epiphany, January 6; Easter Eve and Easter Monday; May 1; Ascension Day, forty days after Easter; Whitsun Eve, forty-eight days after Easter; Whitmonday, fifty days after Easter; Corpus Christi, sixty days after Easter; Assumption Day, August 15; All Saints' Day, November 1; Christmas Eve, December 24; Christmas Day, December 25; December 26.

Chronological list of events in Austria:

JANUARY. Bischofshofen: ski-jumping contests. Innsbruck: ski-jumping contests. Kitzbühel: Hahnenkamm Skiing Race. Lech-am-Arlberg: Westenpokal Skiing Race. St. Anton: Arlberg-Kandahar Skiing Races; Hannes Schneider Pokal Skiing Race. Westendorf: ski-jumping contests.

FEBRUARY. Innsbruck: Austrian skiing championships; winter sports weeks. Kitzbühel: winter sports weeks. Kulm bei Mitterndorf: ski-flying week. Salzburg: winter sports weeks. Seefeld: winter sports weeks. Tschagguns: Austrian junior skiing championships. Vienna: long-distance running race.

FEBRUARY or MARCH. Pre-Lenten Carnivals: Imst, Nassereith, Telfs, Vienna.

MARCH. Bad Gastein: Stubnerkogel giant *slalom*. Seefeld: skiing meet. Vienna: fair.

APRIL. Graz: fair. Reutte: giant *slalom*. Vienna: religious film festival; trotting, usually to June. Zuers-am-Arlberg: giant *slalom*.

MAY. Graz: fair. Salzburg: Zehnerkar giant *slalom*. Solbad Hall: Stempeljoch giant *slalom*. Vienna: Austrian Trotting Derby. Zell-am-See: Austrian gliding championships.

MAY or JUNE. Auto race: Klagenfurt-Graz. Corpus Christi, nationwide; unique observances at Hallstatt, Traunkirchen-Traunsee. Fair: Innsbruck. Modern Music Festival: Vienna.

JUNE. Bregenz: Regatta. Franz-Josef Haus: Grossglockner Glacier skiing race. Friesach: drama festival, to mid-July. Graz: festival, to mid-July. Heiligenblut: Grossglockner Glacier skiing race. Linz: Bruckner Festival. The Wachau: summer solstice. Vienna: Flower Day; rowing races. Western Provinces: Alpine auto, motorcycle races.

JULY. Bad Aussee: Austrian Music Students' Festival. Bregenz: festival, into August; glider meet. Dellach: golf tournament. Dornbirn: fair, into August. Friesach: drama festival. Fulpmes: *Redemption*, to September. Graz: festival; glider meet. Innsbruck: Tyrolean band concerts. Klagenfurt: sports festival. Linz: kayak championships. Pörtschach: sports festival. Salzburg: kayak championships; Salzburg Festival, through August. Styria: glider meet. Thiersee: *Christus*, to September. Velden: sports festival. Vienna: golf tournaments; six-day bike race.

AUGUST. Bregenz: festival. Dellach: golf tournaments. Dornbirn: fair. Fulpmes: *Redemption*, to September. Innsbruck: brass bands contests; fair. Pörtschach: golf tournaments. Salzburg: Salzburg Festival. Styria: Alpine motor races. Thiersee: *Christus*, to September. Vienna: golf tournaments.

SEPTEMBER. Burgenland: wine festivals. Fulpmes: *Redemption*. Graz: fair. Krumpendorf/Wörthersee: yachting regattas. Lower Austria: wine festivals. Salzburg: Austrian tennis championships. South Styria: wine festivals. Thiersee: *Christus*. Tyrol: auto rally. Vienna: fair; Flat racing, trotting; horse riding, jumping tournament.

OCTOBER. Nationwide: Harvest Thanksgiving Festival. Salzburg: motorcycle races.

NOVEMBER. Klosterneuburg: *Fasslrutschen*, St. Leopold's Day Festival, November 15. Vienna: *Fasslrutschen*, St. Leopold's Day Festival, November 15.

DECEMBER. Innsbruck: skiing season opens. Kitzbühel: ice-hockey tournament. Nationwide: St. Nicholas' Day celebrations, December 5, 6. Seegrube: skiing season opens. Vienna: Christmas Eve Service, St. Stephen's Cathedral.

BELGIUM

WHEN ONE studies the list of events that take place annually in Belgium, he is invariably impressed by the tremendous part tradition and religion play in most celebrations. The combination of piety and loyalty to the past has produced some mighty spectacles, such as the pre-Lenten carnival at Binche, the Procession of the Holy Blood at Bruges, and the March of the Penitents at Furnes. It has also inspired many smaller celebrations that give innumerable communities at least one great day each year when old costumes as well as old customs are usually put on display.

Anniversary

In 1830 nine Belgian provinces that had belonged to the Netherlands for fifteen years set up a state of their own. On July 21, 1831, Belgium's first king, Leopold I, arrived in Brussels; so now that anniversary is to Belgians what the Fourth of July is to Americans. There are processions, carillon concerts, sports meetings, special illuminations of buildings, and fireworks displays.

Carnivals

Long before Belgium became an independent nation the people of that part of Europe established a fine reputation for the quality and quantity of their carnivals. Many of the ancient celebrations still survive, and in spite of war and the ravages of time some even prosper. In most instances a religious observance is the underlying factor, even though it is not unusual to find solemn tributes to saints combined with the frivolity of a street carnival. The greatest of all carnivals in Belgium is the pre-Lenten celebration staged by the Gilles of Binche on Shrove Tuesday, the day before Lent begins. The Gilles are famous for their elaborate lace-trimmed, embroidered silk costumes, brilliantly dyed, three-foot-tall ostrich-feather headdresses like those worn by the famous mummers of Philadelphia, Pennsylvania, on New Year's Day, and the fact that they pelt spectators with thousands of oranges while frolicking through the streets. Occasionally the celebrants break into a dance that might be compared with the American Charleston, and the best time to see them in action is in the afternoon when the dancing begins to get hot, or at night when a multicolored shower of fireworks and the sound of thousands of bells pep up the party.

Although folklore authorities point out that the Gilles of Binche originated many centuries ago, there persists a legend that the Gilles began a mere four hundred years ago. According to popular belief, a fancy-dress ball staged by Mary of Hungary on August 22–31, 1549, in honor of her brother Charles V and the heir Don Philippe is supposed to have inspired the Gilles to form their organization. A striking feature of Mary's celebration was the appearance of courtiers dressed as Incas, a reminder of the recent conquest of Peru by Francis Pizarro, and since the long-established Gilles added a few Inca touches to their already elaborate costumes the origin of their annual shindig has been linked with Mary's soiree.

A much more solemn occasion than the carnival at Binche is the Procession of the Large Fire and the Appearance of the Giants at Nivelles on the first Sunday of Lent, usually in February, but sometimes early in March. Similar fires are built in many parts of Belgium—the origin of the custom dating to the days when the fires were believed to be purifying, to lend the reviving sun renewed warmth, and to serve as a safeguard from witches—but the one at Nivelles is probably the best. It features a big carnival, presided over by the four-hundred-year-old giants Largayon, Largayonne, and their son Lolo, and a large fire in the town square.

By mid-Lent even the pious Belgians are ready for some fun, so around March 15—the most popular mid-Lenten feast day being St. Joseph's Day, March 19—De Graaf van Half-Fasten, the Count of Mid-Lent, appears at Arlon with gifts and a giant. The Arlon giant is fairly young, having put in his first appearance as recently as 1934. A queen is chosen at a masked ball to rule over the carnival.

Another popular mid-Lenten party is the Chinel Carnival at Fosse on March 19. The Chinel, with his hump back and front, is a reminder of good and bad luck. The character is said to have been inspired by two hunchbacks who once lived in Fosse. As a rule he is gaily dressed and dances to a sprightly tune written in 1870.

The Ommegang is the big event in Brussels for three days around June 12, usually during years ending in three or eight. When it was inaugurated some five or six hundred years ago, it was a religious procession featuring a statuette revered by the populace for its miraculous powers. According to one legend, the statuette was brought to Brussels by a devout woman of Auvin who said she received her instructions straight from the Virgin. After a while the sacred pageantry was embellished by secular manifestations, and groups began to compete for prizes given for the most imaginative displays and representations of the princes that had ruled the provinces. Eventually a parade of giants from all parts of Belgium and the locally famous horse Bayard joined in the fun. Now the party might include many tableaux and processions of 2,200 handsomely costumed celebrants who march in the wake of some 300 silk banners.

Grotesque figures also dominate two other important Belgian carnivals. They are the *Reuskens,* or Little Giants, who are the stars of the carnival in Borgerhout on the last Sunday in July and the first Sunday in August, and the Giants of Ath, who began parading around Ath as long ago as 1390. The *Reuskens,* who resemble the children of giants and their parents, rule the roost at the carnival of Borgerhout. They ride on top of wagons in a parade and dance to popular tunes every time their wagons stop. The family has four members—the giant, his wife, and their offspring, Kinnebaba and the Dauphin. The procession is halted at least three times to quench the giants' thirst. At one stop the giant's wife presents a bouquet to the mayor. He offers a toast that is served to the giants with the aid of a funnel. At Ath on the Saturday evening before the fourth Sunday in August the "Marriage of the Giants" takes place during the "Gouyase Vespers" sung at the St. Julien Church. The legendary fight between David and Goliath takes place then, too. But on Sunday, which also belongs to the "Ducasse of Ath," or fair, the enthusiasm is at its height. According to the town records the giants are believed to date from about 1450. At that time there also existed a "Horse Bayard" carrying the four sons of Aymon. He disappeared and was missing for centuries, but made a reappearance in Brussels in 1938. A traditional procession of costumed groups features historical tableaux drawn from periods important to the development of the region, and at least seven giants. Prominent among the lumbering figures are the Eagle, Goliath, and Miss Victory. As so often happens at Belgian celebrations, the festival is climaxed by the marriage of Goliath and Victory.

Religion

The fact that Roman Catholicism is the principal religion in Belgium is very evident in the type of festivals that prevail there. The two important performances that dramatize the same event are the Procession of the Holy Blood in Bruges on the first Monday after May 2, and the Passion play *Sanguis Christi,* also enacted in Bruges, but put on only during August in years ending in two and seven. The Procession of the Holy Blood glorifies several drops of the blood of Christ supposed to be in a phial brought back from the Holy Land around 1150 by Thierry of Alsace, Count of Flanders. It was said to have been given to the Count by the Patriarch of Jerusalem because Thierry had distinguished himself in battles under the Walls of Jerusalem. As long ago as 1200 solemn ceremonies were organized to salute the relic. Now men, women, and children in the procession don costumes dating from the Crusades.

The history of the Holy Blood is described by speaking and singing groups that take more than an hour to pass a given point, while other persons afoot and on horseback dramatize the story of humanity, from Adam and Eve to the Crucifixion, with Christ carrying the cross to Calvary. At the very end of the parade is a handsomely wrought casket, an artistic masterpiece worthy of the treasure it was built to enshrine. It is transported from the Chapel of the Holy Blood, where the relic is exposed for the veneration of the faithful every Friday, to the cathedral, where it is placed on the altar and remains throughout mass.

Sanguis Christi, a musical drama based on the passion of Christ and performed in Bruges every five years by a cast of

2,500, a double symphony orchestra, chorus of 800, and a corps of trumpeters, was written in the 1930's by Rev. Jozef Boon, with music by Arthur Meulemans, and given its *première* in 1938. As a rule just six performances are presented on week ends in August every five years. The most recent one was in 1952. The play lasts two hours and fifteen minutes, and its stage is the public square, where full use is made of the famous belfry, windows, balconies, and towers in nearby buildings. Temporary seats accommodate 10,000, while 5,000 may stand. The dialogue and the songs are in Flemish, and even though the theme is familiar to almost everyone, scripts in French, Flemish, and English are available.

Another drama based on a legendary religious experience is the Play of St. Evermard at Russon on May 1. It boasts one of the longest runs in history, since its origin can be traced to the tenth century, and is believed to be staged at the very place where the hero, St. Evermard, and his seven companions were assassinated by bandits in 699.

According to the legend, while St. Evermard and his friends were en route to the Holy Land in 699 they were assassinated by a bandit named Hacco. Some two hundred years later the people of Russon began the game of saints and sinners, and their descendants still play it. The faithful march around the casket, which is believed to contain the remains of the saint. They are joined by eight pilgrims, representing Evermard and his companions, a bevy of angels, and finally two "wild men." Soon about fifty men dressed in white knee breeches, red coats, and derbies trimmed with large red plumes, ride up. Their leader, wearing a gaudy tunic with gold buttons, is the villain Hacco. The whole crowd repairs to the Chapel of St. Evermard, which was built on the site of the murder more than 1,200 years ago. In the afternoon all the villagers take part in the re-enactment of the massacre, and, some say, even a re-volver is one of the props.

There are other noteworthy observances at other times throughout the year and in other places in Belgium. In fact, two spectacles that are intimately linked take place on Trinity Sunday, the eighth Sunday after Easter, at Mons. One is the Procession of the Golden Chariot, the other the Lumecon, or Doudou, colloquial titles given to the dramatization of a knight's fight with a legendary dragon in the perennial struggle between good and evil. Actually, according to the Belgians' definitions of their own words, a Lumecon can be a battle, a parody, or a parade, while the Doudou is the title of a gay song long associated with Mons. The Procession of the Golden Chariot dates to October 7, 1349, when a plague ravaged Hainaut Province. Today the celebration features costumed groups, gold and silver relics, and the casket of Ste. Waudru, patroness of the town. The casket is ensconced on a lavishly decorated early eighteenth-century coach called the Golden Chariot, which is drawn by six white brewery horses that are good to have around for the steep pull up the slope of Ste. Waudru at the end of the parade. The knight who is to be the star of the Lumecon show also takes part in the procession. When it is over, he goes to the town square to stage his performance. This warrior represents the Chevalier Gilles de Chin who, according to a twelfth-century legend, gathered an army of wild men who later became known as Chin-chins and set out to slay a dragon that had been making a nuisance of itself. In the modern re-enactment of the tussle the knight and his followers battle the beast while a crowd of spectators chants the Doudou. If the knight fails to slay the dragon with the traditional sword he merely uses a revolver to finish the job. The pistol shot is also a signal for the local fair to begin.

At a Trinity Sunday celebration that is said to have started in Renaix in the thirteenth century the big attraction is the Procession of the Fiertel. In this parade the casket containing the remains of St. Hermes, patron saint of Renaix, is carried over a twenty-mile route. The climax of the demonstration is a dramatization of events in the life of the saint.

Binche, famous for its pre-Lenten carnival, is also well known for the Procession of St. Ursmer, dedicated to its patron saint, on the Monday following the Sunday after April 18. The treasure of the Collegiate Church at Binche, including relics of the twelfth and thirteenth centuries and handsomely embroidered vestments worn by the clergy, is prominently displayed during the march.

Furnes, in West Flanders, each year has two religious observances that attract multitudes from many countries. The first is the Stations of the Cross, a procession originally staged in 1628 and since repeated every Friday in Lent, and Monday, Tuesday, and Wednesday of Holy Week. Participants recite prayers before each of the eighteen stations or paintings representing the Passion of Christ at strategic places in the streets of the town. Several months later, on the last Sunday of July, the Procession of the Penitents takes place at Furnes. Some folklorists rank it second only to the more elaborate Procession of the Holy Blood at Bruges, and most authorities on the subject are enthusiastic about the parade of the penitents, who come from all parts of Belgium, dress in coarse robes and hoods, and walk barefoot through the streets of the ancient town. Many burden themselves with heavy wooden crosses, and all are obviously devout, humble, and repentant. Gayer aspects of the festival include scenes from the Old and New Testaments, and a fair bright with banners, pennants, and a wide variety of booths.

Maredsous is the focal point of the faithful at Corpus Christi, sixty days after Easter, because the colorful procession there includes companies of soldiers wearing a motley assortment of uniforms of many periods. Since it has long been the duty of these companies to guard processions, they continue to do the honors along the route of march. Occasionally they fire salutes or perform intricate maneuvers under orders from their officers. Visitors also go to Maredsous to pray to St. Benedict, whose feast day is celebrated at the local abbey on March 21. Since the abbey was founded in 1872, the stream of pilgrims has increased steadily. They appeal to the saint to guard them from all misfortune and accidents, and for the protection of the home. The abbey also has a handicraft school of fine reputation.

As almost every motorist knows, St. Christopher is the patron saint of travelers, and millions of them pray to him to ask the Lord to protect them on their journeys. Christopher earned that place in the hearts of the faithful because, according to legend, he was a very strong man who used to carry travelers across a river. One day his passenger was a child who was so heavy that Christopher thought that he was carrying the weight of the world. At journey's end the child revealed himself as Christ. Now blessing automobiles is a popular religious activity in Belgium. If all the motorists who seek the protection of St. Christopher were to congregate in one city for the privilege of driving past a priest sprinkling holy water they probably would create one of the greatest traffic jams in history. Fortunately for all concerned they do not have to do that, because there are usually at least fifty-six pilgrimage places for St. Christopher in Belgium, and for each one there is a definite date prescribed for the blessing of autos. Most of them are staged around the fourth week of July. St. Christopher's Day is July 25.

Between blessing automobiles, animals, and boats the clergy of Belgium are kept very busy. Most of the boat-blessing takes place around June 29, St. Peter's Day, because St. Peter is the patron of fishermen. A typical ceremony takes place at Blankenberge on that date, and sometimes the proceedings are enlivened by re-enactment of heroic deeds by fisherfolk, or their favorite saints. The town records of Ostende show that Blessing of the Sea ceremonies have been performed there regularly on the Sunday following June 29 at least since 1448.

Inland during June, July, and August priests carrying crosses lead their parishioners to the fields for a blessing of the crops, and on November 1 they go to churches and cemeteries to pray for the departed and all saints not mentioned on the calendar. That is why it is called All Saints' Day. Since St. Hubert is the patron saint of huntsmen, St. Hubert's Day, November 3, is a time for blessing horses and dogs. His relics are exhibited at St. Hubert during the annual celebration.

Fairs

Belgium is studded with dozens of small-town fairs, the dates of which are announced regularly by the Belgium National Tourist Office. In the big league of fairs the three leaders are the International Trade Fairs at Brussels and Liége late in April and early in May and the International Trade Fair at Ghent during the third and fourth weeks in September. Businessmen from many countries meet at the fairs to inspect samples, models, designs, and photographs of new products. It is equally interesting for the casual tourist because it is he who will eventually use most of the foodstuffs, furnishings, household appliances, jewelry, plastics, ceramics, glassware, metal, and leather goods on display. The fair at Brussels was inaugurated in 1920 with 1,602 exhibitors from fourteen countries displaying their wares on 210,000 square feet of space. In 1952 at least 4,000 exhibitors from 32 countries spread their goods over 1,130,000 square feet. That year the exhibition was visited by nearly a million persons, of whom an estimated 15,000 were buyers from 60 countries.

The International Fair at Ghent was launched in 1946. Its sponsors always stress certain phases of Belgian and world production, with emphasis on the Belgian Congo Territory.

In 1952 more than a thousand firms used 500,000 square feet of space, and showed their merchandise to more than 500,000 visitors.

Ghent's *Negenmeimarkt,* or "Fair of the Ninth of May," owes its origin to the transfer of the relics of St. Macaire, who used to be held in veneration at Ghent. The transfer took place on May 9, 1067, and since then a big pilgrimage there each year inspired the enterprising merchants to stage a fair at the same time. It was primarily a horse fair, with animals lined up by the thousands, side by side, along the public highway for several miles. However, as recently as 1952 there were signs that the auto is replacing the horse in Belgium, because there were only about a hundred horses there that year.

Bastogne's famous Nuts Fair was a going concern on the third Sunday in December long before the U.S. Army's General MacAuliffe said "nuts" to a demand that he surrender to the Nazi forces during the terrific Battle of the Bulge near Bastogne in December, 1944. However, the General's remark was taken as a good omen by the Belgians, who would have been staging their annual fair then, but for the war. It is called the Nuts Fair because traditionally persons who become engaged there exchange nuts as a token of esteem. Another modern token of esteem in Bastogne is the five-pointed star-shaped monument commemorating the fierce Battle of the Bulge in 1944–45. The monument has forty-eight columns, representing the forty-eight states, to salute the victorious American forces.

Auto Racing

The Grand Prix of Belgium usually takes place around the third or fourth week in June at Spa on the Spa-Francorchamps circuit that has a lap length of approximately nine miles. Enthusiasts consider it a very fast circuit—fast enough for speed demon Lang to establish a lap record of 108.8 miles per hour in 1937. Now the Grand Prix is one of the ten major events that contribute points to the world championship each year. The others are: Argentina, France, Germany, Great Britain, Holland, Indianapolis Speedway, Italy, Spain, and Switzerland.

The exact dates on which festivals will take place in Belgium, as well as the latest travel information pertaining to that country, may be obtained by writing to the Official Belgium Tourist Bureau, 422 Madison Avenue, New York 17, New York.

Bank holidays in Belgium: January 1; Easter Eve and Easter Monday; May 1; Ascension Day, forty days after Easter; Whitsun Eve, forty-eight days after Easter; Whitmonday, fifty days after Easter; July 21, Independence Day; Assumption Day, August 15; All Saints' Day, November 1; Armistice Day, November 11; Christmas, December 25.

Chronological list of events in Belgium:

JANUARY. Arlon: Lovers' Fair. Courtrai: Epiphany fires. Hakendover: *La Treizaine.* Huy: Nativity play. Renaix: All Fools' Monday.

FEBRUARY. Blankenberge: *Bal des Loups.* Lierre: Horse show.

FEBRUARY or MARCH. Pre-Lenten Carnivals: Alost, Binche, Brussels, Eupen, Malmédy, Nivelles, Spa, Termonde.

FEBRUARY, MARCH, or APRIL. Passion Play, Sundays in Lent: Ligny. Stations of the Cross through the streets of town: Furnes.

MARCH. Arlon: Mid-Lenten Carnival. Fosse: Mid-Lenten Carnival. Geel: fair. Maredsous: Feast of St. Benedict. Mons: flower market. Ostend: Mid-Lenten Carnival. Stavelot: Mid-Lenten Carnival. Ypres: fair.

MARCH or APRIL. Holy Week: Nationwide, more spectacular celebrations at Bruges, Furnes.

APRIL. Binche: Procession honors St. Ursmer. Brussels: fair. Hakendover: procession of horsemen. Liége: fair. St. Trond: visits to blossoming apple, cherry, plum orchards. Tournai: flower market. Vise: Festival of the *Gilde des Arbaletriers.* Watermael-Boitsfort: visits to blossoming apple, cherry, plum orchards.

MAY. Bruges: Procession of the Holy Blood. Brussels: fair; Grand Prix for 500 cc racing cars. Chimay: *Grand Prix des*

Frontières, auto, motorcycle races. Écaussines: matrimonial tea party. Geel: pilgrimage honors St. Dymphne. Gembloux: nocturnal procession honors St. Guibert. Gerpinnes: military parade honors St. Rolande. Ghent: *Negenmeimarkt;* regatta. Liége: Benefralux auto rally; fair. Louvain: athletic festival. Mons. Procession of the Golden Car, and the Lumeçon. Ostend: regatta. Renaix: Procession of the Fiertel. Russon: Play of St. Evermard. St. Hubert: pilgrimage, exhibition of relics, honor St. Hubert. Spa-Francorchamps: Grand Prix for standard autos.

MAY or JUNE. Corpus Christi: nationwide; more spectacular celebrations at Blankenberge, Maredsous.

JUNE. Antwerp: Blessing of the River Scheldt; bike race. Blankenberge: Blessing of Boats. Bruges: fair. Brussels: dog show; folklore festival; *Ommegang,* religious-secular celebration, usually in years ending in three or eight. Damme: Procession of the Miraculous Cross. Ostend: Blessing of the Sea. Spa-Francorchamps: Grand Prix of Belgium, auto race. Wepion: strawberry festival.

JULY. Binche: *Ducasse,* procession. Borgerhout: Parade of Little Giants. Brussels: Colonial Day, July 5; *kermesse,* fair, to September. Furnes: Procession of Penitents. Ghent: visits to begonia fields. Nationwide: blessing of autos, usually week end before or after St. Christopher's Day, July 25; Independence Day, July 21; most impressive celebration in Brussels.

AUGUST. Antwerp: *kermesse,* fair. Ath: historical procession. Bruges: pilgrimage honors Our Lady of Pottery; *Sanguis Christi,* staged every five years, usually in years ending in two or seven. Brussels: *kermesse,* fair, to September; planting of the Meiboom, a tradition dating to the thirteenth century. Jambes: Jean Matern Grand Prix professional bike race. Liége: Liége-Rome-Liége auto rally. Ostend: handicap horse race.

SEPTEMBER. Antwerp: flower show. Audenarde: *kermesse,* fair. Brussels: commemorate the 1830 Revolution, around September 27; foodstuffs show; *kermesse,* fair; national pig show. Charleroi: Wallony festivities, procession. Dinant: agricultural, cattle show; auto, motorcycle gymkhana; military festival. Foy-Notre Dame: Final pilgrimage of year honors Our Lady of Foy. Ghent: Fair of Flanders. Hasselt: fair. Hoeilaart: grape fair. Liége: commemorate Revolution of 1830; *Grande Quinzaine Liégeoise.* Louvain: horse, cattle show. Malines: recital of new compositions for carillons. Middelkerke: pilgrimage to Miraculous Cross. Namur: Wallony festivities. Nationwide: commemorate liberation in World War II, early in September. Roisin: pilgrimage honors Verhaeren, the poet. Schoten: flower show. Tirlemont: fair. Tournai: historical procession. Waregem: steeplechase.

OCTOBER. Binche: procession of roses. Boom: horse, cattle shows. Diest: fair. Dison: horse, cattle shows. Duffel: horse, cattle shows. Edegem: candlelight procession. Flobecq: motorcycle races. Forest: horse, cattle shows. Liége: Tour of Belgium, auto race. Lierre: procession honors St. Gommaire.

NOVEMBER. Brussels: solemn mass, colorful ceremonies honor St. Hubert. Herve: fair. Houffalize: fair. Huy: fair. Nationwide: All Saints' Day pilgrimages to cemeteries, churches, November 1; All Souls' Day candlelight processions, November 2; World War I Armistice Day, November 11; most impressive celebration in Brussels. Paliseul: fair. St. Hubert: pilgrimage, exhibition of relics, blessing of dogs and loaves honor St. Hubert, November 3. Vise: patronal festivities of *Gilde des Francs Arquebusiers.*

DECEMBER. Antwerp: pilgrimage honors St. Christopher. Arlon: *Grande Quinzaine Arlonaise;* Lovers' Fair. Bastogne: Nuts Fair. Foy-Notre Dame: Christmas Eve midnight mass. Marcinelle-Villette: Nativity plays. Saint-Severin: Nativity plays. Vosselaar: Nativity plays.

DENMARK

IT LOOKS as though the Danes have decided to concentrate on festivals of a cultural nature. Two years before World War II began in 1939 they launched the Hamlet Festival at Elsinore. As soon as it was possible to do so after the war, they inaugurated the Royal Danish Ballet Festival at Copenhagen, and in 1953 they added a music festival to their list. They named it for Carl Nielsen, the foremost creator of Danish music.

Cultural Events

At least three men of Denmark whose names are known the world over filled their lives with the stuff of which modern festivals are made. One was Hamlet, the legendary Prince Amleth, who was the inspiration for Shakespeare's most familiar play; another was Carl Nielsen, and the third was Hans Christian Andersen.

When the Hamlet Festival is put on it usually takes place in the courtyard of Kronborg Castle at Elsinore for about ten days during the second and third weeks in June. Since 1937 the Shakespearean tragedy has been staged regularly before a capacity audience of three thousand amid the same surroundings that Shakespeare is supposed to have visited and used as a setting for the play. As a rule the players are members of some foreign theatrical company whose version of *Hamlet* has drawn special attention. For example, in 1949 the State Theater of Virginia, U.S.A., was featured. In 1950 the honor went to England's Old Vic Theatre, while in 1951 it was given to Sweden's Norrkoping-Lidkoping Stadsteater. The actor who impersonates the Prince is awarded the Hamlet Medal.

When the Carl Nielsen Music Festival was inaugurated in Copenhagen during the first week in September, 1953, it featured two Danish symphony orchestras, the Royal Opera, the Danish Students Choir, and at least half a dozen soloists. The program included Nielsen's symphonies One, Three, Five, and Six, his opera *Saul and David*, the *Helios* overture, and the overture to *Maskeraden*. Nielsen, who was born at Norre-Lyndelse, on the Island of Füen, June 9, 1864, and died in Copenhagen on October 3, 1931, is considered the foremost creator in the history of Danish music. He joined the Royal Orchestra of Copenhagen on the recommendation of Gade, to whom he dedicated his first quartet, and was appointed assistant conductor in 1904. He became the first Danish composer to depart from the romantic school, and the course of his development as a composer can be traced through a study of his six symphonies, overtures, sonatas, the operas *Saul and David* and *Maskeraden*, and the songs, piano and organ music he wrote during the last twenty years of his life. Nielsen's last public appearance was at a festival at the Royal Opera, where his *Maskeraden* was played exactly one week before he died following a short illness.

Hans Christian Andersen, Danish poet, dramatist, and novelist whose best-known works in English are fairy tales, was born in Odense, Denmark, on April 5, 1805. He died in

1875, yet it was not until 1950 that the first Andersen Fairy-Tale Festival was staged in Odense. That year there were fairy-tale processions along the streets, and open-air performances of Andersen's plays, and ballets in the very settings that inspired their creation. It is planned to stage subsequent festivals there every three or five years, the next one due to salute the 150th anniversary of the writer in 1955. To bridge the gap between festivals the enterprising Danish National Travel Office has arranged a four-day fairy-tale tour of Denmark. The high point of the journey, of course, is a trip to the childhood home of Andersen, now a museum. On April 5 each year a well-known actor or actress sits at the poet's writing table and broadcasts over an international network some of Andersen's best-loved works. The honor has gone to Eva Le Gallienne, the American actress; the English actor Michael Redgrave, and the French actress Jeanne Moreau of Comédie Française.

Copenhagen, where the Royal Danish Ballet Festival takes place during the last week in May each year, has been proud of its Royal Theatre for ballet, plays, and opera since that venerable institution was built in 1748. One of the interesting features of the playhouse is the fact that it is divided into two sections. On the side of the Old Stage, which seats 1,600, plays alternate with opera and ballet. On the New Stage side, which seats 1,100, plays only are performed. The Ballet Festival, which was presented there for the first time in 1950, features classic and modern dances and invariably attracts at least 12,000 visitors. Copenhagen has one of the few permanent ballets in Europe. Its classic Danish ballets (Bournonville) rank high, and the modern ballets produced by several of its *maîtres de ballet* have been well received.

A different type of dancing takes place in parks and meadows throughout Denmark on June 23 when traditional Midsummer Night festivals are held. Bonfires are lighted, and in some places an effigy of a witch is burned, reminiscent of the time during the seventeenth century when everywhere in Europe witches by the thousand were burned at the stake.

About a month later, on July 21, residents and visitors in Nykobing, Zealand, take part in a mammoth Asphalt Ball, as they have almost every year since 1930. Nykobing is the center of an important summer and vacation area, so the Asphalt Ball, complete with pageants, a fun fair, fireworks, and dancing in the street, affords an opportunity for 20,000 visitors to get acquainted.

Every year for three days during the first week in June the people of Frederikssund stage a play on Danish history. In 1953 the play was *Roar and Helge*.

Special Days

There are at least five special days of unusual interest which the Danes celebrate each year. One of them is the Great Day of Prayer, the fourth Friday after Easter. It began during the reign of Christian VII when his prime minister, Struensee, decided it would be best to consolidate all the days of prayer into one. Nowadays, business closes, and churches have special services.

The prayers for liberation uttered by the Danes on Prayer Day in 1945 were soon answered. It was on May 5, 1945, that Denmark regained her freedom from Nazi occupation through the victories of the Allies. The five years of German domination began April 9, 1940. Now Liberty Day is patriotically observed throughout Denmark, and special tribute is paid to the memory of the Danish Freedom Fighters and others who gave their lives in the prolonged struggle. Among the heroes of the conflict was Kaj Munk, a Danish pastor, poet, and dramatist, who was murdered by the Gestapo. One of his sermons delivered during the autumn of 1943, when there was no immunity for words spoken from the pulpit, served as a spur to active resistance.

On June 15 the Danes celebrate Flag Day, to honor the oldest flag in the world. Myth has it that the Danish flag, the *Dannebrog,* fluttered down from heaven on June 15, 1219, and brought victory to the warriors of King Valdemar the Victorious on a crusade against the heathen Estonians. June 15 is also celebrated as *Genforeningsdag* in memory of the reunion of North Slesvig with Denmark in 1920.

Every peaceful year since 1935 several hundred patriotic Danes from abroad have gathered on a June night in the Knights Hall, Kronborg Castle, Elsinore, for a program of reminiscences, speeches, and music. That purely Danish reunion is followed on July 4 by a Danish salute to America's Independence Day in Rebild National Park. Except for the war years the Fourth of July Festival has been held annually since 1912. At least 40,000 persons trek to the section of the park festooned with the flags of all forty-eight states to witness a unique tribute to Danish-American good will, high-lighted by the presence of the King and Queen of Denmark, other members of the royal family, and the American ambassador. There are speeches, of course, and a program of music by artists of the Royal Danish Opera, internationally famous vocalists and instrumentalists, and sometimes a children's ballet. After that the crowd moves on to the city of Aalborg, where there is a banquet, concert and fireworks.

Rebild Park, situated in the heather-covered Rebild Hills, which form a natural amphitheater in the heart of Jutland, was dedicated in 1912 in the presence of the late King Christian X, the late American minister to Denmark, Dr. Maurice Francis Egan, and the father of the project, Dr. Max Henius, of Chicago, a distinguished chemist and fermentologist, who was for many years president of the Chicago Public Library Board. It was a gift to the Danes from Americans of Danish descent. Since 1934 one of the show places of the park has been a Lincoln log cabin built entirely of logs cut in American forests by Danish pioneers. It now houses a Danish Emigrant Museum.

Thousands of Americans and people of many nations who are in Copenhagen late in August or early in September join the Danes in one of the most unusual civic celebrations staged anywhere. It is the unique *Rundskuedagen,* or Look Around Day, which has been sponsored regularly since 1910 by the Copenhagen Journalists' Association to encourage Danes and their guests to look behind the scenes of public buildings and some private places which are usually off-limits to visitors, and also to raise money for social work and scholarships sponsored by the Association. Tickets, which sell for about thirty-five cents each, go on sale at newsstands and tobacco shops about a week before Look Around Day, and often more than 400,000 books of tickets are sold.

At first glance that might suggest that the Danes are mighty curious about what the restricted sections of public buildings look like, but the truth is that most ticket buyers are primarily interested in the tremendous prizes that are given away. The Ministry of Justice grants a special permission for this event. However, no cash can be given away, so each year the list of prizes includes such tempting items as a bungalow, lot, and garden tax free for one year, two round-trip tickets to the Far East, and thousands of dollars in merchandise. Also, the law requires that one-third of the profit be given to charity. The big party at Tivoli Gardens that winds up the affair features internationally famous bands, concerts, and a performance by a prominent young musician who is awarded the Association's prize of the year.

Sports

Tuna fishing, yachting, horse racing, tilting, and association football head the list of sports events in Denmark. Although tuna has been a familiar visitor to Danish waters for many years, tuna fishing in earnest did not start until 1918 off the northwesterly point of Zealand. Game anglers began going there in 1926, and in 1936 the first tuna was caught in the sound near Elsinore. In 1948 one game angler using rod and reel caught 68 tuna having a total weight of 23,324 pounds. Encouraged by increased interest on the part of fishermen from all countries, the National Tourist Association of Denmark, the Municipality of Elsinore, and the Scandinavian Tunny Club in 1950 began staging an annual International Tunny Cup Tournament for three days near the end of August, the height of the season, which runs from about mid-August to near the end of September.

The two big annual yachting events in Denmark are the National Regatta, inaugurated in 1866, and staged in various provincial waters, and Sound Week, which has been celebrated at Copenhagen since 1898. Usually about 150 boats of all classes take part in the National, which lasts for three days in mid-July. Sound Week, sponsored by the Royal Danish Yacht Club for three days in mid-June, attracts about 100 entrants. Cups and trophies are awarded.

Inland, racing enthusiasts turn to the horse tracks at Aarhus, Copenhagen, Odense, and Skive, where races are usually run on Sundays. The season is from the end of April to the beginning of December. The big event of the year is the Danish Derby at Klampenborg Race Course, Copenhagen, on a Sunday during the last half of June. It was run for the first time in 1875.

Another equestrian sport that dates to the time when

knighthood was in flower is the Tilting Tournament at Sonderborg, during the second week in July. The present series of yearly tilts began in 1898, and now attracts at least four hundred horses and riders. It is the largest event of its kind in northern Europe, and is complete with medieval pageantry, a fun fair, and fireworks. Other tilting tournaments take place in Aabenraa and Tonder in June.

Association football season in Copenhagen is from mid-March to mid-June, and again from August to December. In May and June teams of foreign professionals play against selected teams of Danish amateurs.

Fairs

Inasmuch as approximately one million of Denmark's four million inhabitants are engaged in agriculture, the various agricultural, livestock, and poultry fairs are of utmost importance to the Danes. Co-operative farming, which combines large-scale production with full individual ownership, has been firmly entrenched in Denmark since about 1880 and now governs the sale and international distribution of milk, butter, cheese, and bacon. Danish farmers own more than half a million horses, one and a half million dairy cows, three million pigs, and twenty-five million fowl.

It is no wonder, then, that more than 150,000 persons flock to the Funen Farmers Agricultural Fair and Livestock Show, which has been staged regularly at Odense during the second week of July since 1922. Another 80,000 go to Thisted, to the Jutland Breeders Agricultural Fair and Livestock Show, established in 1892, for four days during the third week in July because it is the only show in Denmark that features all the various breeds of cattle. During the first week in July another 150,000 go to the Bellahoj Agricultural Fair and Livestock Show inaugurated in Copenhagen in 1938. The National

Poultry Show, an annual event of long standing, is put on in Odense for two days about the middle of December. It draws about 3,000 exhibits and 20,000 visitors.

Other top-ranking fairs include the Danish Industries Fair, inaugurated in 1913 and staged at Fredericia about the first ten days in August; the International Fair, Copenhagen, late April and early May; Joiners' and Cabinetmakers' Furniture Exhibition, Copenhagen, from about September 25 to October 15; the Danish Textile Fair, Herning, the second week in August; Applied Arts Exhibition, in Copenhagen, from late January to middle of February; and the International Automobile Exhibition, Copenhagen, the first ten days in March.

The exact dates on which festivals will take place in Denmark, as well as the latest travel information pertaining to that country, may be obtained by writing to the Danish National Travel Office, 588 Fifth Avenue, New York 36, New York.

Bank holidays in Denmark: January 1; Holy Thursday through Easter Monday; "*Store Badedag,*" the fourth Friday after Easter; Ascension Day, forty days after Easter; Whitmonday, fifty days after Easter; Constitution Day, June 5; Christmas, December 25; and December 26.

Chronological list of events in Denmark:

JANUARY. Copenhagen: Applied Arts Show, to mid-February. Fur sales.

FEBRUARY. Copenhagen: auto show, February, March.

MARCH. Copenhagen: association football, to June; auto show, February, March; fair; trotting season opens. Nationwide: Birthday of King Frederik IX; most impressive celebration in Copenhagen, March 11; Birthday of Queen Ingrid; most impressive ceremony in Copenhagen, March 28.

APRIL. Copenhagen: fair. Nationwide: Great Day of Prayer, fourth Friday after Easter, April or May. Odense: Hans Christian Andersen Day, April 5.

MAY. Copenhagen: Children's Aid Festival; *Dyrehavsbakken,* fun fair, to mid-August; national championship motor races, May or June; Royal Danish Ballet Festival; Schumann Circus; Tivoli Gardens open, to mid-September; trotting races. Nationwide:

Great Day of Prayer, fourth Friday after Easter, April or May; Liberty Day, May 5. Ribe: tulip festival.

JUNE. Aabenraa: tilting tournament. Copenhagen: athletic meet; Danish horse racing, trotting derbies; national championship motor race, May or June; Sound Week, regattas. Dalby: blossom-time in cherry orchards. Elsinore: Danish homecoming; Hamlet Festival. Frederikssund: Viking festival. Nationwide: Flag Day, June 15; Midsummer Eve, June 23; Midsummer, June 24. Ordruo: amateur bike Grand Prix. Sonderborg: Children's Aid Festival. Soro: rowing regatta. Tonder: tilting tournament.

JULY. A different place each year: national gymnastic marksman-ship contests; national yachting regatta; pirate dinghies national championship regatta; Scandinavian rowing championships. Aal-borg: American Independence Day, July 4. Brande: fair. Copen-hagen: livestock, agricultural fair; national bike championship. Elsinore: national swimming championships. Kildeparken: Amer-ican Independence Day, July 4, Nykobing: Asphalt Ball. Odense: agricultural, livestock show. Rebild Park, near Aalborg: American Independence Day, July 4. Skive: sports festival, fun fair. Sonder-borg: tilting tournament. Thisted: Jutland Breeders' Agricultural Fair, Livestock Show. Viborg: rowing regatta.

AUGUST. Copenhagen: association football, to December; harbor festival, Look Around Day, August or September. Dalby: harvest-time in cherry orchards. Elsinore: Tunny Cup Tournament. Fredericia: Danish Industries' Fair. Herning: Textile Fair.

SEPTEMBER. Aalborg: Visiting Days. Copenhagen: Carl Nielsen Music Festival; Joiners', Cabinetmakers' Furniture Show, to mid-October; Look Around Day, August or September; Tivoli Gardens close. Kvaerndrup, near Svendborg: colts, foals market. Sonder-borg: Visiting Days.

OCTOBER. Aalborg: horticultural show. Copenhagen: Joiners', Cabinetmakers' Furniture Show. Odense: horticultural, flower show.

NOVEMBER. Copenhagen: Velodrome bike-racing season opens.

DECEMBER. Copenhagen: Danish fur sales; six-day bike race. Odense: poultry exhibition.

FINLAND

FINLAND'S principal festivals are
either tributes to famous native sons or are based on rites that
have survived since pagan times. The weather, as it does in all
countries, also helps fashion Finnish festivals. Its influence is
particularly noticeable in the celebration of Midsummer, the
longest day of the year, and the staging of mass christenings,
marriages, and funeral services when the returning sun melts
the walls of snow that often imprison natives of the northern
part of the country.

Cultural Events

Jean Sibelius, one of two world-famous living musicians for
whom important annual music festivals are named—the other
is Pablo Casals, who presides over a festival in France—made
it a rule from the first never to attend in person his country's
Sibelius Festival. At least, he stayed away from the first three
festivals put on in 1951, '52, and '53, preferring, instead, to
listen to radio broadcasts of the performances of his music and
the works of other composers while comfortably seated in his

home about thirty miles from the Finnish capital. The Sibelius Festival usually takes place in Helsinki around the second week in June, at the Festival Hall of Helsinki University, where in 1892 Sibelius conducted the first concert of his works, and where nearly all his symphonies received their world *premières*. Most of the programs are filled with works by Sibelius, and sometimes there are all-Sibelius concerts. Eugene Ormandy, musical director of the Philadelphia Orchestra, had the honor of inaugurating the festival in 1951 with performances of the First and Seventh Symphonies and *Pohjola's Daughter*. Again in 1952 Ormandy was the American representative who conducted the Helsinki City Orchestra and the Radio Orchestra, while in 1953 that privilege went to Leopold Stokowski.

Finland also honors other illustrious sons, among them Johan Ludvig Runeberg, Elias Lonnroth, and J. V. Snellman. Runeberg was Finland's national poet, who died in 1877, and whose work has gone far in interpreting Finland to other nations. On his birthday, February 5, schools close, and shop windows display busts and pictures of the poet against a background of blue cloth and lilies of the valley, blue and white being the colors of Finland's national flag. Special ceremonies are observed at Runeberg's monument in the Esplanade, Helsinki, and the statue is decorated with garlands of pine and spruce, hung between four great torches. In the evening the torches flame brilliantly against the sky, casting shadows on the wreaths of flowers placed around the monument by students who sing the national anthem, which was adopted from Runeberg's *The Tales of Ensign Stal*.

Another great Finnish man of letters, Elias Lonnroth, who published the first edition of the *Kalevala*, Finland's national epic, in 1835, is honored on February 28 in much the same way as the Finns salute Runeberg. February 28 is called *Kalevala* Day because the work is said to have marked the turning point in Finnish literature. Before 1835 little had been written in the language.

On May 12 special honors are paid to the memory of J. V. Snellman, a journalist, patriot, and statesman, at his statue in Helsinki. Snellman, who was born May 12, 1806, helped further the nationalist movement in Finland.

Patriotic Celebrations

Finland's three big patriotic celebrations are Flag Day of the Army, May 19; Flag Day, June 24; and Independence Day, December 6. The Flag Day of the Army is comparable to Memorial Day on May 30 in the United States inasmuch as it honors those who fell in the wars to achieve and preserve their country's freedom. It is observed with military parades and demonstrations, memorial services sponsored by the State in the National Theatre in Helsinki, and the placing of wreaths on graves of war dead. Flag Day on June 24 is marked by a display of the Finnish flag, a blue cross on a white background, while Independence Day, December 6, is celebrated with patriotic festivals, speeches, and concerts. December 6 is the anniversary of the Finnish Declaration of Independence in 1917, when the country was freed from Russian rule.

Traditional Celebrations

One of the oldest traditions in Finland is the pouring of melted tin into a bucket of cold water just before midnight on New Year's Eve. The various forms assumed by the hardening metal are believed to foretell good or evil for the coming year. The custom is said to date at least to medieval times when workers with metal and other persons put great faith in witchcraft and superstition. In Helsinki the year is formally greeted with a concert on the steps of the Suurkirkko, or Great Church, located on the Great Square.

Shrove Tuesday, the day before Ash Wednesday and the beginning of Lent in February or March, is not marked in Finland by costume parades and masking, as in other countries, but by coasting and outdoor sports. Characteristic foods of the day are pea soup, pancakes, and wheat buns, filled with almond paste, and eaten with hot milk.

Some six and a half weeks after Shrove Tuesday the religious Finns observe Good Friday, their strictest church holiday, as the quietest day of the year. Finland is 96 per cent Lutheran, so the vast majority of persons go to 11:00 A.M. Lutheran church services, where the altar rail, normally draped in crimson velvet and white lace or embroidered white linen, is draped in black to commemorate the crucifixion of Christ.

Contrasting with the solemnity of Good Friday is the gaiety of Easter Eve, usually celebrated with family parties where the traditional dish is rye meal mixed with water, flavored, baked in birch-bark baskets, and served with thick, rich cream. The holiday spirit continues through Easter Sunday and Easter Monday, literally Second Easter Day.

May Day, May 1, is important to Finns because it signals the season of returning summer. It is also the day when students of the State University may don their white student caps and wear them until September 30. In Helsinki it is customary for groups of university students to meet early in the morning and march to summer restaurants where they drink *sima,* a special kind of malt ale or mead, and eat *tippaleipia* or *struvoja,* tasty crullerlike cakes. Since May 1 is also the date of the International Workers' Festival, the celebration of which is provided for in Finnish law, laborers also parade in Helsinki on May Day, and take part in demonstrations in parks and public places.

The second Sunday in May is Mother's Day.

Ascension Day, forty days after Easter, is celebrated mainly in Ritvala, a village of Sääksmäki Parish, where folk dances and songs that might have originated in pagan times, and a bonfire on Whitsun Mount, are featured at the St. Helga's Festival.

Midsummer, June 24, is, of course, one of Finland's major traditional celebrations since it commemorates the longest day of the year. Practically everyone deserts Helsinki and large towns throughout Finland to spend the holiday in the country. Before they join in the celebration and dance around the huge bonfires the Finns invariably take a *sauna*, the world-famous Finnish bath. Perhaps the largest bonfires of all are lighted at Rovaniemi, the capital of Lapland and a trading town at the confluence of the Kemijoki and Ounasjoki rivers near the Arctic Circle. Nearby Ounasvaara Hill is the most southerly point from which the midnight sun can be seen that day, and the occasion is celebrated with a carnival, trading fair, a program of athletic events, and music played on a kantele, a three-cornered string instrument like a zither. All Finland, though, is studded with bonfires on June 23. They are built on shores of lakes, on hilltops, and usually consist of boards, fallen trees, and old tar barrels. In the evening these *kokko* fires are lighted as symbolic greetings of joy and renewed life. Young people, usually dressed in national costumes, dance about the blaze. Games and dancing in the fields continue on June 24. Buildings in the cities are brightened by flags then, because June 24 is Finnish Flag Day.

Every year on June 24, the Midsummer Day, lumberjacks from all parts of the vast forests of the north gather in Rovaniemi on the Arctic Circle for their annual competitions. Their exciting logrolling contests and races along chains of logs, the big attractions of this annual festival to celebrate the nightless day, are watched by thousands of spectators who line the banks of the swiftly flowing Ounasjoki River. Throughout the summer other lumberjack competitions are staged in different parts of the Finnish lake district and north Finland, where the green gold, the country's greatest known natural resource and the mainstay of its most important industry, gives employment to thousands of persons. The contests usually take place in June and early July. Wherever possible, they include shooting the rapids on rolling logs, pushing small rapids boats upstream, logrolling, and races over chains of logs. As a rule prizes are supplied by managers of lumber businesses. The date and place of the national championship lumberjacks' competition change each year.

Other thrill-laden events are the rapid-shooting contests held from time to time from June through August in the north Finnish wilderness. But whether there are competitions or not, adventurous visitors may enjoy the experience of racing through the foaming rapids themselves. There are two rapid-shooting routes for tourists in Finland. One located in Suomussalmi on the upper part of the Emajoki River in northeast Finland is maintained by the Finnish Tourist Association. The nine-mile course, which winds through dense forests and typical wilderness, begins at Pello Village and runs along the Tornionjoki River on the Finnish-Swedish border for seven miles. The long, narrow rapids boats used on both routes seat from eight to eighteen passengers. They are handled by skilled and experienced oarsmen who know every stone and boulder along the way. To ensure against the possibility of accident the rides are staged only when there is sufficient water in the rivers to permit easy passage of the boats, which travel at great speed.

Christmas, being an important feast day in the Lutheran Church, is enthusiastically celebrated in church and at home.

In Lapland, northernmost Finland, christenings, marriages and funerals often are scheduled according to the weather.

Those who live in the semiarctic regions must wait until the winter snows begin to melt before they can drive to town, so there are mass ceremonies each spring just as soon as the usually snowbound folks can hitch their reindeer to sleds and drive to town.

Winter Sports

There are at least two internationally important winter sports meets in Finland. One is the Salpausselkä International Skiing Championships at Lahti during February or March, and the other is Ounasvaara International Winter Games Championship at Rovaniemi, capital of Finnish Lapland, during the last half of March. The Salpausselkä championship is always staged at the ski jump and on the terrain surrounding Salpausselkä Ridge. The contests were inaugurated in 1923, one year after the Lahti Ski Club was founded, and have been held regularly since then, except during the war years. A popular feature of the meet is the combination lighting and fireworks display that provides dramatic effects for the ski-jumping on Saturday night. Daytime events include *slalom*, international general, women's, and young people's ski-jumping. In 1952 the Salpausselkä Cup was put up for the first time. Attendance at the two-day meet totals 100,000. The Ounasvaara Games were inaugurated in 1927 to stimulate winter sports in Finnish Lapland. Now some 25,000 persons turn out to see ski-jumping, *slalom*, and cross-country contests.

The exact dates on which festivals will take place in Finland, as well as the latest travel information pertaining to that country, may be obtained by writing to the Finnish National Travel Office, 41 East 50th Street, New York 22, New York.

Bank holidays in Finland: January 1; Epiphany, January 6; Feast of the Annunciation, March 25; Holy Thursday through Easter Monday, March or April; May 1; Ascension Day, forty days after Easter; Whitmonday, fifty days after Easter; Flag Day, June 24; Independence Day, December 6; December 25, Christmas Day; and December 26.

Chronological list of events in Finland:

JANUARY. Nationwide: winter sports contests.

FEBRUARY. Helsinki: Kalevala Day, February 28; Runeberg Day, February 5; speed-skating championships. Jyvaskyla: Finnish skiing championships.

FEBRUARY or MARCH. Salpausselkä skiing championships: Lahti. Shrove Tuesday winter sports meet: Helsinki.

MARCH. Enontekio, Lapland, beyond Arctic Circle: Lady Day. Helsinki: fair. Kuopio: winter games. Nationwide: Good Friday, strictest religious holiday in Finland, March or April. Rovaniemi: Ounasvaara winter games.

APRIL. Nationwide: Good Friday, strictest religious holiday in Finland, March or April. Semiarctic regions: mass christenings, marriages, funerals.

MAY. Helsinki: auto, motorcycle races; dog show; Flower Day, students' festivals, May 13; May Day, May 1; Snellman Day, May 12. Nationwide: Flag Day of the Army, May 19; Memorial Day, third Sunday in May; Mother's Day, second Sunday in May. Porvoo: bike races. Ritvala: Ascension Day, forty days after Easter, May or June; folklore festival. Sääksmäki: folklore festival. Turku: Motorcycle Tourist Trophy Race.

JUNE. Helsinki: Sibelius Music Festival. Jamsankoski: music, song festival. Nationwide: Midsummer, Finnish Flag Day, June 24. Orivesi: music, song festivals. Pello Village: shooting-the-rapids contests, June, July, August. Ritvala: Ascension Day, forty days after Easter, May or June. Rovaniemi: lumberjacks' contests, midnight-sun festival. Suomussalmi: shooting-the-rapids contests, June, July, August. Tammisaari: agricultural show. Vassa: fair.

JULY. Helsinki: Finnish championship bike road, track races; Finnish relay racing championships. Kyro: agricultural show. Lohja: agricultural show. Pello Village: shooting-the-rapids contests, July, August. Raahe: agricultural show. Seinajoki: agricultural show. Suomussalmi: shooting-the-rapids contests, July, August. Tornio: Lapland song festivals.

AUGUST. Helsinki: Finnish championship marathon run, decathlon; Finnish men's, women's track, field championships; Finnish swimming championships. Hyvinkaa: Motorcycle Tourist

Trophy Races. Manttä: Industry Show. Pello Village: shooting-the-rapids contests. Savonlinna: motorcycle races. Suomussalmi: shooting-the-rapids contests. Tampere: Finnish championship trotting races.

SEPTEMBER. Helsinki: dog show; motorboat races. Oulu: fair. Porvoo: rowing regatta. Turku: Rowing regatta.

DECEMBER. Helsinki: concert on steps of the *Suurkirkko,* or Great Church, New Year's Eve, December 31. Nationwide: Independence Day, December 6.

FRANCE

NAME YOUR favorite type of festival and the chances are you will be able to find it in France, where festivals have long been recognized as an integral part of tourism, one of the nation's principal occupations. The French have publicized their annual events so well that now millions of Americans readily associate gaiety with the carnival at Nice, devotion with the pilgrimages to Lourdes, and patriotism with Bastille Day.

Traditional Fetes

Paris, of course, is the most popular tourist attraction in France and one of the greatest in the world. The high tourist season there often opens with the colorful *Quinzaine de la Rose* from late in May to mid-June. During the festival roses are used to decorate shop windows, cafés, and public buildings, and exhibits of prize roses usually can be seen at Bagatelle in the Bois de Boulogne and other rose gardens near Paris. Around the second week in October when the grapes ripen in the only vineyard now growing within the city limits

of Paris, the Montmartre Vine Harvest Festival, which features an auction of grapes and wine, usually brings the high
tourist season to a close.

Next to Paris as a favorite haunt of tourists in France is the
palace at Versailles, the 250-year-old royal residence that cost
$52,000,000 and took 30 years to build under the personal
supervision of Louis XIV during the last half of the seventeenth century. The first great festival he staged there was *The
Pleasures of the Enchanted Isle*. Since then Versailles has been
the personification of regal splendor. Every year it attracts
hundreds of thousands of visitors who stroll through the Hall
of Mirrors, where Woodrow Wilson and other dignitaries
signed the Peace Treaty ending World War I on June 28,
1919, and gaze at the Royal Chapel, the Grand and Petit Trianon, and Marie Antoinette's Hamlet. But most of all the
crowds flock to Versailles when the fountains are turned on.
As a rule the Grand Fountains in the park of the palace spout
in all their splendor for the first time each year on the first or
second Sunday in May, then regularly on the first Sunday in
each month from June through October, the fourteenth of
July, and on special occasions. The fountains in the Trianon
Garden play on the third Sunday of every month from May
through September, while those at Neptune Basin are turned
on at night on the first Sundays of June, July, August, and
September. What's more, in addition to seeing the happy combination of gaily colored lights and Neptune's graceful jets of
water, visitors are entertained with a band concert and a ballet
performed on the fringe of the dramatically lighted stately
grove of trees where French royalty used to frolic. Now when
the nocturnal fountain displays are scheduled, some 50,000
commoners begin crowding into the area at sunset and wait
patiently for the show to start. Fountain displays may also be
seen at St. Cloud on the fourth Sunday of each month between
May and September.

It was around 1950 that officials of the French Government took definite steps to make several of the country's world-famous tourist attractions work overtime in the high season by adding a night shift to their schedule. In addition to the well-established night fete once a month at Neptune Basin there now are regular presentations of a spectacle called *A Toutes les Gloires de la France* in the palace and gardens of Versailles on Wednesday nights and most Sunday nights during July, August, and September. It features the reading in French of descriptions of the glories and splendors of Versailles during the past three hundred years, written by Jean Cocteau, Jacques Ibert, director of the Academy of France at Rome, and André Maurois, of the French Academy. Visitors hear these explanations as soon as they enter by the Cour de Marbre, and continue to hear them as they cross the Galerie Basse, and come out on the great terrace of the palace. The lighting effects are very theatrical indeed!

In 1951 for the first time the handsome châteaux of the Loire were floodlighted to attract additional crowds of tourists. Apparently the plan worked, because it was credited with drawing at least 50,000 more sight-seers to the region that year. Now the regular schedule is from June 15 to September 30, with additional displays at Easter and Pentecost. Many visitors in Paris leave there late in the afternoon, see such famous castles as Azay-le-Rideau, Chenonceaux, and Villandry drenched with golden light, and return to Paris early the next morning.

Without a doubt the most important annual festival of all in France is Bastille Day, July 14, when everyone commemorates the storming of the Bastille by the people of Paris on July 14, 1789. Now on that anniversary Frenchmen and their guests stage parades, dance the whole night through, and shoot fireworks, especially in Paris, where the celebrations often last for several days.

Next in importance on France's list of traditional festivals is the carnival at Nice, usually in February. No one knows exactly when it began, but it is believed to be the outgrowth of a pagan festival. Existing records do show that in 1866 the celebration was visited by the Emperor of Russia, Liszt, Meyerbeer, and Alexandre Dumas. King Carnival of 1899 arrived at the party aboard a yacht, and was met by the Prince of Wales, later King Edward VII, who touched off the fireworks. The Lord of Misrule that year was the twenty-seventh member of a line of kings that began in 1873 when a carnival committee, now known as the *Comité des Fêtes, des Arts et des Sports,* tied together the loose ends of an unwieldy festival. After that the well-organized celebrations were interrupted only by the wars of 1914–18 and 1939–45. King Carnival LXII revived the celebration in 1946, and now each year about eight major floats and six smaller ones, a couple of dozen horsemen and trumpeters, several thousand mummers, masqueraders, and "big heads"—the huge comic figures of animals, clowns, and public personalities—parade behind the float on which rides a big, gaudily dressed straw figure with a beaming baby face. They prance and caper to the tune of "Carnival," the official song of the celebration. Each year there is a different theme. In 1954 it will be "The Kingdom of Toys." The city-wide party starts two Thursdays before Shrove Tuesday, or Mardi Gras, with the arrival of King Carnival. Ordinarily, there is a big parade on the following Sunday, a battle of flowers on the second Thursday, a carnival review, fireworks, and battle of confetti and serpentine the second Sunday, and another parade *Bataille de Confetti en Platre* (colorful powdered confetti), a fireworks display, burning of the Buffoon King condemned to the fire by Lent, and a masked ball at the Municipal Casino on the climactic Shrove Tuesday. Often a second battle of flowers is staged a few days after the carnival season to accommodate tourists who missed the

A scene from Hugo von Hofmannstahl's *Everyman,* performed regularly at the Salzburg Festival, Salzburg, Austria. *Austrian State Tourist Department*

The intricately wrought metal casket in which a few drops of the blood of Christ are kept is paraded through the streets of Bruges, Belgium, during the Procession of the Holy Blood in May. *Official Belgian Tourist Bureau*

Michael Redgrave and members of the Old Vic Company of London are shown in a scene from *Hamlet*, which they performed in the courtyard of Kronborg Castle, Elsinore, Denmark, at the annual Hamlet Festival. *Danish National Travel Office*

Folk dancing is traditional at Whitsuntide and Midsummer festivals in Finland when the returning summer sun casts long shadows. *Finnish National Travel Office*

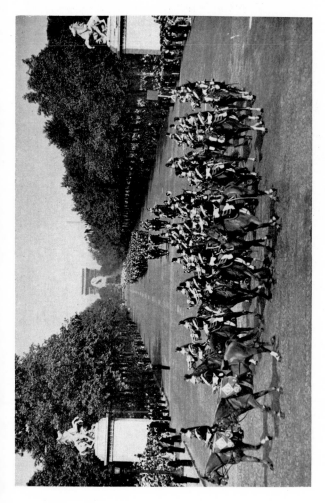

One of the big attractions of Bastille Day in Paris, July 14, is a full-dress military parade through the heart of the city. *French Government Tourist Office*

The Wagner Festival at Bayreuth, Germany, is once again the most important musical event in Germany. This is a scene from a modern interpretation of *Parsifal*. *German Tourist Information Office*

The Military Tattoo is one of the most exciting events on the elaborate program of the Edinburgh Festival, Edinburgh, Scotland. *British Travel Association*

A typical procession in Greece, where religious festivals are widely celebrated. *Executive Research, Inc.*

Stage plays in the open-air theater at Bloemendaal are a popular part of the Holland Festival in the spring. *Netherlands National Tourist Office*

Celebration of National Day in Reykjavik. *Icelandic National Tourist Office*

Horse Week in Dublin, Ireland, early in August, invariably attracts skilled riders from many countries and an international audience. *Irish Tourist Bureau*

William Faulkner receiving the Nobel Prize for Literature for 1949 in Sweden from the Crown Prince, now King Gustavus VI Adolf. *Swedish National Tourist Office*

This is a dramatic moment in a performance of *William Tell*, a summer attraction in even years at Interlaken, Switzerland. *Swiss National Tourist Office*

Two students don traditional costumes to perform an *Erzurum* dagger dance, a familiar attraction at Youth Day celebrations, Ankara, Turkey. *Turkish Information Office*

The saber dance is performed by Macedonian dancers at festivals in Opatija, Yugoslavia. *Yugoslav State Tourist Office*

first one, and to encourage those already there to linger a little longer on the Côte d'Azur.

A country as old as France is bound to be filled with traditional celebrations. However, from *mi-carême,* mid-Lent, to Christmas, there are several dozen that are particularly distinctive. For instance, the only surviving joust in France dates from the thirteenth century and is usually staged at Champagne during Holy Week. Before they proceed to a hill where the combats are staged, young men on horseback carrying long lances and accompanying a large wooden statue of Christ ride in procession through the town to church, where they attend mass.

The village of Pont-de-Cervières in the Alps is one of the last in France to have preserved the tradition of the sword dance. On or about August 16 nine unmarried men come in single file wearing white robes and red belts, and swords at their sides. They dance forty-five figures and simulate the execution of one of the dancers, and then his resurrection. Meanwhile, young girls chant a tune traditional to the celebration. The festival is intended as a tribute to St. Roch, the healer of cattle and protector of harvests.

Ribeauvillé's big day is the first Sunday in September when it celebrates the six-hundred-year-old fete of Pfifferdaj, Fifers' Day, with a torchlight procession through the old streets by uniformed fifers and drummers playing tunes that date to medieval times and a costume play on the Place du Marche. Women wear crimson skirts, embroidered velvet bodices, and headdresses of huge black silk bows, and there is much eating and wine drinking.

In 1953 tourist officials and the wine makers of France combined their talents and plotted two well-defined courses through wine-producing territories to encourage tourists to drive among the vineyards and buy their favorite wines where they are produced. One of the circuits is the scenic Route du

Vin d'Alsace, and the other the Route du Champagne. The narrow country roads that wind through those and the other fabulous grape-growing regions of France are particularly popular in September and October, because that is harvest-time in Alsace, Anjou, Bordeaux, Burgundy, Champagne, the Charente cognac district, Touraine, and the Rhone Valley. At Fontainebleau the harvest festival of the King's Vine is the center of attraction, and there is even a wine harvest festival at Montmartre, the famous Parisian quarter of night spots and artists' studios, both in October. At other times of the year one may sample all sorts of plain and fancy wines at regional *foires aux vins,* such as the ones at Angers and Vouvray in January, Saumur in February, Brignoles in March, Ribeauvillé and Belley in May, and Reims in June, and Chagny, Colmar, and Macon in August.

In Burgundy on the Saturday, Sunday, and Monday after November 11 the towns of Nuits-St.-Georges, Beaune, and Meursault celebrate the glories of Burgundy wine with the festival of *Les Trois Glorieuses,* as they have done in all peaceful years since 1933. In Nuits-St.-Georges the Chevaliers du Tastevin, who named their fraternity for the little flat cup of silver from which wine is tasted, don their red robes and square caps to receive their new members and to enjoy a banquet. They make a colorful sight as they march across town headed for a fancy meal of pork, wine, and other delicacies. The next day, the most important day of the three for visitors, the party transfers to Beaune, where the big public attractions are the traditional auction of vintage wines in the courtyard of the ancient Hospice de Beaune, which was founded in the fifteenth century, and tents where samples of all sorts of local wines may be tasted for a fee. The third day, observed in Meursault, is devoted to a dinner mainly for those who have taken part in the work in the vineyard.

The Festival of St. Catherine of Alexandria, which is celebrated mainly in Paris by *midinettes,* or dressmakers, is observed on November 25 with parties in the dressmaking establishments and dances at night. Mass for the Catherinettes is celebrated at Notre Dame de Bonn-Nouvelle. Though St. Catherine is the protector of all spinsters, she was taken over long ago by the Paris *midinettes* as their particular patroness. On her anniversary work in the ateliers stops, and all employees devote themselves to feasting, merrymaking, and dancing, which often lasts far into the night. Guests of honor at the parties are the Catherinettes, girls who have reached the age of twenty-five without having found a husband. Coifed with elaborate green and yellow hats that they concocted for the occasion, they preside at festivities in the *couture* houses and then, according to tradition, sally forth on the streets in search of a husband. Tradition accords them the privilege of proposing marriage to a man on that day, the way spinsters in America may propose during leap year, every year divisible by four. Today the Catherinettes' public parades are much less boisterous than they were before a ruling made by the police in 1928 put a stop to their practice of kissing unattached males they met in the streets, and now the parties are more private. The police objected to the too ardent responses girls usually received.

Film Festivals

One of the firmly established annual events in the cinema world is the Film Festival at Cannes each spring. Inaugurated in 1948, it usually lasts for two or three weeks in April and May. As a rule at least two dozen countries send their choice entries to compete for the top awards, because winning a prize at Cannes has wonderful box-office appeal elsewhere, and American motion-picture makers are among those who participate most enthusiastically. In addition to the showing of the preferred films there are also a number of meetings of international film organizations. Since this is usually the first film festival of the year it invariably gets the jump on others in pointing up new trends. For example, for the first time at any festival interest will be focused on three-dimensional films at Cannes in 1954.

The latest community to sponsor a film festival is the town of St.-Jean-de-Luz on the Basque coast of southern France. Throughout the first two weeks in September, 1953, it staged the first International Festival of Love Films.

Music, Dance, Drama Festivals

Although the annual calendar of events in France has many music and drama festivals, the principal ones are at Aix-en-Provence, Arles, Avignon, Besançon, Bordeaux, Lyons-Charbonnières, Menton, Nîmes, Orange, Prades, Royaumont, Sceaux, and Strasbourg. One of the first and greatest of the French music festivals is the one at Aix-en-Provence during the last three weeks in July. Inaugurated in 1948, it is presented in the famous theater built by Cassandre in the court of the archbishop's palace. Typical programs include *The Marriage of Figaro, Cosi fan tutte, The Barber of Seville,* about three orchestral concerts, and eight concerts of French, German, and Italian modern music.

Another music festival of the vintage of 1948 is the one at Strasbourg during the second and third weeks in June. The music of Bach, Beethoven, Haydn, Mozart, and contemporary composers is played at the cathedral, in the churches of St. Guillaume and St. Thomas, Municipal Theater, and Palais des Fêtes.

As famous as any music festival in the world these days is the Casals Festival, usually presented at Prades during the last half of June and the first week in July. The annual program of classical music, organized by Alexander Schneider in 1950 to commemorate the two hundredth anniversary of Bach's death, featured Pablo Casals because he was one of the foremost exponents of Bach. The inaugural program was such an overwhelming success that Casals agreed to take part in a festival of six concerts of chamber music and six orchestral concerts featuring the music of Bach, Beethoven, and Mozart at Perpignan in 1951. In 1952 he played his cello or conducted the orchestra in performances of music by Bach, Brahms, Schubert, and Schumann in the abbey of St. Michel de Cuxa. In 1953 the concerts were returned to Prades in the Pyrénées Orientales, where Casals lives. There were five orchestral and five chamber music programs, with Bach, Beethoven, Mozart, and Schubert the featured composers. Soloists included William Kapell, Joseph and Lillian Fuchs, Martial Singher, Arthur Grumiaux, Rudolf Serkin, Myra Hess, Eugene Istomin, and Mieczyslaw Horszowski.

Le Mai Musical, inaugurated in Bordeaux in 1950, and staged in the cathedral, the Château de la Brède, the Grand Theater, and the Public Gardens, usually takes place during the last two weeks in May. In 1953 the program included *Christophe Colomb,* by Claudel, religious music, and symphony concerts. An art exhibition devoted to the works of a single artist or a school begins when the music festival starts, and lasts for three months. For example, in 1951 the art show was devoted to paintings of Goya, in 1952 to Mediterranean primitives, and in 1953 to El Greco.

Every Saturday and Sunday afternoon in June, in the lovely setting of a Cistercian abbey founded by St. Louis at Royaumont, some two hundred miles from Paris, music of many nations is presented.

In June and July the concerts organized by the *Nuits de*

Sceaux, and played in the Orangerie of the Parc de Sceaux, include vocal selections as well as orchestral works of Bach, Debussy, Fauré, and Mozart.

In August, 1953, the people of Menton revived their traditional Festival of Chamber Music in the square in front of the church of St. Michael, and in Besançon, during the first two weeks in September, as they have done every year since 1948, musicians and music-lovers gather for their annual celebration, which includes selections by Bach, Beethoven, Mozart, Ravel, Schumann, Richard Strauss, and Wagner. One of the important activities of the Besançon Music Festival is the awarding of a cash prize worth about $250 to the outstanding young conductor. In 1953 the winner was Peter Traunfellner, a twenty-three-year-old Austrian, who is a composer as well as a conductor.

At least four of the top-ranking cultural events in France emphasize drama and dancing, or give it equal place with the musical portion of the program. The festival that takes place for about five days in June at Nîmes is staged in an ancient amphitheater made for animal and gladiator combats. Typical programs have included Shakespeare's *Julius Caesar, Andromaque,* by Racine, and *Les Mouches,* by Sartre.

The festival of music, drama, and dancing at Lyons-Charbonnières during the last week in June and the first week in July takes place in a wide range of halls and auditoriums—in the Roman theater, the Cathedral of St. John, the inner court of the Musée des Arts Decoratifs, and at Charbonnières Casino.

Shortly after the festivities at Lyons-Charbonnières, Avignon plays host at a Festival of Dramatic Art during the last two weeks in July, as it has done regularly since 1947. In the setting of the Palais des Papes, in its Court of Honour, and the Urban V Gardens capacity crowds have cheered performances of such classics as *The Choephoroi,* of Aeschylus; Shakespeare's *Henry IV* and *Richard II; Le Cid,* by Corneille;

L'Histoire de Tobie et de Sara, by Paul Claudel; and André Gide's *Aedipus.*

In Orange on the last four or five days of July there is drama, music, and dancing in the ancient theater that King Louis XIV, in a burst of enthusiasm, once described as "the finest walls in the kingdom."

At Arles, during the first week in July, the *"grande fête artistique et régionaliste"* is a combination of drama, a parade of Provençal costumes, dancing, singing, and bullfights. The drama, ballet, and opera take place in the Roman theater. In the Roman arena are the Spanish style bullfights—which means the bull is killed—and a *"course Royale de la Cocarde d'Or,"* in which a cockade must be picked from between the bull's horns.

Biarritz is often the scene of an international folklore festival during the second week in April and plays host to dancers of many lands. Bayonne and Biarritz are also pleasant places during the first week in August, because the Gascon vivacity, regional traditions, and Spanish enthusiasm combine to recall the great folk fests of the past. Basque boys and girls dance the vigorous fandango, the *arin-arin,* and the *mascarade.* The girls wear hoods, pleated skirts, and brilliant shawls, while the boys sport red vests, berets, and short trousers of white wool. Pyrenees guides display their expert horsemanship, and there are championship games of pelota, a kind of handball played with baseballs and wicker scoops, which is to the Basque country what baseball is to the United States.

Religion

Of the approximately six dozen religious observances which take place regularly throughout France, perhaps the most distinctive are the six Brittany "Pardons," long pilgrimages on foot that provide a display of regional costumes and music as well as pious devotion. They usually take place at Tréguier, in May; Rumengol in May or June; Locronan and Auray in July; Plonévez-Porzay in August, and Le Folgoët in September. The first pardons took place many years ago. The Pardon of St. Yves, at Tréguier around May 19, is dedicated to the patron of lawyers everywhere, so each year they come from many nations to pay tribute to their guardian. Symbols of their recognition are several magnificent banners. The big Pardon to Notre Dame de Tout Remède, the pardon of the singers, takes place at Rumengol always on Trinity Sunday. The pilgrims arrive singing on the evening before the main celebration, bringing offerings of flowers, hams, and animals, which are auctioned the next day. On leaving many of the faithful take home bottles of water from a fountain considered sacred.

The Pardon called *Petite Troménie,* covering about six miles, or *Tour de la Montagne,* is centered in Locronan on the second Sunday in July. It honors Ronan, a Breton hermit, who gave his name to the locality in which he was buried. The procession passes through places associated with events in the life of the saint. However, since the participants do not wish to annoy him as he sleeps they walk in absolute silence around a huge dolmen—a sepulchral monument consisting of a large unhewn stone resting on two or more others—where the Druids are said to have sacrificed, and where the saint preached. In 1953, as happens every seven years, there was a *Grande Troménie,* a pilgrimage covering the ten miles the saint walked every year as a penitence. The Grand Pardon of St. Anne d'Auray at Auray about July 25, 26, is believed to stem from a peasant's discovery of a wooden statue in 1623. As a rule, on July 25 the basilica is illuminated, and there is a torchlight procession. On the last Saturday and Sunday in August the important pilgrimages are the Pardon of the Beggars of St. Anne la Palud, and Grand Pardon of St. Anne la Palud, both at Plonévez-Porzay. St. Anne is the patron saint of Brittany, and legend has it that she was married to a wicked and jealous lord who hated children and chased his wife away from home. She left at night, went down to the sea, and boarded a boat that, guided by an angel, brought her to Judea, where she met the Virgin Mary. She returned to Armorica by the same route and was greeted with joy, for the power to appease the elements and cure sickness was attributed to her.

The second of the two pardons that week is considered as important as those of St. Anne d'Auray and the Troménie of Locronan. The chapel is decorated with garlands of ivy and bunches of roses. The men wear their traditional costumes embroidered in very bright colors, and behind them walk the widows whose husbands died at sea, their costume gray cloaks and dark veils.

Number six among the foremost pardons in Brittany is the Grand Pardon to Our Lady at Le Folgoët around September 7 and 8. This pilgrimage was inspired by the legend that concerned a pious beggar who roamed about Le Folgoët repeating, "Hail Mary, I greet you, Mary." Soon after his death a lily bearing the words "Ave Maria" in golden letters grew on his grave in winter. John V, Duke of Brittany, was so impressed that he built the Notre Dame Basilica over the beggar's grave.

There are at least half a dozen other religious celebrations in other sections of France that are of special interest. Among them are the three pilgrimages to Lourdes, around March 25, August 15, and December 8. Lourdes became a place of pilgrimages soon after the Blessed Virgin is believed to have appeared to Bernadette Soubirous, a fourteen-year-old girl who was gathering firewood with two companions on February 11, 1858. Later a spring gushed out beneath the child's fingers, and the waters from it have been credited with healing the sick. Nowadays visitors to the grotto see hundreds of tapers lighted in thanksgiving, as well as crutches and other aids discarded by those who have been cured of ailments.

A Procession of Penitents at Saugues during Holy Week, in March or April, dates from the twelfth century. On the morning of Holy Thursday the penitents proceed to their chapel, where mass is celebrated. In the evening a crowd gathers from afar to attend the procession, which is lit by torches, lanterns, and candles. The cross is borne by two veiled, barefooted penitents dressed in red and girt with ropes. Children carry the implements of the Passion, while other marchers chant psalms and shake rattles, which replace the bells that have "departed for Rome."

Domrémy, where Joan of Arc was born in 1412, reveres the memory of the girl who raised the siege of Orléans on May 8, 1429, had Charles VII crowned at Reims, and on May 30, 1431, died at the stake at Rouen. On May 8 or the Sunday after there is a pilgrimage to her birthplace, a little peasant cottage in Domrémy, and on May 30 in Rouen there are ceremonies in the cathedral and at the monument that marks the spot where she died.

Gypsies from all parts of the world converge on the village of Stes.-Maries-de-la-Mer on May 23–25 to worship St. Sarah, their patron saint, who, according to legend, landed there with Ste. Marie Jacobé, the mother of James and John, and Ste. Marie Salomé, sister of the Virgin. Relics of the three women are said to have been discovered and re-enshrined in 1448 by René of Anjou, Count of Provence. The reliquary of the Maries is stored in the attic of a church, and each year it is lowered through the ceiling. On the second day the images are carried to the sea and dipped into the water by gypsies. Girls wearing a variety of colorful regional costumes chant while men on horseback, whose everyday job is the breeding of bulls for bullfights, raise their tridents and salute the saints. From his place on a boat near shore the Bishop of Aix blesses the sea, the gypsies, and the guardians of the images. The saints are posed, hands folded, in a blue boat on a tufted platform about three by six feet.

On May 31 and December 8 pilgrims crowd the famous cathedral at Chartres, which was built between 1194 and 1225 and is therefore the oldest church of Our Lady in France. The pilgrimage in May is made up primarily of students from all the universities in France, who go there to venerate Notre Dame du Pilier, a sixteenth-century *Vierge noire*. On December 8, the Feast of the Immaculate Conception is observed with a torchlight procession to the crypt where Our Lady of the Underground is worshiped. One of the important relics in the cathedral is believed to be the tunic of the Blessed Virgin, called the Tunic of the Annunciation, which was sent by the Emperor of Byzantium to Charlemagne in 792.

Corpus Christi, of course, is celebrated in all Catholic churches sixty days after Easter. Three places where the ceremonies are unusually colorful are Itxassou, Helette, and Bidarray in the Basses-Pyrénées. The celebrations have their pious and their joyous sides, with processions of young people in charming traditional costumes singing and dancing right up to the doors of the church, and young Basque men parading in the uniform of sappers and grenadiers.

Pilgrimages to the grave of St. Theresa of Lisieux during the last week in September and the first week in October take the devout to the third largest church in Europe. It is superseded in size only by St. Peter's in Rome and St. Paul's in London. The basilica contains the relics of the saint and many ex-voto offerings from those who are grateful to her.

Those who want to see a very moving and sincere ceremony in simple surroundings trek to Les Baux for the Midnight Mass on Christmas Eve. There shepherds and shepherdesses approach the church carrying candles while tambourines are sounded. At one point a ram pulls a chariot bearing a beribboned lamb that is to be offered as a sacrifice; then all the shepherds offer gifts.

Fairs

Trade fairs are an ancient institution in Europe, and many of the contemporary ones are merely streamlined versions of the commercial caravans that roamed from city to city a few centuries ago. Today France presents many exhibitions of all sorts of merchandise. Those that draw the greatest attendance are in Bordeaux, Dijon, Lille, Lyon, Marseille, Paris, and Strasbourg. Paris, of course, leads with about six outstanding exhibitions. For example, around the second week in March the International Show of Agricultural Machinery is staged at Porte de Versailles; for two and a half weeks in May the famed Paris International Samples Fair, launched in 1904 with 486 exhibitors and now boasting more than 10,000 exhibitions from 32 nations, fills its own gaily decorated permanent exhibition grounds; the International Aeronautical Show at Le Bourget Airport in the last week of June and the first week in July is climaxed by exhibition flights and an aviation festival; the Leather Goods Show, featuring leather goods from French colonies such as Morocco, is the big event during Leather Goods Week in Paris around the third week in September, and boats and automobiles hold the spotlight in different parts of Paris annually during the first ten days in October.

The current International Fair at Lyon was inaugurated in 1916, but it is linked, at least by its publicists, to a fair that flowered there some 550 years ago. The show at Lyon during the second and third weeks in April is a trade exhibition where business is negotiated entirely between manufacturers and merchants for the benefit of export and trade between the nations of the whole world. Covered exhibits fill 1,135,000 square feet of space, while outdoor exhibits cover 5,000,000 square feet.

An important fair was going full tilt in Bordeaux in the fourteenth century, but the present one, usually staged during the second and third weeks in June, is less than forty years old. It is famous for its exhibits of craftsmanship from the colonies, agricultural machinery, and displays of automobiles from many nations of the world.

In the fifteenth century a commercial fair flourished in Lille, at which time the streets of the fair were named for the subjects displayed on them, such as Cheese Street, Chicken Street, and Tanners' Street. The present international fair held during the third and fourth weeks in June is famous for agricultural produce and breweries' stands.

Industries that thrive in and around Strasbourg have been put on display at the Strasbourg Fair during the first two weeks in September almost every year since 1923, because the city is a center for trade with many countries.

The stands featuring products of France's colonies are most popular at the fair in Marseille during the last two weeks in September, probably because Marseille is one of the most important gateways through which colonials and their handicrafts enter France.

Just how popular automobiles are in Paris is proved every year when the annual Auto Show is staged at the Grand Palais early in October. At the fortieth exhibition in 1953 more than one hundred auto makers from eight countries displayed their latest models. The sensation of the show was a small car that had four motors inside the wheels. They were fed current by a generator turned by a four-cylinder gasoline engine. The auto was built by two French brothers, Casi and Maurice Loubière.

Colonials, residents of France, and foreigners all head for Dijon during the first three weeks in November, because that is when the Gastronomique Fair offers the best in food and wines for which Burgundy is famous. This fair, inaugurated in 1920, was the brain child of M. Gaston Gerard, the gourmet mayor of Dijon. The city is a traditional focal point for everyone who is interested in wine and food and the numerous accessories to the fine art of eating and drinking. It also continues the tradition of the fair on St. Martin's Day, November 11, and usually has booths where one may sample some of the delicacies and vintage wines for a small fee.

Sports

Even before spring comes to Paris the horses begin leaping the hurdles at Auteuil racecourse. First of the top-flight steeplechases is the Prix d'Auteuil on a Sunday in mid-March, Sunday being the favorite day for horse races in France. But the most important event of the steeplechase meeting in the spring is the Prix du Président de la République at Auteuil on the first or second Sunday in April. Inaugurated in 1895, it is a handicap event over a distance of 4,500 meters, about three miles.

The principal race in the first half of the season for horses more than five years old is the Prix du Cadran, run over a distance of about two and a half miles at Longchamp racecourse, in May. It dates to 1838, and some authorities on racing compare it with the Gold Cup at Ascot, England.

Around the last week in June the Grand Prix de Paris, with stakes worth approximately $12,500, is run over a mile and seven furlongs at Longchamp racecourse. It is an international race open to three-year-olds of all breeds and countries. Founded in 1863 with a stake of 100,000 francs, it has become the most important equestrian event on the Continent, and marks the high point of the Paris season.

But the race meetings that have the reputation for being the most elegant of the Paris season are the Prix de Diane at Chantilly around the first Sunday in June, and the Prix des Drags or Journée des Drags during the last week in June. The Prix de Diane dates to 1843 and is the top contest reserved for fillies. They compete for about $5,000 over a distance of a mile and half a furlong. The Prix des Drags was inaugurated in 1883 by the Prince de Sagan, a reigning leader of fashion. Ever since then it has been the style to arrive at the racecourse in drags, or horse-drawn coaches. What is more, many men who attend the event still wear the type of top hats and tails that were in vogue in the 1880's, while women dress up in the voluminous dresses of that period.

Chantilly is also the site of the race that is the favorite of many breeders and owners. It is the Prix du Jockey Club, usually run on the second Sunday in June, and it has been favorably compared with the Derby in England. The distance is a mile and four furlongs; the prize, approximately $7,500.

At Deauville the fashionable season is brought to a close with the running of the Grand Prix du Deauville around the last Sunday in August. Inaugurated in 1871, the stakes of at least $5,000 are competed for over a mile and five furlongs.

The autumn counterpart of the Grand Prix de Paris is the Prix de l'Arc de Triomphe at Longchamp about the first or second Sunday in October. The race was created in 1920, and now stakes are valued at approximately $12,500. The distance is a mile and four furlongs.

On a Sunday during the last half of October at Longchamp racecourse the Prix du Conseil, inaugurated in 1893, is worth about $5,000 to the winner. This mile-and-four-furlongs event, which was inaugurated in 1893, used to mark the climax of the autumn season, but now it must share that honor with the Prix de l'Arc de Triomphe, which is run earlier in the month.

Steeplechasing returns to Auteuil early in November. The

three big contests that month are the Grand Prix d'Automne over a distance of about three miles for a prize of almost $4,000 on the first Sunday of the month, the $5,000 Prix La Haye-Jousselin on the third Sunday, and the Grand Prix for three-year-olds on the fourth Sunday.

Bicycling, of course, is dear to the hearts of most Frenchmen. The three annual cycling events that generate the most interest are the six-day race in Paris in March, the championship of France, which is usually staged on an autodrome in Paris in June, and Le Tour de France in July. The tour of France is probably the top event of the three. Inaugurated in 1903 by Henri Desgrange, a Paris law clerk, it generally begins in the provinces in mid-July and ends in Paris about four weeks later. The first race consisted only of six laps lasting nineteen days, with ample rest periods between laps, and avoided any terrain that even slightly resembled a mountain. It was not much of a success, either, for just a few of the country's best cyclists entered. But M. Desgrange did not lose faith. He made the race even longer than it was at first, increased the publicity, and made the event a fixture. Now each year thousands of fans take up points of vantage for miles along the countryside waiting patiently to watch the cyclists scoot by, and to get a glimpse of the one who pedals more than three thousand miles in the shortest time.

The greatest of all French automobile races, and one of the foremost automotive contests in the world, is the twenty-four-hour test for sports cars at Le Mans. Inaugurated only in 1923, the twenty-first contest was staged June 13–14, 1953. The fast, unbanked course through the countryside near the resort city has a lap length of approximately 8.4 miles. In 1952 the racers, who endured normal conditions of fog, rain, and blinding sun, were watched by a crowd of more than 200,000 that came to the event in 25,000 cars and 60 private or chartered aircraft. Only 17 of the original 57 racers finished the grueling contest that year. In 1953 quite a few Americans participated, and a British Jaguar driven by Tony Rolt and C. Duncan Hamilton set a Le Mans distance record of 2,535 miles. The Jaguar's average speed, 106 miles per hour, was almost ten miles an hour faster than the record of 96.7 miles per hour set in 1952 by a German Mercedes Benz.

Another major racing circuit in France is the Albi, at Tarn. It is the site of the Grand Prix d'Albigeois, which is usually run during the last week in May. The circuit is approximately five and one-half miles in length, and is roughly triangular in shape. Lap speeds exceeding 100 miles per hour have been achieved. At Montlhery, about fifteen miles southwest of Paris, the circuit known as the Brooklands of France is about 7.75 miles long, while the circuit five miles west of Reims, where the French Grand Prix is usually staged during the first week in July, is considered the second fastest course in Europe. Among the remaining outstanding auto-racing events in France are those that take place at Nîmes, late in March; Marseille, the third week in April; Bordeaux, the first week in May; Orléans, the last week in May; Rouen, the fourth week in June; and Reims, the first week in July. The French Grand Prix is one of the ten major events that contribute points to the world championship each year. The others are: Argentina, Belgium, Germany, Great Britain, Holland, Indianapolis Speedway, Italy, Spain, and Switzerland.

A 3,350-mile automobile Tour de France, first held in 1951, is an international touring competition that begins and ends in Nice during the second and third weeks in September. It is usually divided into three stages: Nice–La Baule, La Baule–Reims, and Reims–Nice. Classifying tests are held in certain towns during each stage, and it is at such times that spectators usually can get a good look at some of the participants in the race. Among the more famous participants in the contest in 1953 was the thirty-year-old Prince Rainier III of Monaco. He had a brush with death, but escaped unhurt when the car he was driving crashed into a tree during a fog.

Tennis

In all probability only a few of the thousands of spectators at the International Tennis Championships in Paris in April know that the authorities on the game regard France as its true home. Sports historians report that tennis used to be called *Le Paume,* the palm, because the palm of the hand was used instead of a racket. Originally, it was an outdoor game, but as long ago as 1230 A.D. there was a public indoor court in France. The sport fascinated the English, so they imported it to England around 1360 and called it tennis because they had heard the French say *ten-ez,* resume, when they played. By 1600 there were about two thousand tennis courts in France, and the sport prospered in France and England until crooked gambling in connection with the matches during the seventeenth century caused it to be banned first in France, then in England.

Air Show

Le Bourget Airport near Paris is known to most Americans as the place where Charles Augustus Lindbergh landed in 1927 at the end of his history-making nonstop transatlantic flight from New York. The field is known to aviation enthusiasts throughout the world as the site of the Paris Air Show, which was inaugurated in 1909 and is now the oldest aviation event of its kind. At the annual exhibition during the first week in July, 1953, the newest types of jet fighting planes shocked Paris and its suburbs with a series of "sonic booms," which sounded like exploding bombs as the planes dived faster than the speed of sound. Jet fighter planes that took part in the demonstrations were the U.S. F-86 Sabre jet, Britain's Hawker Hunter and Submarine Swift, and France's Dassault Mystère IV. The demonstrations were witnessed by more than 100,000 spectators at the field. When the visitors were not watching the latest types of aircraft perform in the sky, they inspected the newest models of all types of planes on the ground. In some ultramodern transports all seats for passengers were installed with the backs toward the front of the plane on the theory that fewer casualties occur in emergency landings when passengers are riding backward, because at such times they are normally propelled toward the front of the craft.

The exact dates on which festivals will take place in France, as well as the latest travel information pertaining to that country, may be obtained by writing to one of the following French Government Tourist Offices: 610 Fifth Avenue, New York 20, New York; 307 North Michigan Avenue, Chicago, Illinois; 1014 Kohl Building, San Francisco, California; 448 South Hill Street, Los Angeles, California; 1170 Drummond Street, Montreal, Canada.

Bank holidays in France: January 1; Easter Monday; May 1; Ascension Day, forty days after Easter; Whitmonday, fifty days after Easter; Bastille Day, July 14; Assumption Day, August 15; All Saints' Day, November 1; Armistice Day, November 11; Christmas, December 25.

Chronological list of events in France:

JANUARY. Alpe d'Huez: skiing contests. Alsace: Route du Vin d'Alsace open all year. Auron: skiing contests. Champagne: Route du Champagne open all year. Mégève: skiing contests. Montgenèvre: skiing contests. Pau: riding tournament. Vouvray: wine fair.

FEBRUARY. Angers: wine fair. Barcelonnette: skiing contests. Bordeaux: Grand Pardon of the Terre-Neuvas. Chamonix: skiing contests. Fécamp: Grand Pardon, Blessing of the Sea. Lourdes: Feast of St. Bernadette. Menton: Lemon Festival. Nice: fair. Paris: Prix Robert de Clermont-Tonnerre, horse race. Saint-Malo: Grand Pardon, Blessing of the Sea. Saumur: wine fair. Serre-Chevalier: skiing contests.

FEBRUARY or MARCH. Pre-Lenten Carnivals: Bailleul, Bayonne,

Bordeaux, Châlon-sur-Saône, Limoux, Nice. Six-day bike race: Paris.

MARCH. Arles: Bullfights. Brignoles: wine fair. Limoges: pilgrimage, festival every seven years (1953, 1960, etc.). Lourdes: pilgrimage. Nantes: Mid-Lenten festivals. Nîmes: auto races. Paris: agricultural machinery show; housekeeping show; Mid-Lenten festivals; Paris–Saint-Raphaël auto rally; photography show; Prix Agitato, Prix d'Auteuil, Prix Murat, and Prix Troytown, horse races; steeplechases. Pau: steeplechases. Saint-Raphaël: Paris–Saint-Raphaël auto rally. Toulouse: agricultural machinery show.

MARCH or APRIL. Basque Easter, folklore festival: Biarritz. Holy Week, nationwide; more spectacular observances at Burzet, Celles-sur-Belle, Champagne, Perpignan, Sartene (Corsica), Saugues, Thann.

APRIL. Arles: bullfights. Bayonne: sale of famous Bayonne hams. Béziers: bullfights. Cannes: Film Festival, to May. Lyon: fair. Marseille: auto race. Paris: camping, sporting equipment show; Prix du Président de la République, horse race; steeplechase; tennis championship; tulip show at Parc de Bagatelle.

MAY. Bayonne: bullfights. Belley: wine fair. Bernay: pilgrimage to Notre Dame de la Couture. Biarritz: folk festival. Bordeaux: auto races; folklore festival of St. Estelle, at Bordeaux or Toulouse; *Le Mai Musical,* May Music Festival. Cannes: air show; Film Festival, April, May. Cermont-Ferrand: religious procession. Chamonix: *Coupe des Amethystes,* downhill skiing race. Chartres: students', other pilgrimages. Domrémy: pilgrimage honors Joan of Arc. Grenoble: fair. Limoges: fair. Macon: fair. Menton: festival. Monteux: ten-mile relay race honors St. Gens. Nice: Europe–Côte d'Azur Tourist Rally, international bus race. Nîmes: bullfights. Orléans: auto races. Paris: fair; French Cup final, football; Prix du Cadran, horse race; *Quinzaine de la Rose,* to mid-June. Ribeauvillé: wine fair. Rouen: pilgrimage honors Joan of Arc. St. Anne d'Auray: Grand Pardon of St. Anne d'Auray. St. Brieuc: Grand Pardon, torchlight procession. St. Cloud: fountain displays, specific Sundays, holidays, to October. St. Emilion: wine festival. St. Tropez: Feast of St. Tropez. Saintes-Maries-de-la-Mer: Gypsies' pilgrimage. Tarn: Grand Prix d'Albigeois, auto race. Toulouse: Folklore Festival of St. Estelle, Toulouse or Bordeaux. Tours: festival. Tréguier: Grand Pardon of St. Yves. Versailles: fountain displays, specific Sundays, holidays, to October.

MAY or JUNE. Corpus Christi: nationwide; more spectacular observances at Bidarray, Geispolsheim, Helette, Itxassou. Grand Pardon to Our Lady All Healing, Singers' Pilgrimage: Rumengol.

JUNE. Angers: air show; dramatic art festival, at the Castle; fair. Angoulême: ramparts circuit auto race. Bagnéres-de-Luchon: midsummer bonfires, festival. Beaune: fair. Beauvais: historic celebration. Bordeaux: fair. Chamonix: rhododendron festival. Clamart: folk music, liturgical chant. Laforce: Protestant celebration. Le Mans: Le Mans Twenty-four-hour Grand Prix auto endurance test. Lille: fair. Lyon-Charbonnières: music, drama festival, June, July. Nîmes: music, dance, dramatic art festival. Paris: air show, June, July; bike championship of France; classical games, bullfights, dramatic performances in amphitheater of Lutèce, June or July; French fencing championships; Grand Paris Steeplechase; Grand Prix de Paris, Prix de Diane, Prix des Drags or *Journée des Drags,* Prix du Jockey Club, horse races; horse show; *Quinzaine de la Rose,* May, June; rose show. Prades: Casals Music Festival. Provins: midsummer bonfire, festival. Reims: wine fair. Rouen: auto races. Royaumont: Music of Many Nations, music festival. St. Amarin: midsummer bonfires, festival. St. Cloud: fountain displays, specific Sundays, holidays, to October. St. Germain: Bol d'Or, auto, motorcycle meet. St. Jean-de-Luz: midsummer bonfire, festival. Saint-Jean-du-Doigt: Grand Pardon, bonfires. Sceaux: *Nuits de Sceaux* concerts. Semur: tilting at the ring. Strasbourg: music festival. Tarascon: festival. Thann: St. Thiébaut Festival. Toulouse: procession of relics of St. Sernin. Tours: châteaux of the Loire illuminated, through September. Versailles: festival; fountain displays, specific Sundays, holidays, to October.

JULY. Aix-en-Provence: music festival. Arcachon: pelota championship. Arles: bullfights; dance, drama, music festival. Arles-sur-Tech: procession of relics of SS. Abdon and Sennen. Auray: Pardon of St. Anne d'Auray. Avignon: drama festival. Bagnères-de-Luchon: torchlight procession of Luchon Guides. Bayonne: festival. Besse-en-Chandesse: ascent up the mountains. Camaret: Blessing of the Sea. Carcassonne: performances in ancient theater of the fortress. Chamonix: *Le Brevent,* ski meet. Deauville: polo, July, August; steeplechase, horse races. Estaing: Feast of St. Fleuret. Evian: Evian–Mont Blanc–Mégève auto rally. La Pointe-du-Raz: Pardon of Our Lady of the Shipwrecked. Locronan: *Petite* or *Grande Troménie,* depending on the year. Lyon-Charbonnières: drama, music festival, June, July. Mégève: Evian–Mont Blanc–Mégève auto rally. Mont-de-Marsan: Cow-baiting, July, August. Nancy: fair. Nationwide: Bastille Day, principal celebration in Paris, July 14. Orange: dance, drama, music festivals. Paray-le-Monial: religious celebration. Paris: air show, June, July; Bastille Day, July 14; classical games, bullfights, dramatic performances in amphitheater of Lutèce, June or July; finish of spectacular *La Tour de France,* bike race. Quimper: festival. Reims: Grand Prix auto race. St. Cloud: fountain displays, specific Sundays, holidays, to October. St. Malo: dance, drama, music festivals. St. Véran: pilgrimage. Tours: châteaux of the Loire illuminated, through September. Versailles: *À Toutes les Gloires de la France,* through September; fountain displays, specific Sundays, holidays, to October.

AUGUST. Amélie-les-Bains: folkloric festival. Ars: pilgrimage honors St. Jean-Marie Vianney. Basses-Pyrénées region: Basque sports meet. Bayonne: bullfights; festival. Boulogne-sur-Mer: religious procession. Chagny: wine fair. Chamonix: Festival of the Guides. Chartres: Feast of the Assumption, August 15. Collioure: religious procession, festival. Colmar: wine fair. Concarneau: Festival of the Blue Nets. Deauville: Grand Prix du Deauville, horse race; polo, July, August. Evian: dog show. Le Mans: onion fair. La Délivrande: pilgrimage to the Dark Virgin. Lisieux: Feast of the Assumption, August 15. Lourdes: Feast of the Assumption, August 15. Macon: wine fair. Menton: chamber-music festival; dahlia festival; battle of flowers; illuminations. Mont-de-Marsan: cow-baiting, July or August. Plonévez-Porzay: Pardon of Beggars, and Grand Pardon of St. Anne-la-Palud. Poitiers: pilgrimage to tomb of St. Radegonde. Pont-de-Cervières: sword dance, *Bacchu-Ber.* Roquebrune-Cap-Martin: Procession of the Passion. St. Cloud: fountain displays, specific Sundays, holidays, to October. St. Odile: Feast of the Assumption, August 15. Tours: châteaux of the Loire illuminated, through September; music festival. Versailles: *À Toutes les Gloires de la France,* through September; fountain displays, specific Sundays, holidays to October.

SEPTEMBER. Arles: bullfights. Bayonne: bullfights. Besançon: music festival; National Clock, Watchmaking Show. Biarritz: horse show. Bordeaux: auto rally. Calvi (Corsica): Feast of Notre Dame de la Serra. Camaret: Pardon to Notre Dame de Rocamadour. Carnac: procession, blessing of animals. Casamaccioli (Corsica): Feast of the *Santa du Niolo.* Céret: bullfights. Dax: bullfights.

Deauville: Golden Cups, golf matches. La Baule: horse show. Lavasina (Corsica): pilgrimage. Le Folgoët: Grand Pardon to Our Lady. Le Mas-Soubeyran, near Mailet: Commemoration of Protestant Martyrs. Luchon: torchlight procession of the Luchon Guides. Marseille: fair. Mont-Saint-Michel: pilgrimage. Nice: *Tour de France,* auto race, begins, ends at Nice. Nîmes: bullfights. Paris: French junior tennis championships; Leather Goods Show. Ribeauvillé: *Pfifferdaj,* Fifers' Day. St. Cloud: fountain displays, specific Sundays, holidays, to October. St.-Jean-de-Luz: Love Film Festival. Strasbourg: fair. Tours: châteaux of the Loire illuminated. Versailles: *À Toutes les Gloires de la France;* fountain displays, specific Sundays, holidays, into October.

SEPTEMBER or OCTOBER. Grape, wine festivals, harvesttime: Alsace, Anjou, Bordeaux, Burgundy, Champagne, Clos Vougeot, Cognac, Fontainebleau, Montpellier, Paris, Rhone Valley, Touraine. Pilgrimage to shrine, relics of St. Theresa at third largest church in Europe: Lisieux.

OCTOBER. Lourdes: Pilgrimage of the Rosary. Metz: fair. Paris: auto show; horse jumping contests; Prix de l'Arc de Triomphe, horse race. St. Cloud: fountain displays, specific Sundays, holidays. St. Denis: pilgrimage honors martyred first bishop of Paris. Saintes-Maries-de-la-Mer: Religious festival. Versailles: fountain displays, specific Sundays, holidays.

NOVEMBER. Beaune: *Les Trois Glorieuses,* three days celebrating the glories of Burgundy wine. Dijon: gastronomic fair. Meursault: *Les Trois Glorieuses,* three days celebrating the glories of Burgundy wine. Nuits-Saint-Georges: *Les Trois Glorieuses,* three days celebrating the glories of Burgundy wine. Paris: Feast of St. Catherine of Alexandria, patroness of Catherinettes, girls unmarried at twenty-five, and *midinettes;* Grand Prix d'Automne, Grand Prix steeplechase for three-year-olds, and Prix La Haye-Jousselin, all steeplechases. Pontigny: pilgrimage honors St. Edme.

DECEMBER. Brancion: Christmas Eve midnight mass. Chartres: Feast of the Immaculate Conception, December 8. Les Baux: Christmas Eve midnight mass, famous for procession, offerings by shepherds. Lourdes: Feast of the Immaculate Conception, December 8. Luceram: Christmas Eve midnight mass for shepherds, shepherdesses in traditional costumes. Marseille: fair, famous for clay models of personages of the Nativity. Perouges: Christmas Eve midnight mass with torchlight procession. Strasbourg: fair.

GERMANY

TRADITION is a mighty power in Germany. For that reason the vast majority of German festivals stem from circumstances that prevailed many years ago. Incidents inspired by various degrees of heroism have been plucked from the records of wars and pestilence and fashioned into a motley array of pageants and folk plays. Many of the cultural events are based on works of the older masters, yet the new Germany is drawing heavily on the works of composers and writers of the recent past, and also on those of today. The religious festivals most certainly date to antiquity. However, in the field of industrial fairs and exhibitions of mechanical devices the Germans rarely dwell on the past. Instead, they divide their attention between now and the day after tomorrow.

Music, Drama

When the cornerstone of the Bayreuth Festspielhaus was laid on May 22, 1872, the fifty-ninth birthday of Richard Wagner, he presided and conducted Beethoven's Ninth Symphony. Numerous notables were present, and there were many wishes for the success of that new festival, which was always to be devoted primarily to the authentic representation of Wagner's works. Little did the most ardent well-wisher dream that the new type of musical festival in Germany would become the country's foremost annual festival some seventy-five years later. Bayreuth has become a shrine for Wagnerites, so as many of them as can do so flock to the Wagner Festival, which is staged there each year from about the last week in July through the third week in August. It was suspended during World War II, yet when it was revived in 1951 Beethoven's Ninth was repeated, to emphasize and reinforce the link with the past. An innovation that year, however, was the presentation of Astrid Varnay, a soprano from the Metropolitan Opera Company of New York, as the festival's first American Brünnehilde in *Die Walküre,* and the first to undertake all three roles in the "Ring" cycle at Bayreuth. The current series of festivals is being staged by Wieland and Wolfgang Wagner, grandsons of the composer, who have reconciled their duty to tradition with the demands of modern tastes and circumstances, including economy. They have streamlined the operas as much as they dare. Among the notable changes are spotlighting scenes ordinarily played under bright lights, and the projection of colors. The reactions of seasoned operagoers to all the changes are varied. Some like it old, some like it new. Nevertheless, even though the methods of staging the music dramas are novel, one can readily recognize such familiar works as *Tristan und Isolde, Rheingold, Walküre, Siegfried, Gotterdammerung, Meistersinger, Parsifal,* and *Lohengrin.*

Every year at ten in the morning on the day the Wagner Festival begins there is a small commemorative ceremony at the grave of Richard and Cosima Wagner in the park behind their former home at Bayreuth. Their tombstone is heaped with flowers, and the simple, solemn ceremony is attended by members of the family, musicians, singers, and visiting artists. A short eulogy is usually delivered by the director of the orchestra.

Throughout Germany during the spring and summer there are at least a dozen music festivals worthy of special consideration. For example, the international Bach Week at Ansbach has shown continuous progress since it was inaugurated in 1947. Usually presented late in July and early in August, a typical program might include the Mass in B Minor, Passion of St. John, the six Brandenburg concertos, and other well-known works of the master.

Open-air performances of operas and operettas at Augsburg from June to September include the music of Wagner, Verdi, Puccini, Mascagni, Zeller, and Benatzky.

The annual Beethoven Festival of the city of Bonn takes place during the first two weeks of May. It is Bonn's annual reminder that Ludwig van Beethoven was born there in a small house that still stands and can be visited at the back of the Bonngasse, in the oldest point of the former Roman castle on December 16, 1770. Well-known conductors, soloists, and organists combine their talents to present a cross section of Beethoven's music.

In 1949 the Modern Chamber Music Festival was organized by the city of Brunswick, and every November since then it has presented such unusual fare as the compositions of master students of German music colleges in first performances by master students of German conservatories, as well as compositions of Malipiero, Stravinsky, and Martinu.

Another gathering place for persons interested in contemporary music is Donaueschingen during the first week in October. There the newest compositions of composers from many lands are played, some of them for the first time.

More music of our times is offered at Dusseldorf during the third week in May when the hundred-year-old Lower Rhenish

Music Festival features works by Béla Bartók, Paul Hindemith, and Hans Vogt.

The International Music Festival at Konstanz during the second and third weeks in July reflects the co-operation in the field of music that exists in that region between Germany and Switzerland, for often the program is made up of works by composers from both countries, and they are performed by nationals of the two nations.

At Marburg the Organ Week inaugurated in 1949, and usually presented during the second and third weeks in June, is designed to provide an outline of music for that instrument by the scientific music seminary of the Philipps University, and features leading German organists at different organs, particularly at the magnificent instrument in the St. Elizabeth Church, erected seven hundred years ago.

Munich times its annual Opera Festival to take advantage of the crowds of music-lovers that pass through the city en route to Bayreuth in July and August. There one might hear such familiar operas as *Meistersinger, The Flying Dutchman, Tannhauser,* and *Rosenkavalier,* one or two Mozart operas, and less well-known works like *Elektra* and *Arabella* by Richard Strauss, as well as operas by the moderns Karl Orff and Hans Pfitzner.

In 1953 the fourth International Opera Festival at Wiesbaden during May offered performances by the National Opera of Vienna, the Teatro San Carlo of Naples, the English Opera Group of London, and the Municipal Opera of Berlin.

The Mozart Festival in Wurzburg during the second and third weeks in July makes use of the Park of the Residence, the Emperor's Hall of the Residence, and St. Stephen's Church. In 1953 the festival opened with a serenade in the Hofgarten by the Bavarian National Academy of Music, and the program included two chamber music concerts, four symphonic concerts, and sacred music.

The Summer Music Festival at Hitzacker during the last week in July is usually concerned with the development of chamber music from the baroque to the present. Eminent German and foreign artists take part.

Yodeling, singing, blowing the alpenhorn, and clog dancing by Austrians, Germans, and Swiss enliven the town of Aschau in the Upper Bavarian Chiemgau Region at the annual Alpine Choral Festival about seven weeks after Easter. The international song fest was inaugurated in 1938 and now attracts hundreds of enthusiasts in regional costumes who perform for visiting Americans, British, and French, and, of course, for Germans and visitors from other countries.

The latest cultural conclave to be launched in Germany is the Berlin Festival, usually held late in August and throughout most of September. The project, initiated at a London meeting of Western Foreign Ministers in May, 1950, was inaugurated in 1951 by the western powers to display their artistic vitality with a lavish program of ballet, opera, stage shows, and exhibitions. The Big Three underwrite the festival, although it is a Berlin affair. The principal attractions at the second Berlin Festival in 1952 were the New York City Ballet Company and *Porgy and Bess,* the American folk opera by George Gershwin in which Cab Calloway played Sportin' Life and William Warfield was Porgy. Leontyne Price, who became Mrs. William Warfield, was Bess. The British were represented by Sadler's Wells Ballet, while the French exhibited works of Picasso and other well-known modern artists. Wilhelm Furtwängler and Eugene Ormandy conducted, the Hamburg Opera Company performed, and Alexander Brailowsky, the American pianist, played. In 1953 the program stressed opera, and included a German *première* by the Städische Opera of *Prozess* ("The Trial") by Gottfried Von Einem, Shaw's "Don Juan in Hell," Molière's *The Miser,* and Buchner's *Danton's Death* by the Théâtre National Populaire of Paris.

In 1951, too, Berlin joined the other European cities that sponsor film festivals each year. The Berlin Film Festival usually takes place for about ten days during the second half of June, and aims to show the development of films in all democratic countries. Early in 1953 twenty-six countries signed up, each nation being allowed to show from one to three feature films and two to four art films, the exact number depending on its annual production. Competing films are screened in two modern motion-picture houses on the *Kurfürstendamm*. Other attractions of the festival include showings of classic silent films, tours of Berlin's film studios, two outdoor performances in the Waldbühne, and the International Film Ball, which is usually attended by many actors, producers, and directors.

Of course, it is a far cry from the modern film to the staging of the traditional Passion Play at Oberammergau every ten years. The next presentation is scheduled for 1960, at which time the drama will be 326 years old. It dates back to 1634, when it was first put on in fulfillment of a pledge made by the people of Oberammergau, who vowed that if they survived a plague that was raging then they would re-enact the sufferings of Christ every ten years. Their descendants have stuck to that schedule as much as possible, too, permitting postponements only in time of war. For example, no performances were given in 1870, at the time of the Franco-Prussian War, in 1920 following World War I, or in 1940 during World War II. Each performance lasts from 8:30 A.M. to 6:30 P.M., with two hours out for lunch. The big scene, of course, is the crucifixion, when the person representing Christ is suspended from the cross for almost half an hour. In 1950 there were at least 33 performances from May through September in the Passion Play Theater, which seats 5,000. The theater, itself, has become a goal of sight-seers even during the years when the Passion Play is not being presented. For example, an average of 7,000 persons a month visited the theater during June, July, and August, 1953.

The Germans have a fondness for drawing on historical events when looking for themes for their festivals. Typical samples of that are "The Master Draught" and "Shepherds' Dance," which are staged regularly during Pentecost, seven weeks after Easter, at Rothenburg-on-Tauber. "The Master Draught" commemorates the feat by which ex-burgomaster Nusch kept the imperial field marshal General Tilly from turning the town over to his soldiers for pillage and burning during the Thirty Years' War. Nusch emptied at one draught the great state beaker which held four quarts of wine. Now the master draught is re-enacted in the forenoon in the large Assembly Room of City Hall, where it happened. That afternoon, and at various times throughout the summer, the Shepherds' Guild exercises its privilege of dancing in the square. That right was given to them many years ago because a guildsman who was the first to see Tilly's troops approaching the city sounded the alarm. The dance was originally a tribute to the shepherds' patron saint, St. Wolfgang.

Every July the town of Dinkelsbühl presents a history play called the *Kinderzeche* in memory of the time during the Thirty Years' War when children's prayers saved their home town from fire and plundering. After a musical reveille the children in period costumes re-enact the historic episode and turn the conqueror's wrath to mercy. Outside the town there is a folk festival.

Nördlingen is another of the many medieval towns that recall events of the Thirty Years' War. For at least a quarter of a century the play *Anno 1634* has been presented there every July, peace permitting.

At Landshut every two or three years on three Sundays in June and July the Royal Wedding is staged. It is the re-enactment of a sumptuous wedding feast in 1475 when Duke

George, son of Ludwig the Rich, married Hedwiga of the Polish Royal House of the Jaguellonen. The memory of this wedding has been kept so alive, and perhaps embellished, through the centuries that the pompous procession includes 900 burghers dressed in elaborate period costumes. Official records show that at the original wedding 333 oxen, 275 pigs, 40 calves, and 12,000 geese were eaten. The procession and a festival play are the high lights of the modern celebration.

Every year from July to August three classical works by German and other European dramatists are staged in the Knights' Hall of the castle of Burg, on the Wupper River. The presentations are noted for two things: the accurateness of the period costumes, and the fact that there are no wings for the stage.

Carnivals

Although the fabulous festivities of pre-Lenten carnivals are usually associated with Latin countries, Germany, too, is carnival-conscious. The Mainz Carnival, which reaches its climax just before Ash Wednesday, is one of the nation's great celebrations. It gets underway in January and builds steadily until the Rose Monday procession of elaborate floats and "Tomfool Infantry," dedicated to the perpetuation of good humor and merrymaking.

Among the outstanding carnivals are the ones at Cologne, Düsseldorf, and Munich, where there are dozens of fancy-dress balls to which visitors are invited, and parades. Other important carnivals are at Berlin, Bonn, Hamburg, Munich, and Wiesbaden. The oldest carnival society in Bonn was inaugurated in 1826. In 1952 more than a quarter of a million spectators are said to have watched the spectacular Rose Monday parade, which satirized current political and other events.

In Wiesbaden the carnival was started only in 1949. Even

so, its "Three Lilies Girls' Guard" is already an established attraction.

Every seventh year at the Munich celebration the coopers, very important craftsmen in this city famous for beer, present a dance introduced some five hundred years ago. It is performed by twenty-five coopers clad in red jackets, black shorts, white socks, a light leather apron, and a green velvet cap with light blue feathers. They swing a hoop of fir branches, and beat time to a tune all their own on beer barrels. As a matter of fact, the exact movement of the coopers' dance can be seen every day at 11:00 A.M. on the belfry of the City Hall, where it is performed by carved figures. Individuals and clubs may order a coopers' dance, and during the carnival season the coopers receive more orders than they can fill.

Another private organization that brings the carnival spirit to Germany at different times of the year is the Union of Bavarian Costume Clubs, which comprises 650 groups with 70,000 members. In Bavaria national dress clubs are recognized as cultural organizations. Throughout the year the different groups arrange costume festivals, the biggest of all being staged at the *Oktoberfest* in Munich late in September.

Customs

It is customary in many places in Germany to light an Easter fire on a crest of a hill on Easter Sunday evening. But that is not enough for the people of Lügde. They take huge oak wheels measuring seven feet in diameter and weighing eight hundred pounds, fill them with straw, put fire to them, and let them roll blazing down the hill.

In some districts, like the Harz Mountains, when the people want to chase away witches they get after them by banging on drums, pots, pans, and even pipes.

On Corpus Christi Day, sixty days after Easter, religious

processions are held in every Catholic community. Really tremendous ones in the wake of an image of Our Lord are staged in Cologne and Munich, and there is an unusual procession on Lake Chiemsee in Upper Bavaria. The water parade begins at the old church of the Frauenwörth Monastery on Frauen Island. The devout get aboard gaily festooned boats, sail to the four corners of the island, where they sing the four Gospels, then return to church. A similar procession is staged on Lake Staffel.

Bavarians celebrate two church consecration festivals a year: the general one on the third Sunday in October, and a local one on the anniversary of their saint. Most of the celebrations consist of church sermons followed by a fair, and much eating and drinking.

In the early part of July miners from the famous industrial Ruhr District carry fire from their furnaces in solemn procession to the grave of Bishop Ketteler, eminent social reformer buried in the cathedral at Mainz.

A much more elaborate pilgrimage is the showing of holy relics in Aachen every seven years. The most recent one was in July, 1951. Called the Germans' oldest national church festival, the observance attracts the faithful who want to see the four great relics accumulated by Charlemagne: the gown the Holy Virgin is said to have worn in the Holy Night, the swaddling clothes, and a loin cloth of Christ, and the cloth on which John the Baptist was beheaded. Until the first half of the thirteenth century the pilgrims saw only the "St. Mary's Shrine" in which the treasures were kept.

Around the first week end in September, as a rule, Germans and their guests bid a fiery welcome to autumn with the traditional Rhine Aflame Festival on the Rhine River near the famous Lorelei Rock between St. Goar on the left bank and St. Goarshausen on the right bank. Thousands of spectators line the banks of the stream, while others crowd into all sorts of craft and cruise along the river to see the bonfires ablaze on hilltops, and belfries, castles, and towers flooded with light. The celebration is climaxed with a tremendous display of fireworks.

Fairs

At least a half-dozen festivals and as many fairs of international importance are staged in Germany from time to time throughout the year. The one that is probably the most fun of all is the famed *Oktoberfest*, which usually begins in mid-September and lasts into October. It started on October 17, 1810, the wedding day of King Ludwig I, for whose bride, Theresa, the fairgrounds known as Theresa Meadow were named. When the *Oktoberfest* is on, the meadow is aswarm with Americans, Austrians, Bavarians, Swiss, and other nationalities, many of whom are dressed in their regional costumes. And the king of the festival is Munich beer, of which some two million quarts were drunk at a recent *Oktoberfest*. Beer is given a royal welcome the very day the fair opens by the festival hosts and their buxom waitresses who prance around the place, while beribboned brewery horses draw decorated trucks with heavy loads of beer through the lanes. The feast is considered officially opened when the tap faucets are ceremoniously driven into the first barrels, the very first one usually by the chief burgomaster. From then on, according to custom, beer is dispensed only from barrels and only in steins holding at least a quart. Favorite food at the fair includes whole roast chicken, sausages of many lengths and widths, fried fish, and oxen roasted on a spit. For amusements there are a midway, sports events, riding tournaments, and a grand costume pageant three miles long. In the line of march are historical groups, guilds in medieval costumes, crossbow societies, and other organizations.

Among the international trade fairs the principal ones are at Frankfurt, the fourth week in February and the second week in September; at Hanover, the first week in March, and the last week in April and first week in May; and at Cologne the last week in February, the second week in March, and the first and second weeks in September. These and the following dates are approximate, and often vary slightly according to circumstances.

The Frankfurt fairs were going concerns in the thirteenth century. Now at least 27 kinds of consumer goods are on display by about 3,000 German firms. The Hanover International Trade Fairs show the wares of more than 3,000 exhibitors from Germany and abroad, and they also attract a multitude of buyers. For example, just 4,000 foreign buyers appeared there in 1947, but by 1952 the total had swelled to 60,000. They went to buy textiles, clothing, glass, china, ceramics, gold- and silverware, as well as musical instruments and toys. The three fairs at Cologne concentrate on household articles, hardware, textiles, clothing, furniture, photography, and machinery. The 4,100 exhibitors sell to 100,000 buyers.

The *Photokina,* a gigantic photography fair inaugurated in 1950, and usually held in Cologne late in April and early in May during even years, is of particular importance because of Germany's fine reputation for making cameras. Thousands of visitors go there to get information, to buy and sell, and to see the latest developments in the field of photography.

German handicrafts have their own fair in Munich during the first three weeks in July. Started in 1949, the fair's 1,150 exhibits now attract craftsmen and their works from 50 countries, and thousands of visitors.

Leipzig, of course, has been the scene of fairs for seven hundred years. Now, usually in September, businessmen, technicians, and engineers inspect the newest things in printing machinery, public conveyances, textiles, musical instruments, ceramics, and the most extensive exhibition of Soviet industry outside the Soviet Union.

Posters, too, have a fair all their own. The travel posters for which Europe is famous are only a part of the International Poster Exhibition, which covers all phases of poster publicity. The first show was put on in 1952. Since then exhibitions have been staged regularly during the last half of September in the huge City Exhibition Hall of Karlsruhe.

When the annual International Book Fair was staged at Frankfurt during the last week in September, 1953, the customary period for this important cultural activity, almost 500 publishers from 13 countries joined 465 German publishers to display their newest and best works.

Berlin Green Week, usually staged during the first week in February, gives a comprehensive picture of the production program of German industry, manufacturing, agricultural machinery, and tractors in addition to a demonstration of European agriculture and cattle breeding by the Food and Agricultural Organization of the United Nations, and exhibits by Belgium, the Netherlands, Switzerland, and the United States. Berlin is once again becoming a center for conventions and fairs. In 1950 there were just 12 conventions, yet in 1952 there were 140.

The *Salad Kermis* in Ziegenhain is one of the real folk fairs of Germany, which are picturesque as well as big and merry. Perhaps even more appropriately it might have been called the *Potato Kermis,* because early in the eighteenth century the landgrave Carl of Hesse had a large patch of potatoes planted, and to promote the popularity of the vegetable that was not so well known in his domain, Carl invited the populace to a salad and potato party in Ziegenhain. To commemorate the event the town has staged a *Salad Kermis* two weeks after Whitsunday regularly since 1728.

The inventor of movable printing type, and therefore the

father of modern printing, Johannes Gutenberg, was born Henne Gensfleisch about 1400 in Mainz. So now on St. John's Day, June 24, the city stages a scientific exhibition and expositions dealing with printing, art, musical and literary events, and folk dancing.

On St. Michael's Day, September 29, the big attraction of the fair at Augsburg is the *Tura Michele*. In the foundation of the Perlach Tower at the City Hall there has been, since 1526, a group of figures representing the archangel Michael with the devil at his feet. On St. Michael's Day the angel appears every full hour, and with each sounding of the hour it stabs the struggling devil.

Mayence's Wine Mart around the last week end in August and the first in September combines good business with pleasure, and the wine usually flows freely. Grapes and wine also have their days along the Rhine each fall when a grand procession of floats depicts the development of wine from grape to glass at Bingen, and at Rüdesheim during the first week in September. There is a dance under the linden trees, and a flower *corso* on the river. In addition to these celebrations there are innumerable smaller wine and vintage festivals in September and October in the various wine-growing districts of Western Germany.

The German Industries Exhibition, on an attractive fairground around a radio tower that has become a landmark, is staged in the beginning of October. Both heavy and light industries are displayed.

When Christmas rolls around the annual Christ Child Fair at Nuremberg is opened by a youngster who impersonates the Christ Child, and two angels, who appear on the gallery of the Church of Our Lady to invite everyone to visit the fair and buy the famous Nuremberg toys, gingerbread, and tinsel angels. The so-called gold-leaf angel is the symbol of the Nuremberg Christmas Fair. It stems from a medieval practice of giving the Christ Child away to children as a doll. That original meaning was forgotten after the Reformation, and by and by angels were substituted. Today at the fair children have a homemade-lantern parade on December 21. They start at the Fleisch Bridge and wind up at the castle singing Christmas carols.

Sports

Automobile racing has made a terrific comeback in Germany since the end of World War II, and much of the credit for that has been given to an American, Colonel Vollrath, a former scoring official at the famous Indianapolis Speedway. The Grand Prix of Germany is raced over the many curves, hills, and fast straightaways of the 14.14 mile Nürburgring in the heart of the Eifel Mountains between Coblenz and Cologne during the first week in August. It is one of the ten major events that contribute points to the world championship each year. The others are: Argentina, Belgium, France, Great Britain, Holland, Indianapolis Speedway, Italy, Spain, and Switzerland. Other important German automobile races include the Rhine Cup, Hockenheim, the second week in May; the Eifel Meeting, Nürburgring, late in May; the Avus Meeting, Berlin, second week in July; and the 1,000-kilometer race, Nürburgring, late in August.

Junior speedsters are also having their day now in Germany, just as they are in the United States. Since the end of World War II and the arrival of American military and civilian personnel in Germany the Germans have adopted some of the activities of the Americans. For example, in the field of sports the purely American Soap Box Derby, which originated in 1933 as a newspaper's test promotional event in Dayton, Ohio, is now very popular with German youngsters under fifteen years of age. In 1953 about 10,000 of them competed in local contests throughout Western Germany during June and July, and the 120 regional winners took part in the national finals at Duisburg, in the British Zone. At least 35,000 spectators of all ages lined the rails to see the streamlined "crates" whiz by at speeds approaching thirty miles per hour, then come to a halt in loosely piled straw just past the finish line. The winner received an educational grant worth about $1,200 and a free trip to Akron, Ohio, to compete in the American Soap Box Derby finals. The winner of the second prize received a scholarship valued at about $750, and third prize was a scholarship worth approximately $500.

Germans, as almost everyone knows, are also very keen about gliding, and they are very adept at it, too. They began to concentrate on developing their skill for riding the air currents not long after World War I, when the victorious Allies forbade them to fly motorized craft. Their training ground was Orlinghausen Field in Westphalia, and from that seemingly insignificant plot of ground came the core of the formidable Luftwaffe. After the Allies defeated the Nazis in World War II, the Germans once more were forbidden to fly. This time the restrictions included gliding. However, the ban on gliding was lifted in 1951, and within the next two years some 850 gliding clubs are reported to have sprouted wings. After two years of trial flights the Germans were ready to stage the first renewal of their prewar annual National Gliding Championship. It was staged for two weeks in August, 1953, and was so successful it probably will be held in August from now on, right at the old training ground, Orlinghausen Field. The two dozen pilots who competed in the contests in 1953 were cheered by a crowd estimated at 50,000. However, when it came time to cheer the champion the bravos were not for a German but for twenty-five-year-old Gerard Pierre, of France, who piloted his French-built Air 102 glider at an average speed of 35.8 miles per hour over a 62-mile triangle course. The Germans vowed to do better in the future.

In the field of winter sports the most important places for international contests are Oberstdorf, famous for its ski-flying contests, and Garmisch-Partenkirchen, where the International Winter Sports Week is staged annually late in January. It usually features a combination ski jump and *slalom* for men and women, long-distance run for men, jumping for men, downhill for men and women, and a bob-sleigh race that counts in the year's world championship. The Feldberg in the Black Forest is the site of the Black Forest Ski Championships in the second week in February, and Hahnenklee/Bockswiese and St. Andreasberg in the Harz Mountains where a top-flight ski meet is held in mid-February, and auto ski races are staged later in the month. Night ski jumping is the big attraction at Reit im Winkel during March.

Horse racing in Germany starts around Easter. There are tracks in all major cities in West Germany and Berlin. The outstanding events are the German Derby in Hamburg, near the end of June, and the famous Iffezheim Week at Baden-Baden around the end of August, which was inaugurated more than a hundred years ago.

Schützenfests, a kind of target practice that originated centuries ago when citizens' guards were necessary to keep order in town and for protection from marauders, are still held in Germany. Three important ones are at Goslar in the Harz Mountains every July, at Schliersee in Bavaria late in July, and Xanten/Rhineland, the last week in July and the first two weeks in August.

The exact dates on which festivals will take place in Germany, as well as the latest travel information pertaining to that country, may be obtained by writing to one of the following German Tourist Information Offices: 500 Fifth Avenue, New York 36, New

York; 11 South La Salle Street, Chicago 3, Illinois; Elkin Gunst Building, 323 Geary Street, San Francisco 5, California; 1176 Sherbrooke Street West, Montreal, Canada.

Bank holidays in Germany: January 1; Good Friday; Easter Monday; May 1; Ascension Day, forty days after Easter; Whitmonday, fifty days after Easter; Repentance Day, third Wednesday in November; Christmas, December 25; and December 26.

Chronological list of events in Germany:

JANUARY. Braunlage: skiing, to May. Dortmund: six-day bike race, indoor sports festival. Düsseldorf: women's fashions show. Feldberg: skiing, to May. Freudenstadt: skiing, to May. Garmisch-Partenkirchen: skiing, to May. Munich: riding, driving tournament. Oberammergau: skiing, to May. Oberstdorf: skiing, to May. Schleching: skiing, to May. Schliersee: skiing, to May. Wildbad: skiing, to May.

FEBRUARY. Berlin: Green Week. Düsseldorf: radio, television show. Frankfurt: fair. Hahnenklee: skiing championships; German bobsled championships. Offenbach: Leather Goods Fair. St. Andreasberg: skiing championships.

FEBRUARY or MARCH. Fairs: Cologne, Hanover. Pre-Lenten carnivals: Berlin, Bonn, Cologne, Düsseldorf, Hamburg, Mainz, Munich, Wiesbaden.

MARCH. Frankfurt: auto show. Gimmeldingen: almond-blossom festival. Heidelberg: procession. Munich: riding, driving tournament.

MARCH or APRIL. Bach's *St. Matthew's Passion*, Holy Week: Bremen, Dortmund, Düsseldorf, Hamburg, Lügde, Munich, Oberhausen. Rolling Fiery Easter Wheels: Lügde.

APRIL. Cologne: Equestrian spring trials; *Photokina*, April, May, in even years. Frankfurt: fur fair. Hamburg: horticultural show. Hanover: German Industries' Fair. Harz Mountains: Walpurgis Festival. Mannheim: procession. Munich: *Auer Dult*, giant rummage sale, folk festival, April, May; German Handicrafts Fair.

MAY. Aachen: Present Charlemagne Prize. Adenau/Eifel: Eifel races on the Nürburgring, for autos. Bayreuth: Franconian Festival of Arts. Berlin: Avus motorcycle races. Bonn: Beethoven Festival. Cologne: Modern Music Festival; *Photokina*, April, May, in even years. Düsseldorf: Lower Rhenish Music Festival. Heidelberg: concerts in castle courtyard. Hanover: German Industries' Fair. Munich: *Auer Dult*, giant rummage sale, folk festival, April,

May; bike race, Zurich–Munich. Murnau/Staffelsee: Alpine costume festival. Nuremberg: Modern Theater Week. Oberammergau: Passion Play, to October, usually in years ending in zero. Pforzheim: goldsmiths', jewelers' trade show. Ruhpolding: Ride of St. George. Schwab-Hall: plays on great stairway of St. Michael's Cathedral. Weingarten: "Blood Friday" with "Blood Ride." Wiesbaden: opera festival; play festival; riding, jumping tournament.

MAY or JUNE. Alpine Choral Festival: Aschau. Corpus Christi: Cologne, Lake Chiemsee, Lake Staffel, Munich. *The Master Draught,* Shepherds' Dance, Hans Sachs plays, historical procession: Rothenburg. Salad *kermis,* salad fair: Ziegenhain.

JUNE. Augsburg: operas, operettas, the Red Gate, to September. Berlin: film festival. Burg: drama festival, to August. Hamburg: German Derby, horse race. Kiel: sports contests, congresses, exhibitions. Koblenz: operetta festival, to mid-September; vintners' festival in Wine Village, to September. Landshut: Royal Wedding, June, July, every two or three years. Luisenburg: plays at the castle, June to August. Mainz: Gutenberg Book Printing Week. Marburg: Organ Week. Oberammergau: Passion Play, to October, usually in years ending in zero. Recklinghausen: Ruhr festival plays, into July. Stuttgart: Mozart Festival.

JULY. Aachen: Display of the Great Relics (loin cloth, sweat cloth, grave cloth of Christ) every seven years (1951, 1958, etc.); riding, driving, jumping tournament. Ansbach: Bach Week. Augsburg: operas, operettas, the Red Gate, to September. Bad Hersfeld: festival plays in ruins of a monastery. Bayreuth: commemorative ceremony at grave of Richard and Cosima Wagner on morning Wagner Festival opens; Wagner Festival, July, August. Berlin: Avus sports car races. Burg: drama festival, July, August. Constance: music festival. Duisburg: soap-box derby finals, July or August. Feuchtwangen: festival plays, July, August. Dinkelsbühl: *Die Kinderzeche,* historical play. Goslar: *Schützenfests,* marksmanship contests. Hanover: Grand Marksmen's Festival. Hitzacker: summer music festival. Hohenschwangau: Wagnerian concerts in Neuschwanstein Castle, July, August. Jagsthausen: plays in the Götzenburg, to mid-August. Kaufbeuren: Peasants' dance festival. Koblenz: operetta festival, to mid-September; vintners' festival in Wine Village, to September. Landsberg: Reuthen Festival, features children in historical costumes. Landshut: Royal Wedding, June, July, every two or three years. Luisenburg: plays at the castle, July, August. Mainz: miners' procession. Munich: German Handicrafts Fair; opera festival, July, August. Nördlingen: *Anno 1634,* a play. Oberammergau: Passion Play, to October, usually in years ending in zero. Recklinghausen: Ruhr festival plays. St. Goar: Hansen Festival, Rheinfels Castle. St. Goarshausen: Lorelei Festival. Schliersee: *Schützenfest,* marksmanship contests. Schotten: Round Schotten motorcycle races. Stuttgart: motorcycle solitude race. Wurzburg: Mozart Festival. Xanten/Rhineland: *Schützenfest,* marksmanship contests.

AUGUST. Adenau/Eifel: Grand Prix of Germany, auto race. Augsburg: operas, operettas, the Red Gate, to September. Baden-Baden: Iffezheim Week. Bayreuth: Wagner Festival, July, August. Berlin: Berlin Festival, through September. Burg: drama festival. Cologne: fair. Düsseldorf: radio, television show. Duisburg: soapbox derby finals, July or August. Feuchtwangen: festival plays, July, August. Freiburg: sports-car race. Hamburg: German gymnastic festival; tennis championships. Hohenschwangau: Wagnerian concerts in Neuschwanstein Castle, July, August. Jagsthausen: plays in the Goetzenburg. Kassel: *Zissel,* folk festival. Koblenz: operetta festival, to mid-September; vintners' festival in Wine Village, to September. Luisenburg: plays at the castle. Mainz: wine market. Munich: opera festival, July, August. Oberammergau: Passion Play, to October, usually in years ending in zero. Oberwesel: wine market. Offenbach: Leather Goods Fair. Ulm/Donau: *Schwörmontag,* festival play at Town Hall. Waldshut: costume festival. Westphalia: national gliding championships, Orlinghausen Field.

SEPTEMBER. Adenau/Eifel: a twenty-four-hour race for sports, touring cars. Augsburg: fair; operas, operettas, the Red Gate. Bad Dürkheim: sausage market, wine festival. Berlin: Berlin Festival; German Industries' Fair; German Trotting Derby. Cologne: textile fair. Dinkelsbühl: Bavarian shepherds' day, pageant, dance. Düsseldorf: German Music Fair. Frankfurt: Book Fair; Trade Fair. Hamburg: fair. Hanover: machine tool show. Heidenheim: shepherds' race, dance. Karlsruhe: Poster Fair. Koblenz: operetta festival; vintners' festival, Wine Village. Leipzig: fair. Lübeck: Bach Festival. Munich: *Oktoberfest,* to October. Oberammergau: Passion Play, to October, usually in years ending in zero. Oberwesel: wine market. Rothenburg: Hans Sachs plays, in Emperors' Hall. Rüdesheim: wine festival.

OCTOBER. Bavaria: General Church Day, third Sunday. Donaüschingen: music festival featuring original first performances. Düsseldorf: synthetic fabrics fair. Munich: *Oktoberfest,* September, October. Oberammergau: Passion Play, usually in years ending in zero.

NOVEMBER. Bad Tölz: Leonhardi Ride. Bonn: St. Martin's Festival. Bremen: Gerhart Hauptmann Festival. Brunswick: Modern Chamber Music Festival. Dülken: St. Martin's Festival. Düsseldorf: Modern Music Week; St. Martin's Festival. Hamburg: *Dom,* grand folkfest, to mid-December. Schliersee: Leonhardi Ride.

DECEMBER. Bonn: Kris Kringle Mart. Hamburg: *Dom,* grand folkfest to mid-December. Munich: Kris Kringle Mart. Nuremburg: Kriss Kringle Mart. Stuttgart: Kris Kringle Mart.

GREAT BRITAIN

MOST people outside Great Britain seem to believe that unless the British are being titillated by festivities as tremendous as a Coronation or the Festival of Britain they do not concern themselves with festivals. What a mistaken belief that is! Why, just one glance at their long list of annual events will show how much fun and frivolity the fifty million British pack into approximately 95,000 square miles, an area about the size of Oregon or Wyoming, and prove that the British are very festive indeed!

Changing of the Guard

For many travelers dignified, conservative old London invariably exudes an air of festivity, even when there is no extraordinary event in the offing. Perhaps that is because it is a royal capital, or because pomp and pageantry dress up so many ordinary activities there. Take, for example, the simple ceremony of the Changing of the Guard, which usually is performed in the forecourt of Buckingham Palace every other day when the sovereign is in residence, and at St. James's Palace when the sovereign is away from London. Its very title tells you that one group of soldiers is relieving another, as happens regularly in front of public buildings and monuments in other parts of the world wherever soldiers stand guard. Yet this routine shifting of military personnel in London is an event. The centuries-old ritual is performed by guards provided by the five regiments of foot guards: the Grenadiers, Coldstream, Scots, Irish, and Welsh. The new guard, headed by a Guards' Band, marches into the palace forecourt at 10:30 A.M., and when the ceremony has ended the old guard marches out to the music of the band. Visitors to London can find out about the correct dates and places of the Changing of the Guard by getting in touch with the Tourist Information Centre, Queen's House, 64/65 St. James's Street, London, S.W.1.; telephone, MAYfair 9191.

Mounting of the Guard

At about 10:50 A.M. on weekdays, 9:50 A.M. Sundays, the Household Cavalry Guard rides past Buckingham Palace on the way to Whitehall for the Mounting of the Guard at Horse Guards at 11:00 A.M. on weekdays, 10:00 A.M. Sundays. The regiments taking part are the Life Guards, bedecked in scarlet tunics, scarlet cloaks, and white plumes, and the Royal Horse Guards (The Blues), resplendent in blue tunics, blue cloaks, and red plumes.

Trooping the Colour

The annual Trooping the Colour by the Brigade of Guards is the outstanding military spectacle of the year in London. Trooping the Colour means saluting by drumbeat. It is an enlarged version of guard mounting, and is usually staged around June 10 on the broad expanse of Horse Guards Parade, site of Tudor Tiltyard where combatants on horseback used to indulge in the medieval military pastime of attacking each other with lances. The colour trooped is the sovereign's colour, not to be confused with the Union Jack. Specifically, it is the sovereign's colour of the battalion furnishing the guard for that day. Also, this is supposed to be the only occasion on which the Regimental-Sergeant-Major draws his sword in peacetime, and the Drum Majors wear their State uniform, which is actually the livery of the Royal household. The earliest known mention of a ceremonial trooping the colour on the Horse Guards Parade was an order by the Duke of Cumberland dated May 15, 1755. The present version was introduced on June 2, 1805, when the sovereign's birthday celebration was officially set for a day in spring because the weather is apt to be at its best then for a public manifestation. That year five officers and 229 other ranks trooped the colour in honor of George III. Since 1820, when George IV ascended the throne, the continuity of this annual event has been broken only during the two World Wars, and to gaze upon this military spectacle that is unsurpassed anywhere in the world thousands of visitors go to London even to witness the two dress rehearsals during the week before the final performance. On the big day thousands crowd the Mall for hours before the parade leaves Buckingham Palace around 10:30 A.M., and many stay there until it returns at noon. Normally the sovereign rides in from the Mall escorted by a Sovereign's Escort of Household Cavalry and attended by the royal procession. Then follows the inspection of the troops by the sovereign, and the marching and countermarching to the music of massed bands, with the Guards immaculate in full-dress uniform of black trousers, red tunics, and enormous bearskin hats. The actual inspection lasts about twenty minutes. When it is over the Colour Escort moves out, halting opposite the colour, which is taken over by an officer and trooped down the line.

After the ceremony the sovereign rides away at the head of the guard along the Mall to Buckingham Palace. A relieving ceremony takes place in the forecourt of the palace, and the remaining Guards march past and return to barracks. On June 11, 1953, when the newly crowned Queen Elizabeth II took the salute while mounted on horseback at Horse Guards Parade, she wore a scarlet tunic as Colonel-in-Chief of the five regiments of Foot Guards. The First Battalion of the First or Grenadier Regiment of Foot Guards, of which Her Majesty was colonel before her accession, furnished the Queen's Guard, and the colour to be trooped. It was the new Queen's colour that she had recently presented personally to the battalion. Eight guards paraded, each composed of three officers and seventy-six other ranks, and for the first time the Duke of Edinburgh rode in the parade. Attired in the full dress of a field marshal, he rode close behind the Queen. At the actual inspection the Queen rode round the motionless ranks. After that the Grenadier Guards Colonel commanding the parade gave the command: "Troop!" Immediately the massed bands of hundreds of musicians stepped off in slow time to their playing of selections from Meyerbeer's *Les Huguenots,* then "swept grandly across the front of the line of five Guards." The impressive military maneuvers that are an integral part of this tradition-bound ceremony were culminated with the taking of the salute by the young Queen, and the formation of the parade, which she led back to Buckingham Palace. It rained rather heavily that day, but the Queen braved the downpour majestically. At the palace she took up her position outside the center gateway and took the salute as the troops marched by. Then she went indoors to get to the balcony where she acknowledged the cheers of the multitude gathered around Victoria Memorial, and watched a fly-past of thirty-six Canberra jet bombers.

Lord Mayor's Show

The City of London, a square mile in area, which starts at Ludgate Hill and includes St. Paul's Cathedral, the Bank, and the business district, has been ruled by a Lord Mayor since 1189 when Henry Fitz-Aylwin, who served for life, was placed in that exalted position in an effort to improve relations between king and commoners. The ancient rivalry has faded, but the traditional distinction between the City and the king's realm of Westminster remains. The sovereign must still formally seek the permission of the Lord Mayor before entering the City. In 1215 King John, in return for financial and other services, granted the City guilds the privilege of electing their mayor every year, which is done on Michaelmas, or St. Michael's Day, September 29. However, the King made the condition that the chosen aldermen should appear at the Palace of Westminster for royal approval beforehand. That led to an inaugural procession through the streets annually on November 9, and for many years it even included a parade of decorated barges on the river Thames.

Around the middle of the seventeenth century Puritans under Cromwell's leadership put a stop to such frivolity, but it was revived when the monarchy was restored. With the exception of the war years Lord Mayor's Day remained one of London's most colorful yearly events until 1951 when austerity and twentieth-century traffic jams combined to strip it of some of its traditional pageantry. Despite the fact that he is called Lord, the Lord Mayor is not a member of the peerage. He need not be a member of one of the guilds, or even a native of England, as was demonstrated in 1951 when Sir Leslie Boyce, a fifty-five-year-old Australian-born barrister and former Conservative member of Parliament, became the first man from the Commonwealth to assume the office. The Lord Mayor should be wealthy, however, because he serves without salary and must foot the bills for numerous receptions during his one-year term. To attain his exalted position the aspirant must first be elected one of 25 aldermen chosen by about 10,000 liverymen of the guilds who are entitled to vote at elections in Common Hall. Then he must be elected sheriff by the liverymen, who later nominate two of the sheriffs as Lord Mayor. The Court of Aldermen makes the final choice, casting their votes on September 29 after they attend services in Wren's old church of St. Lawrence Jewry and march to Guildhall, each carrying a bunch of flowers.

In 1951 at the inaugural banquet in historic, war-scarred Guildhall Winston Churchill, the guest of honor, who had been returned to office as Prime Minister in a general election just two weeks before, began a sober summing up of the state of the world with a brief summary of his own colorful career by saying: "Though I have very often in the last forty years or so been present at your famous Guildhall banquets to salute the new Lord Mayor, this is the first occasion when I have addressed this assembly as Prime Minister. The explanation is convincing. When I should have come as Prime Minister Guildhall was blown up, and before it was repaired I was blown out. I thought at the time they were both disasters."

Drama, Literature, Music

When William Shakespeare was earning his livelihood as a playwright between 1590 and 1610, many of his now famous works were first presented at the Globe Theatre located on the rowdy south bank of the Thames in London because the aldermen considered the theater an outcast. Today the Shakespeare Festival at Stratford-upon-Avon, where Shakespeare was born April 23, 1564, and died April 23, 1616, is the longest annual festival in the world. It begins as early as March and continues through October. Although David Garrick, the great English actor, organized a Shakespeare Jubilee in the eighteenth century, credit for launching the present one belongs to Charles Flower, who blithely ignored the slurs of his contemporaries in 1864 and began to make Stratford a center of pilgrimages for Shakespearean devotees. In 1874 he not only campaigned for a Shakespeare Memorial, he also donated a two-acre site for it on the banks of the Avon. The first Memorial Theatre, built in Gothic style, opened with a Shakespeare Festival in 1879. It was granted a Royal Charter of Incorporation by King George V in 1925; then in March, 1926, the building burned down. That mishap, however, did not stop the festival. The plays were presented in a local cinema until the present modern theater was built. Almost a quarter of a million pounds— the equivalent of at least a million United States dollars then —were raised for it through a world-wide campaign. Americans donated more than half the total amount. The new theater was opened by the Prince of Wales on April 23, 1932.

An annual Festival of Contemporary Literature launched at Cheltenham in 1949 usually features an exhibition of books considered the best published in England during the year, lectures by well-known authors, and play and poetry readings by famous actors and actresses in the Town Hall in October.

Some five or six thousand brass bands in Britain run choral groups a close race for honors as the largest amateur music-making movement in the British Commonwealth. The high time of the year for the musicians is the National Band Festival, which usually takes place in London around the second week in November. The first contest is believed to have been staged at Burton Constable, near Hull, in 1845. Five bands competed, each limited to twelve players. Drums were prohibited. In 1949 at least 482 bands representing some 12,000 bandsmen entered for the area championship. From that number 17 were chosen to compete for the national championship at Royal Albert Hall, London.

Perhaps the oldest music festival of its kind in Europe is the Three Choirs Festival held annually in Gloucester, Worcester, or Hereford, in that order, for almost a week early in September. There are records of performances being given by the Three Choirs as long ago as 1715. The 226th took place at Gloucester in 1953. In the beginning the recitals were just yearly gatherings of musical clubs in the three cities. The participants invariably belonged to the local church choirs, and their concerts were staged in the great naves of the cathedrals. By 1838 there were ten principal soloists, a band of 110, and a chorus of 181 voices. In 1951 there were 13 principals, the London Symphony Orchestra, and a chorus of 300 voices. As a rule the program of choral and orchestral works follows long-established custom, a blending of old and new. Handel's *Messiah* has been sung at every performance since 1757. Haydn's *Creation*, Bach's *St. Matthew Passion*, Brahms' Piano Concerto No. 2 in B Flat, Handel's Organ Concerto in F Major, and Elgar's *Dream of Gerontius* are perennial favorites. New works might include such numbers as Fantasia on the "Old 104th" Psalm Tune by Vaughan Williams, *Intimations of Immortality* by Gerald Finzi, and *Hymnus Paradisi* by Howells.

With the exception of the war years an Opera Festival has been held annually since 1934 in a specially constructed opera house on the grounds of the beautiful manorial estate named Glyndebourne, near the small village of Glynde, Sussex, about fifty miles from London, from early in June until late in July. The organizer and patron is John Christie, an ardent lover of music, scientist, builder, and former master at Eton. Mrs. Christie, who was Audrey Mildmay, a singer, was his copartner until she died in 1953. They hired singers and musicians from all parts of the world, and critics have called the results "the most satisfying Mozart to be seen and heard anywhere." Originally the theater accommodated three hundred, but the festival attracted such patronage that Mr. Christie doubled the capacity of the intimate little opera house in 1938, and it was still further enlarged in 1953. Yet the demand for tickets still invariably exceeds the supply.

Another musical festival in Sussex is the increasingly popular week-long series of concerts in the two concert halls in White Rock Pavilion along the Promenade at Hastings during the second week in May. There the classical tradition prevails, and each year since it was first presented in 1949 the programs have been filled with the choral, instrumental, and orchestral compositions of two masters. In 1951 a typical program was shared by the works of Beethoven and Elgar.

Ever since the summer of 1925 those who enjoy pre-seventeenth-century music have gone to Haslemere Hall, Haslemere, Surrey, where Arnold Dolmetsch founded a festival especially to give practical expression to his research in the field of early music. It features professional musicians and is usually staged during the third week in July.

In sharp contrast to the program of early music at Haslemere is the Festival of British Contemporary Music at Cheltenham, where modern works are interlarded with the classics, usually for two weeks beginning on the last Monday in June.

Also in the modern manner, every summer since 1948 Aldeburgh on the Suffolk Coast has staged a Festival of Music and the Arts around the third or fourth weeks in June, primarily to show off one of their famous fellow citizens, composer Benjamin Britten, his works, and the English Opera Group, which he founded. *Albert Herring* had its first performance at an Aldeburgh Festival. Visitors can expect to hear modern operas as well as classical choral and instrumental concerts in the parish church and local halls.

In the history of modern cultural festivals no celebration

has made greater strides toward international acceptance than the Edinburgh Festival. It is usually staged during the last ten days in August and the first ten in September, and from the outset it acquired such tremendous stability and authority that one finds it difficult to believe that the first Edinburgh Festival was staged as recently as 1947. It was the pet project of Rudolf Bing, who became general manager of the Metropolitan Opera in New York City in 1950, and from the day he launched this many-sided celebration with the help of influential Edinburghers, everything was done in the grand manner. Only top-ranking drama groups, the foremost opera companies and ballet dancers, first-rate symphony orchestras, star soloists, and the cream of small musical ensembles have been invited to participate. To that rich array each year has been added the Edinburgh Film Festival, art and crafts exhibits, and a magnificent military tattoo, a pageant reinforced with military color, precision, and timing. One year when eleven famous battle-honored regiments took part, seven of them Scottish, massed pipe bands of royal regiments marched in the white beams of glaring searchlights, setting the pace for superb performances by the kilted, white-coated Highland dancers and the mounted band of the Life Guards. The word tattoo means a drumbeat or bugle call, usually sounded about 9:30 P.M. to summon soldiers back to their quarters. It is also used to define a military entertainment, such as the spectacle at the Edinburgh Festival, with the same workaday tattoo embellished with music or military exercises. The dress tattoo is usually performed at night with torches or other artificial illumination. The word is believed to have originated late in the seventeenth century when British troops were campaigning in the low countries of Europe. When winter approached it was customary for active outdoor operations to cease, and the troops were billeted in nearby towns and villages. To kill time the soldiers headed for the nearest inn, so it was necessary for the drummer to beat a call at 9:30 every night to get the troops back in their quarters, and also to signal the innkeepers to stop selling liquor to the men. In the Dutch language that became known as *Doc Den Tap Toe*. Later is was corrupted to *taptoe,* and then tattoo.

The National Gaelic Mod of *An Comunn Gàidhealach* is a festival of singing, drama, and poetry similar to the Welsh Eisteddfods. It has been staged at a different place in Scotland around the first week of October during peaceful years since 1892. The Mod is really a great event in the life of the Gael, for there choirs and soloists from Highland crofts, island villages, and cities compete in Gaelic, their native tongue. When the first Mod was staged at Oban in 1892 there were only forty competitors. Now there are more than a thousand in the senior section alone. Duet and solo singing attracts at least 800 contestants, many of them being sent by fellow villagers who pay their candidate's way by raising funds for his expenses. There are some eighty classes for literary and music competitions, as well as four Celtic art competitions, which are organized by the Art and Industry Committee of *An Comunn*. One of the unusual prizes in that division is the trophy for the best example of homespun suit length. In October, 1953, the Mod returned to Oban to celebrate its fiftieth jubilee. One of the important musical events there that year was the singing of the *Òran Mór,* or great songs, the heroic songs of the Gael. Some are centuries old. One competition in this music was for men, another for women. On view that year was the ancient crozier of St. Moluag of Lismore, which had miraculous powers ascribed to it. The crozier was lent to the Mod by its hereditary custodians, Livingstone of Bachuil and the Duke of Argyll.

It was the Romans who discovered the medicinal properties of the hot springs at Bath; and it was Beau Nash, dubbed "the King of Bath" during the first half of the eighteenth century, who popularized the spa. A series of assemblies in his famous

Pump Room caused Bath to become a synonym for elegance. People of fashion congregated there, so many of the houses in this fine example of eighteenth-century cities are associated with persons who were famous two hundred years ago. Since 1948 a serious attempt has been made to recapture the glory that was Bath's. During the last half of May an annual festival called the Bath Assembly features stage plays and films, ballet, symphonic concerts, church music, lectures, serenades, folk dancing, marionette shows, fireworks, and the Bath Assembly Ball, a period costume affair in the famous chandelier-lit Pump Room. The party-goers dressed up as kings and queens in 1953.

As might be expected, an almost overpowering program of religious music and drama is featured at the Canterbury Festival in the historic cathedral, usually late in July and early in August. The first church erected where the Canterbury Cathedral now stands is said to have been dedicated by St. Augustine around 597. At one of the early celebrations of this festival the big attraction was the first performance of T. S. Eliot's play *Murder in the Cathedral,* which dramatized the killing of Archbishop Thomas à Becket by four knights in the northwest transept of Canterbury on December 29, 1170. New operas, too, have been composed for performance by festival choristers, and in 1951 there was a new ballet based on Chaucer's *Canterbury Tales.* In 1953 two new plays, *His Eminence of England,* by Hugh Ross Williamson, and *The Prodigal,* by Richard Church, were written for the celebration, and Shakespeare's *The Tempest* was performed in the Archdeacon's garden.

Every year in Wales there are two big eisteddfods. Originally the term meant "sittings" or "sessions," but now it means competitive festivals of music and literature. One of two big ones staged in Wales each year is national in scope; the other is international. The International Musical Eisteddfod, which always takes place in Llangollen around the second week in July, was organized in 1947. It is the meeting place of choirs and folk-dance teams from Europe and the Americas, as well as from Great Britain. Ironically, while the celebration is a home-grown idea intended to show off the fine qualities of Welsh choir singing, Continentals often get the prizes. The contests take place in a hillside pavilion seating 10,000 spectators. The contestants are amateurs whose only rewards are prizes that include a first prize of about $300. As a rule each unit—male, female, or mixed—must sing two set pieces and one of its own choosing. The set selections might be sixteenth-century songs in Latin, English, or a modern foreign language, while the free choice is usually a folk song of the land of the contestants.

The Royal National Eisteddfod of Wales, a traditional festival of music and poetry accompanied by ceremonies deeply rooted in the past, is usually held in August but in a different community each year. Normally each town has an opportunity to play host about once in thirty years. The host town must organize the official Eisteddfod Choir, which forms the backbone of the festival concerts. The choir numbers about 500 persons and draws its membership from towns within a radius of twelve miles. First prize in one of the musical divisions for singers aged eighteen to twenty-five is a scholarship and a trophy.

In Ireland a celebration similar to the Welsh Eisteddfod is called a feis. The one in Newry, Northern Ireland, was launched in 1928 and is customarily staged in mid-April. As many as 5,000 amateurs take part in dancing, music, and verse-speaking contests. Dancers perform single, double, or treble jigs, reels, and the hornpipe.

The degree to which festival fever has risen in Britain is shown by the appearance of several new ventures. One, a Festival of Music in Warwick for three days in mid-May, in

1953 featured Handel's *Messiah,* orchestral concerts, organ recitals, choral services, and singing from the top of the tower of St. Mary's Church on Ascension Day.

Another newcomer to the field of music and arts festivals is the one at St. Ives, Cornwall. Michael Tippett, prominent contemporary composer, takes a leading part in the preparation of the program of choral, orchestral, and chamber music, madrigals, Shakespearean plays, lectures by authorities on the arts, and the festival ball. It takes place during the second week in June.

The Drama Festival at Pitlochry from early in May until late in September offers a potpourri of comedy plays as well as symphonic and choral concerts. In 1953 visitors to the "theater in the hills" saw *The Rivals, Hay Fever, The Importance of Being Earnest, Mr. Bolfry, Marigold,* and *Charley's Aunt.*

Barnstaple and Bideford, in Devonshire, combined their talents to stage a festival of the arts, and named it Taw and Torridge after their respective rivers. The English Opera Group handles the artistic direction of the fete, and in 1953 offered *The Beggar's Opera, Let's Make an Opera,* and *Don Juan,* a new play by Ronald Duncan, as well as choral and orchestral concerts, silver band, procession of boats, lectures by distinguished visitors, a festival ball, and a musical soiree with Benjamin Britten at the piano. The festival takes place during the second and third weeks in July.

At King's Lynn, Norfolk, the Festival of the Arts during the last week in July in 1953 included concerts, recitals, music by the Netherlands Chamber Choir, Dickens readings by Emlyn Williams, and talks by Sacheverell Sitwell and other authorities.

Lichfield, Staffordshire, just about closes the festival and high tourist season with its Festival of Music and Drama during the last ten days in September and the first ten days in October. The stars of the celebration are the City of Birmingham Symphony Orchestra, the Hallé Orchestra, and the B.B.C. Midland Orchestra. Other attractions are solemn evensong and a festival play performed in the cathedral, chamber music, and an art exhibition.

Dancing

The English Folk Dance and Song Society, which holds its annual festival at the Royal Albert Hall, London, in January, was founded around 1911 by Cecil Sharp. The festival is one of the most enthusiastic expressions of national and international folk dancing and singing in the world. One year Miss Jean Thomas, the "Traipsin' Woman" of Ashland, Kentucky, who organized the American Folk Song Festival in 1930, escorted backwoods fiddlers and singers to the gathering in England, where American square dance sets are also popular. Another folk festival is staged at Stratford-on-Avon during the first two weeks in August.

Fairs

When Prince Albert conceived the idea of assembling under one roof the best products of all nations and promoted the Great Exhibition of 1851 in London, he gave the world a new pattern for international fairs. The public nicknamed the hall "the Crystal Palace," because the building, which was made of glass, iron, and steel, resembled a huge conservatory. It was officially opened by Her Majesty, Queen Victoria, and her consort, Prince Albert, on May 1, 1851, and closed October 11, 1851. During that time some 1,700 exhibits were on view, among them the first sewing machine ever seen in England, and a "shocking" nude, the life-size statue of a slave girl by Hiram Power, an American sculptor. More than six million visitors paid anywhere from one to five shillings admission.

Now even the 1951 Festival of Britain, the twentieth-century counterpart of the Great Exhibition, is history. It was officially opened by King George VI and Queen Elizabeth on May 3, 1951, and closed October 11, 1951.

The British Industries Fair was organized in 1915 to "combine business with pleasure." It has now become so large that the 1,000,000 square feet it occupies fill Earl's Court and Olympia in London, and Castle Bromwich in Birmingham. At least 3,000 manufacturers display the products of 90 industries in these three gigantic show cases. Between 1947 and 1950 almost 80,000 overseas visitors attended. Many of them used the special air service that connects London with Castle Bromwich's own airfield. The fair usually takes place during the first two weeks in May.

Every year since the Ideal Home Exhibition sponsored by the *London Daily Mail* was revived following the close of World War II more than a million persons have flocked to Olympia and its twelve acres of floor space during four weeks in March to see the show. They go to gaze at the newest gadgets they hope to incorporate into their dream homes, and to walk the streets of a model village filled with sample homes open to all visitors. In 1951 this village contained a house built and furnished to incorporate the collective ideas of four hundred thousand housewives. There are also two acres of indoor gardens, and a playland where youngsters revel for free while their parents roam.

The London Motor Show, inaugurated in 1902, usually draws half a million visitors to Earl's Court for about ten days in September or October, while thousands of Britishers who never expect to own an airplane flock to the air show at Farnborough, in Hampshire, the oldest field in Great Britain, in September.

The Model Engineer Exhibition staged annually late in August at the New Horticultural Hall, London, is probably the only national exhibition of its kind. It is the high point of the year for the 120,000 modelmakers who live in Great Britain, many of whom belong to the 750 clubs and 12 societies devoted exclusively to the interests and requirements of the amateur craftsman. Among the principal attractions are miniature railways, a small-scale train to transport passengers about the hall, and sometimes a tank filled with water to eye level for showing off the latest model radio-controlled boats. Light tools, construction sets, and accessories are displayed.

Other paraphernalia dear to the hearts of young people fills the Horticulture Halls in London when the National Schoolboys' Own Exhibition is installed there during the first two weeks in January. The first one took place around 1927, and ever since then it has become a fixture of the post-Christmas season. Its prime purpose is to help keep the family happy and amused, inexpensively, in the aftermath of Christmas festivities. At least one hundred thousand schoolchildren, both boys and girls, might be captivated by a completely equipped, electrically operated gauge "O" model railway with five hundred feet of track shown by British Railways; the *Daily Mail* Sports Arena, where boxing, cricket, fencing, football, swimming, and other activities are demonstrated; a model tank-racing track run by the War Office so that boys may maneuver miniature tanks by radar and use mine detectors; a demonstration of farm life; a pet's corner for free advice about birds and animals; a rifle range; puppet show; motion pictures; a library; and information on planning careers.

Flower, Farm Shows

The rose is the emblem of England. As a rule it is seen at its incomparable best amid the regal surroundings it so richly deserves when the annual Royal Windsor Rose Show is staged on the private grounds of Windsor Castle early in July. That is the one time when the sovereign permits the private grounds to be opened to the public. Other annual flower festivals of note are the traditional Chelsea Flower Show on the grounds of the Royal Hospital in the Chelsea District of London for three days around May 20, the Flower Show at Southport, Lancashire, late in August, and the Battle of Flowers Parade at Guernsey, Channel Islands, early in September. The show at Southport in August is among the largest in the world. It also offers gymkhana events and sheep-dog trials as added attractions.

The big attraction at the Royal Counties Agricultural Show, which is staged around the third week in June at a different town each year, is the coaching marathon. Just about every team of four-in-hands in the region competes over a five-mile marathon course, and in this exciting event the old is vividly contrasted with the new. The gleaming harness, crackling whips, and immaculate coaches filled with passengers wearing styles of the nineteenth century show the twentieth-century motorists how the elegants of old attended the fair.

The famed Smithfield Show has been a fixture in London since Napoleonic times. Now it takes place in Earl's Court in the first or second week in December, and emphasis is placed on Britain's fine reputation as a breeder of Aberdeen-Angus, Devons, Galloways, Herefords, Shorthorns, Welsh, Highland, and other breeds of cattle.

Sports

It is difficult to believe that cricket, which many consider the national game of England, was outlawed in the 1470's by Edward IV because he felt it interfered with the compulsory practice of archery. The ban held, too, until around 1550. Then, during the next three hundred years it gradually superseded all other sports in popularity. There was a time when

England's position in the cricket world was supreme; however, for some time now her teams have had to battle vigorously against opponents from Australia, India, New Zealand, Pakistan, South Africa, and the West Indies. Test matches with those teams usually take place in spring and summer.

Although croquet is believed by some sports authorities to have been the forerunner of cricket in England, it was not until around 1868 that croquet was soundly organized there. Now at least six main matches take place in London between May and September.

Soccer is another British favorite. There are eleven men on a soccer team. Ten of them are permitted to use only their feet and heads to propel the ball, but the goalkeeper may use his hands also. The exact origin of the game is lost in antiquity, but records of the sport since 1863, when it was formally organized in Great Britain and became known as association football, are readily available. The Football Association Challenge Cup competition was started in 1871. Some fifteen clubs participated during the first season. The annual entry now exceeds five hundred clubs.

They begin competing for the championship early in September, and the season lasts until near the end of April, at which time a capacity crowd of 99,000 spectators fills Wembley Stadium to see the Association Cup Finals. In Scotland as many as 135,000 spectators jam Glasgow's Hampden Park for the Scottish Cup Final around the last week in April. Soccer has been called "the world's most popular game," yet its history as an international sport dates only to 1872, when England and Scotland played the first international match. The game went professional in 1885, with the blessing of the Football Association.

It is a well-documented fact that Rugby is the offspring of soccer. One day in 1823 a young student at the English Public School of Rugby named William Webb Ellis was playing soccer. He decided to pick up the ball and run with it to the goal instead of kicking it as the rules of soccer provide. That is how the game of Rugby football is supposed to have been born, and from it grew the strenuous American version of the game. By 1860 most public schools in Britain had Rugby teams. The English Rugby Union was formed in 1871, and the first overseas match was played in 1888, when a team from New Zealand visited England. Today the only international trophy in British Rugby is the Calcutta Cup, competed for annually in mid-March by England and Scotland since 1879. It is of Indian design made from melted silver rupees, the accumulated funds of the Calcutta Rugby Football Club when it was temporarily disbanded in 1878. The contest is played alternately at Murrayfield, Edinburgh, and Twickenham. Royalty often go to Twickenham when the game is there.

Other important international Rugby matches usually take place between January and April, and invariably follow this schedule: England plays Wales in January, Ireland in February, Scotland in March, and France in April; Wales plays Scotland in February, Ireland in March, and France in March; Scotland plays France in January and Ireland in February; Ireland plays France in January. There are two versions of this type of football. One, the Northern Union or Rugby League Game, is played almost entirely by professionals. There are thirteen men on each side, and while the game is closely related to "Rugger" the rules are different. In Rugby, or "Rugger," there are fifteen men on each side, amateurs only. Both hands and feet may be used, as in the American version, where there are eleven men per team.

Although some authorities on the history of golf believe that the game was invented by the Dutch, the British long ago practically made it their own. A parchment in the library of St. Andrews University, Scotland, dated 1553, tends to prove that the game was played in Scotland at least in 1413, when the university was founded. Perhaps that head start gave the Scots the edge they needed. At any rate, for many years past the Royal and Ancient Golf Club of St. Andrews, founded in 1754 as the St. Andrews Golf Club and given its present title by King William IV in 1834, has become the spiritual and governing home of golf because of its historical associations and the influential and widely representative character of its membership. It framed the code of laws for the game and in response to questions and disputes on the rules gives decisions that are accepted by golf clubs throughout the world. Today two of the four major titles in golf are the British Amateur and the British Open. The other two are the United States Amateur and Open. The British Open was instituted by the Prestwick Golf Club in 1860 and was played there for ten years. Gradually other clubs were added to the list, and the annual contest rotated among them. This high light of the British golfing season usually takes place around the first week in July.

The British Amateur Championship, open to contenders of any nationality, was inaugurated in 1886 by the Royal Liverpool Golf Club and played at St. Andrews that same year for the first time. It is played on a different course each year, usually during the last week in May.

The English Amateur is limited to players born in England, the Channel Islands, the Isle of Man, or the sons of parents born in those places. It usually takes place in the last week in April.

The Scottish Professional Championship is played around the first week in June. The Scottish Amateur, restricted to amateurs of Scottish birth, or those whose parents were born in Scotland, usually takes place during the second week in July, while in Wales the professional golfers settle their championship early in June. Welsh amateurs, who must be native Welshmen or descended from parents born in Wales, stage their title match about the first week in September.

Three of golfing's world-famous international contests are the Curtis, Ryder, and Walker Cup Matches. The Curtis Cup for women amateur golfers of Britain and the United States, played for in September in even years, was contributed by Harriet and Margaret Curtis of Boston, Massachusetts. The first formal match was staged in 1932. Harriet Curtis was U.S. Women's Champion in 1906. She was defeated for the title in 1907 by sister Margaret. The Ryder Cup, put up by Samuel Ryder, a wealthy seed merchant of St. Albans, England, as an incentive for professional golfers born in England or the United States to join in an international match, was first competed for in 1927 at Worcester, Massachusetts. The match is played alternately in each country, usually in October during odd years. The Walker Cup presented by George H. Walker, a past president of the U.S. Golf Association, came into being as the result of a conversation between Mr. Walker and Norman Boase, a member of the Royal and Ancient Golf Club, about the feasibility of staging an international match for teams of amateur golfers in Great Britain and the U.S. The first Walker Cup Match was played in 1922. The contests are staged biennially, usually during September in odd years.

Lawn tennis as we know it today is believed to have got its start at the All England Club around 1874, a year after it was introduced at a lawn party by Major Walter C. Wingfield, a British Army officer, who also tried to patent the game. It began as a breakaway from the indoor game of rackets and court tennis, and continued to prosper until it became perhaps the most international of all sports. In 1900 Dwight F. Davis, an American tennis enthusiast, put up the Davis Cup for play, open to teams of all nations. That was probably the boost that the game needed to help it achieve its present international status. Now thirty or more nations are represented in the annual Davis Cup contests, which take place in the country that won the preceding Davis Cup matches.

The first of the now famous Wimbledon Tennis Championships was staged at Old Club Ground, Worple Road, Wimbledon, in 1877. The contests were transferred to the All England Club, their present location, in 1922. Now all sixteen of the club's grass courts, which experts consider the finest in the world, are in play during championships. Each day of the two-week tournament late in June the matches are watched by about thirty thousand spectators, at least fifteen thousand of whom can be accommodated in the center court. There are five events: men's singles and doubles; women's singles and doubles; and mixed doubles. The club is about a half hour's ride by subway from central London. Gates usually open at twelve noon. Play begins at 2:00 P.M. and continues until 9:00 or 10:00 P.M. Great Britain's Junior Championship also takes place at Wimbledon, usually late in September. Hard Court Tennis Championships of Great Britain are an annual event at Bournemouth around the end of April, and the British National Covered Courts Open is a fixture at Torquay in October.

Every thoroughbred race horse in the world is said to descend in direct male line from one or another of only three out of nearly two hundred Arabian, Barbary, or Turkish steeds imported into England during the seventeenth and eighteenth centuries. They are the Darley Arabian, the Godolphin Arabian or Barb, and the Byerley Turk. A Briton's love of racing is no mere on-again, off-again affection. It is a deep-rooted, perennial enthusiasm that finds its gratification in flat racing from March to November and steeplechases from September into May. The first big event of the flat racing is the Lincolnshire Handicap, inaugurated in 1849 and run over a straight mile at Lincoln on the third day of the opening meet during

the third week in March. The only horse to win that race two
years in succession was the French-bred Ob, in 1906 and 1907.
Its first victory gave rise to one of the classic mistakes of Aus-
tralian journalism when the telegraph report that listed the
names of the win, place, and show horses read: "Lincoln. Ob,
Dean Swift, Roseate Dawn," and was written up this way by
a misguided rewrite man: "The death of Dean Swift, of Lincoln, author of the famous hymn 'The Roseate Hues of Early
Dawn,' was announced today."

The Derby at Epsom Downs early in June is to England
what the Kentucky Derby is to the United States. The English
Derby was dreamed up at the Oaks, an old alehouse on Ban-
stead Downs that had been converted and enlarged and used
as a shooting box by Edward, twelfth Earl of Derby. The house
had already given its name to "The Oaks," another important
event of Derby Week, when one evening after dinner the Earl
and Sir Charles Bunbury planned a new race. In a mellow
mood the two men plotted a fixture for three-year-olds, colts
and fillies, and eventually came to the point of naming the
event. Casting false modesty aside, they agreed that it should
be named for one of them, and that the honor should be decided on the turn of a coin. Sir Charles called, as a sovereign
was spun in the air. Lord Derby won, and that is why this
world-famous race is called the Derby instead of the Bunbury
Stakes.

The first running of the Derby over one mile straight took
place on May 4, 1780. It was won by Sir Charles's entry,
Diomed, the wonder horse of the era. In 1798, when the horse
was twenty-one years old, Sir Charles sold him to an American
who resold him to a Colonel John Hoome, of Virginia. At
stud Diomed had a great influence on the breeding of American thoroughbreds, and when the horse died in 1808 at the
age of thirty-one, Virginians, who have a boundless affection
for thoroughbred horses, mourned his passing. At present the

Derby course covers one mile, four furlongs, and five yards. It is uphill and bends to the right for the first half-mile, then sweeps in a wide curve to the left downhill to Tattenham Corner, and finally takes a sharp turn into the last straight four furlongs, which end uphill at the finish line. This is a race for the blue bloods of British and continental horsedom. A half-million spectators jam Epsom Downs to see them run. In the crowd are fortunetellers, gypsies, one-man bands, and the gayest garbed of all, the coster folk from the East End of London who strut about in the glittering, beplumed costumes of the Pearly Kings and Queens and lesser royalty of their realm. Just before the running of the Derby in 1953 Jockey Gordon Richards, a forty-nine-year-old Englishman who had ridden at least 4,670 winners in his long career, many more winners than any other jockey has ever ridden, received the first knighthood ever conferred on a jockey. That year, too, after having tried for twenty-seven years to win the Derby, he rode his first Derby winner, Pinza. The horse nosed out Aureole, owned by the newly crowned Queen Elizabeth II, who had knighted Sir Gordon a few days before as part of her coronation celebration.

The most fashionable race meeting of the year is the Royal Ascot, on Ascot Heath in Berkshire, around the second week in June. For that is the event traditionally honored by the presence of the Royal Family, who make a grand entrance and ride in state down the course in open landaus drawn by the famous Windsor Greys past the stands and the Royal Enclosure en route to the Royal Box. All in all the Royal Meeting at Ascot is a great day for top hats and pretty frocks, and, incidentally, a time of outstanding horse races. The trophy for the main event is the famous Gold Cup. The cash prize, based on today's money values, might be worth as much as $35,000. Ascot was founded by Queen Anne in 1711, the first meeting being held on August 11, 1711, when seven horses raced for a plate valued at approximately $150. It was not until William

IV ascended the throne, however, that the course came into its own. He introduced the Royal Procession, and Queen Victoria encouraged the tradition, which still prevails. Among the famous horses that have competed at Ascot were St. Simon, one of the great horses of the nineteenth century, who won the Gold Cup as a three-year-old in 1884. His son, Persimmon, won the Derby at Epsom in 1896, then copped the Gold Cup in 1897. Between that year and 1951 no horse duplicated that feat! Of course, there were no Royal Meetings during the two World Wars, but since the close of World War II there have been Ascot Heath meetings in addition to the Royal Meeting at Ascot. Normally they are held on the fifth day of the Royal Meeting in June, at the end of July and the end of September, and in mid-October.

The oldest racecourse in England is the Roodee, Chester. Horse races were held there as long ago as 1540, during the reign of Henry VIII. The Chester Cup, founded in 1824, is the only fixture there now. It is a handicap race of two miles, two furlongs, and seventy-seven yards run early in May.

Newmarket has been the headquarters of the turf since the reign of Charles II. During the flat-racing season there are eight meetings: the Craven Meeting, in mid-April; the First Spring Meeting early in May; the Second Spring Meeting two weeks later; the First and Second July Meetings; the First and Second October Meetings; and the Houghton Meeting in November.

Among the more important and fashionable race meetings in the north of England is the St. Leger, a classic for three-year-olds run in September on the Town Moor at Doncaster in Yorkshire over a mile and six furlongs. The famous Doncaster yearling sales are held annually in the mornings and evenings of the meet.

The flat-racing season comes to a close during the third week in November at Castle Irwell, Manchester, with the running of the mile-and-one-half November Handicap founded in 1876.

The first steeplechase on record is believed to have taken place in Ireland in 1752 when a Mr. Burke was challenged by a Mr. O'Cellaghan to a four-and-one-half-mile cross-country race from Buttevant Church to St. Leger Church. During the entire sprint the St. Leger church steeple served as a goal and guide, hence the term steeplechase. Sometime in the 1830's William Lynn, an innkeeper at Aintree, hit on the idea of leasing an area near his Waterloo Hotel for "a selling sweepstakes of 10 sovereigns each with 80 sovereigns added." He promoted that meet, and it was so successful that a second one, featuring a steeplechase, was arranged over the same course in 1839, with the town of Liverpool chipping in an added hundred sovereigns.

The world-famous Grand National Steeplechase staged on the Aintree Course, Liverpool, around the fourth week in March dates its origin from that hurdle race in 1839. It has been a handicap event since 1843, and is beyond a doubt the greatest and most spectacular steeplechase in the world today. The four-and-one-half-mile course over which it is run includes some very formidable fences, natural ditches, and a very sharp turn at the canal just before Valentine's Brook. Becher's Brook, too, provides a thrill for contestants as well as spectators because the fence is nearly six feet high, and the running brook below is nearly six feet wide. What is more, the landing side is about six feet lower than the take-off, so the horses actually fall nearly twelve feet after they have cleared the top of the fence. All told there are sixteen fences. Fourteen of them must be cleared twice as the horses complete two circuits. The all-time record-holder is a horse named Manifesto. He ran in eight races between 1895 and 1904. During that period he won twice, came in third three times, and finished fourth once!

The principal prize at the National Hunt Meeting at Cheltenham, where meets began around 1833, is the Cheltenham Gold Cup, run over a distance of three miles, two furlongs, early in March. Cash prizes are valued at approximately $6,000.

The name "point-to-point" was long ago given to that type of racing indulged in by amateurs who ride their hunters, which have been ridden to hounds throughout the season, across the open country from one point to another in friendly competitions to round off the hunting season between February and May. From vantage points on hillsides where most countryfolk view the contests, the races might seem unorganized. Nevertheless, they are conducted under rigid rules intended to safeguard the general public, owners, and riders.

In the years to come a few hundred American veterans of World War II will regale their grandchildren and cronies with stories of the time they saw Princess Elizabeth, now Queen Elizabeth II, and Princess Margaret Rose compete for the first time in any show. It happened in May, 1944, during the climactic period of preparation before the epic invasion of Europe by Allied troops. The occasion was the Royal Windsor Horse Show staged in connection with a "Wings for Victory Week" organized by the National Savings Movement to help that cause as well as War Registered Charities, and to entertain the public. King George VI and Queen Elizabeth, now Queen Mother, were there, and they beamed with parental pride as Princess Elizabeth with her sister as passenger competed in the class for best Single Private Driving Turnout, and took first prize driving a pony phaeton with "Hans," a purebred Norwegian dun in the shafts. The phaeton, itself, was a royal curiosity, having been built seventy years before for Queen Victoria to use in the grounds of Windsor Castle. Next the Princesses competed in the wartime Utility Driving Class.

Margaret held the reins that time and handled her dad's fell pony "Gypsy" so expertly she was awarded first prize, a silver cup that the King presented to her. By 1946 the annual show was so successful it was increased to two days, and it is now a three-day affair from Thursday through Saturday during the second week in May, as a rule. The show is staged in Home Park, with the gray stone walls of Windsor Castle and a grove of chestnut trees in the background. In 1948 a coaching marathon was introduced. In that event, after preliminary inspection a coach-and-four-in-hand is put on the road for a five-mile drive through Windsor before returning for final judging. Often other features include hackney and jumping classes for children's ponies, trade and agricultural turnouts, and a musical ride carried out by the Household Cavalry. In this spectacle a contingent of the Life Guards and the Royal Horse Guards (The Blues) in full-dress uniform parade to music provided by the excellent band of the Royal Horse Guards.

The International Horse Show, staged at White City for six days during the last week in July, might well be called a Royal show because the Royal Family has emphasized its keen interest in the affair ever since it was inaugurated around 1907 by awarding several exquisite trophies, which are among those most coveted by the international horsy set. The three principal prizes are the King George V Gold Cup, a handsomely wrought statuette of St. George slaying the dragon awarded to the supreme international jumping champion; the Edward, Prince of Wales Cup, given to the best international team of riders; and the Queen Elizabeth II Cup for the lady rider who jumps her horse over the difficult course fences with the least faults. Hundreds of horses from many countries converge on London to compete in approximately five dozen events. Many types of horses—the Arab, the child's pony, the cob, the hack, the hunter, and the aristocratic polos—participate. Even the little ponies and donkeys that pull the gaily painted carts of the costers, the pearl-buttoned, ostrich-plumed folk of London's East End, sometimes take part.

A new type of event for Britain is the Horse of the Year Show, the country's only indoor show. It was launched in 1949 at Harringay Arena, London, and has since been staged regularly early in October. To qualify for this unique competition, which is similar to some regional blue-ribbon shows in the United States, horses must accumulate points at smaller meets between May and September. This all-inclusive enterprise even admits the husky Clydesdale, Percheron, Shire, and Suffolk, those heavy work horses of Britain, arrayed in their honorable working dress. Pit ponies are led by their friends the miners, while other ponies demonstrate the work for which they were first intended: Shetland mares carry baskets of peat, and Highlands carry baskets of game. These and other lesser breeds prance proudly with the traditional show horses, the thoroughbred Arab, Hackney, and Shire, in the great Cavalcade of Horses that brings the exhibition to a dramatic close. The winner of the grand finale is quite properly recognized as the undisputed champion of the year.

Coursing

Authorities on coursing, the pursuit of game by dogs, are quick to point out that this field sport is among the most ancient of all, and that many of the forms and methods used as long ago as the second century are still in vogue. Nevertheless, it was not until the English became coursing enthusiasts during the reign of Queen Elizabeth I that the first authentic code of rules for judging the activities of greyhounds chasing hares was compiled. Those rules were in effect until about 1825, but since then many changes and new regulations have been introduced. The first coursing clubs were formed during the first

Elizabethan Age, the very first being founded by Lord Orford at Swaffham, in Norfolk, and for the past hundred years the chief prize of the coursing season between September and mid-February in England has been the Waterloo Cup. The Waterloo Cup Meet is also known as the Altcar Classic, because it has always been run on the Altcar estate of Lord Sefton, the site of the famous Altcar Coursing Club. The event is to coursing what the Derby is to horse racing. It has been copied by many countries, which is a fine tribute to its character, because the meet was launched very unpretentiously. In 1836 the proprietor of the Waterloo Hotel in Liverpool improvised an eight-dog stake that he styled the Waterloo Cup. Evidently he had a real genius for launching sports events that eventually became fixtures, because also in the 1830's as a promotion stunt in behalf of his hotel he promoted a sweepstakes for horses that developed into the world-famous Grand National Steeplechase on the Aintree Course, Liverpool. By a happy coincidence, the founder of the Waterloo Cup was the first winner. In 1837 the Cup was increased to sixteen runners, and in 1838 to thirty-two. The current sixty-four-dog stake was introduced in 1857. Now the running takes place usually in mid-February, when frost does not interfere, and lasts about three days. To win the Waterloo Cup a greyhound must defeat six opponents. The event has been run continuously since its inauguration, except during the two World Wars. Famous winners and the years they won include Master M'Grath, 1868, 1869, and 1871; Fullerton, half a win in 1889 since it divided the honor with another dog, and complete wins in 1890, 1891, and 1892, and Golden Seal in 1927. Golden Seal, a puppy not quite twenty months old, became the youngest dog ever to have won the Cup. In 1953 the prize went to Holystone Lifelong. The official time of the final was thirty-four seconds. However, the hare was even faster than the hound, escaping over the bank several jumps in the lead.

In the realm of dogdom sheep-dog trials attract the attention of town- and countryfolk alike during the summer months. The first trials were held around 1880, and today the principal ones in Great Britain are the English, the Scottish, and the Welsh, usually staged in August at different places each year, and the International in September, also at a different place each year. Although they are fascinating to watch, entertainment is not the main purpose of the trials. They are primarily utilitarian since the principal object is to test the capabilities of border collies used on large sheep farms for everyday work. The tests include gathering a small flock of sheep from a point about four hundred yards in front of the farmer or shepherd. To do that the dog guides the sheep in a more or less straight line, steers them round a post, then drives them diagonally to a pair of hurdles about two hundred yards away to the left. Between the hurdles is a gap through which the sheep must be passed, turned, and driven crosswise to another pair of hurdles about two hundred yards away, and then brought back to the shepherd, who, with his dog, directs the sheep into a small pen. Favorite sites for trials during July, August, and September are Aberdeen, Dunbar, Dunoon, Hayfield, Isle of Man, Keswick, Llandudno, and North Berwick, in July; Callandar, Denbigh, Helensburgh, Hathersage, Hope, Patterdale, and Rydal, in August; Bala, Llandovery, Longshaw, and Rhayader, in September.

Cruft's Great Dog Show at Olympia, London, around the second week in February was founded in 1886 by Charles Cruft. Since then it has become not only a meeting place for all breeds, but the premier dog show of Great Britain, and one of the foremost in the world. In 1953, the centenary of the birth of Mr. Cruft, a record number of 6,040 dogs were entered in 12,448 classes. The show filled the entire area of the Grand and National Halls of Olympia. What's more, the contestants were competing for big money in addition to the usual silver trophies, because a winner at Cruft's can be worth as much as $4,500. One fox-terrier puppy valued at $150 before entering the ring in 1948 brought $1,200 immediately after gaining the judges' decision.

A typical Briton's love for horses and dogs is matched only by his fondness for boats. Just mention "The Boat Race" to an Englishman, and the chances are he will know right off that you must mean the annual University Boat Race between crews from Cambridge and Oxford. That classic rowing event is staged annually on the river Thames from Putney to Mortlake, in the heart of London, usually late in March or early in April. The race is so popular that an estimated one million spectators line the riverbanks along the four-and-one-half-mile course to watch it. Meanwhile, the British Broadcasting Company not only describes every stroke and splash, but also records a description of the event for rebroadcast in forty languages! The initial contest between sweep swingers from the two senior universities in England grew out of a challenge issued by a Mr. Stanniforth of Christ Church College, Oxford, to a Mr. Snow, of St. John's College, Cambridge, in 1829. The first meet was staged at Henley, where the now-famous Henley Regatta takes place each year, and some 20,000 spectators are said to have witnessed it. The fixture was transferred to its present site in 1845. Two years before that, however, Oxford won at Henley with only seven men, instead of the customary nine. To perpetuate the memory of that triumph a part of the winning boat was made into a chair, which is still in use at Oxford. Through 1953, however, Cambridge won most of the races. The total at that time: Cambridge 53, Oxford 44, with 1 dead heat in 1877. Cambridge also holds the speed record for the course, having covered the distance in 17 minutes 50 seconds in 1948.

Thousands of sports-loving Americans who admittedly know little about rowing are well aware of the Henley Royal

Regatta. This super-social, four-day rowing event on the river Thames between Maidenhead and Reading, some thirty-five miles west of London, is usually staged during the first week in July. Yankee oarsmen have been taking part in it since 1872, when E. Smith, of New York, tried to capture the Diamond single sculls. He failed; but during the next eighty years other Americans have triumphed in that event, and also in four-oar and eight-oar contests. The first of several American crews since then to row to victory was a team from Columbia College in 1878. It won the Visitors' Trophy. In 1920 John B. Kelly, of Philadelphia, who had won the American single sculls crown for two years hand running, tried to enter the Henley single sculls competition, but was barred. Unofficially, it was intimated that he was rejected because a part-time bricklaying job he filled during vacation had given him a muscular advantage over his opponents. In 1946 his nineteen-year-old son John B. Kelly, Jr., entered the Diamond Sculls event, but was beaten in the finals. If he had won, he would have been the first to hold the triple crown of singles rowing, since he had already won the American and Canadian singles titles. It was a third Philadelphian named Joe Burk who established a mark for all contenders to shoot at by winning the Diamond in 1938 and 1939. In the 1938 contest his time of eight minutes, two seconds, set a record for the route. The Henley Royal Regatta, which dates to 1839, is an extension of the annual Wingfield Single Sculls competition inaugurated in 1830. The Wingfield is still staged, being one of the regular races on the Henley card. The most important event is the Grand Challenge Cup for eights. It was originated in 1839 and is open to all amateur rowing clubs. The Stewards Challenge Cup for coxswainless fours, introduced in 1841, is the premier four-oar event. The Diamond Challenge Sculls, which started in 1854, ranks third in importance with Britons; yet it is the favorite with foreigners who probably hold it in greater esteem than the Stewards Cup. The Silver Goblets for double sculls date to 1845. Other outstanding events include the Ladies' Challenge Plate for eights from British College Schools; the Thames Cup, which is attracting more and more entries from abroad, particularly the U.S.; the Visitors' Challenge Cup and the Wyfolds, both for coxswainless fours. Ordinarily the straightaway course of approximately a mile and one third is idyllic.

Headquarters for salt-water sailing in Britain is Cowes on the Isle of Wight where organized yacht racing began August 10, 1826. Cowes Week in August is still a major event in international yachting circles, with the Royal Corinthian Yacht Club, one of the world's very exclusive clubs, playing host.

Back in 1804 and 1805 when Napoleon threatened to invade England one of the defense works created to thwart the attack was the Royal Military Canal, which runs for some twenty-three miles from Seabrook, the eastern district of Hythe, to Rye, just over the Sussex border. Hythe is one of the Cinque Ports. The others are Dover, Hastings, Romney, and Sandwich. To celebrate the fiftieth anniversary of the invasion that did not come off the people of Hythe in 1854 put the canal to a frivolous use by staging their first Venetian Fete. Since then the celebration has been staged frequently in mid-August. It is the only event of its kind in aquatic-minded Britain, and when it is held, some 25,000 visitors loll in comfort on the banks of the placid, tree-lined canal while some three dozen gaily decorated boats float serenely by. One year the open section for tableau boats depicted scenes from Kentish history, "the county where history started." Entries in the floral section emphasized Kent's position as the Garden of England. There were humorous sections, too, and a number of illuminated boats that competed for special prizes. The Corporation of Hythe Challenge Trophy, a small silver replica of a galley, is awarded to the boat judged best exhibit in the festival.

Britons are also very motor-conscious. Their activities in the field of sport and pleasure driving have been prodigious for almost a century. For example, we take pretty much for granted the freedom of the roads enjoyed by automobiles in England as well as the rapid transit those vehicles provide there. Yet both freedom and speed were achieved only after a tedious thirty-year battle that began soon after Parliament passed the ultraconservative Locomotive Act of 1865. It ended with the repeal of the act on midnight, November 13, 1896. The memory of the nation-wide celebration that marked the end of that long-drawn-out fight is kept green by the Royal Automobile Club each November 14, when it sponsors the restaging of one of the high lights of the first Emancipation Day, the historic ride from London to Brighton, which turned out to be the first motor trial ever held in England. Probably there would have been no need for either a fight or the subsequent celebration if those who wished to perpetuate the horse and buggy age had not incorporated into the act such restrictive measures as limiting the speed of vehicles to two miles per hour, causing each car to be preceded by a man carrying a red flag in order to warn people that a dangerous vehicle was approaching, and making it mandatory for the automobile to stop instantly if signaled to do so by persons on horseback or in carriages. No wonder the British motorists campaigned to repeal the Locomotive Act!

On November 14, 1896, the emancipated motorists started out from London for Brighton about 10:30 A.M. after symbolically tearing up the accursed red flag. The parade was led by a pilot car, but apparently it went too slowly to satisfy the ancestors of today's hot-rodders who were anxious to see what their buggies could do, because when the pilot car stopped at Brixton to cool off many of the others did not. They shot past the parked pilot and continued on to Brighton nonstop, accelerators pressed to the floor, or wherever accelerators were pressed to in those days. The annual jaunt has become known as the Veteran Car Run, limited to cars built before the end of 1904. It is not to be confused with a race or contest, because now the ancient autos travel at a set speed over a specified route.

Motor trials have changed a lot since the first one was staged between London and Brighton on November 14, 1896. Now Ulster, the most northerly of the four provinces of Northern Ireland, and the Isle of Man are the favorite meeting places for devotees of trials as well as auto races in Britain, because they are the two remaining areas where sections of the public roads can be closed off and converted into race tracks or circuits. Among the new developments of this kind is the approximately 7.5 miles long Dundrod Circuit on the outskirts of Belfast. It has been described by racing enthusiasts as "potentially the finest road-racing circuit in all Europe." It is the home of the Tourist Trophy Race, around the third week in September. That world-famous open-road race was sponsored by the Royal Automobile Club for the first time in 1905, and since its inception has been an excellent proving ground for production models of European cars, just as the Memorial Day Speed Classic at Indianapolis, Indiana, has been the principal public testing place for American models.

At Douglas, on the Isle of Man, the biggest postwar motorcar racing events have been the British Empire Trophy and Manx Cup Car races on the circuit that measures approximately 3.83 miles. They are organized by the British Racing Drivers Club, and usually take place in mid-June. Since 1948 the first big international racing meet of the season has taken place on Easter Monday at Goodwood, a circuit 2.4 miles long on the Duke of Richmond's private property at Chichester, Sussex. Other important British circuits are the one with a lap length of 3.2 miles at St. Helier, Jersey, and Silverstone, about sixty miles northwest of London, where the perimeter track is approximately three miles. The approximately two dozen racing and speed events on the British calendar include the Goodwood Meeting in April; the Silverstone, Dundrod, Brands Hatch, Goodwood, and Boreham Meetings in May; the Empire Trophy and Bo'ness and Prescott Hill Climbs in June; the Rest-and-be-thankful Climb, Jersey Road Race, British Grand Prix, and Bouley Bay Hill Climb in July; the Boreham, Brands Hatch, and Charterhall Meetings, and Goodwood nine-hour race, in August, and the Brighton Speed Trials, Tourist Trophy Race, Brands Hatch Meeting, and Goodwood Meeting in September. The British Grand Prix inaugurated in 1948 is usually run at Silverstone during the third week in July. It is one of ten major events that contribute points to the world championship. The others are: Argentina, Belgium, France, Germany, Holland, Indianapolis Speedway, Italy, Spain, and Switzerland.

Laws forbidding racing on public highways in England, Scotland, and Wales, or the closing of roads for such purposes in those countries, apply to motorcycles as well as to automobiles. So the International Tourist Trophy Motorcycle Race, inaugurated in 1907 to develop stamina in motorcycles when the industry was just gaining headway, has been installed on the Isle of Man and is usually staged around the first week in June. The present Shaefell Mountain Circuit, where the races were held for the first time in 1911, is almost 38 miles around the tiny Manx island in the Irish Sea. The course has many hazards, and within a space of seven miles it climbs from sea level at Ramsey to 1,400 feet by way of the shoulder of Staefell. There are races for juniors and seniors. The fastest average prewar speed for a senior race was 89.38 miles per hour for seven laps, or 264 miles. The record for the 38-mile lap was 91 miles per hour.

Even greater speeds are attained by daredevil motorcyclists of many nations who take part in the Ulster Grand Prix, the premier event in the calendar of Irish motorcycling competitions at Clady Circuit about six miles from Belfast, Northern Island, during the third week in August. The speed record over the prewar 246-mile course was an average 97.85 miles per hour, one lap being covered at 100.03 miles per hour. Since the war the contests have been staged on a shorter course. The initial meet in 1922 was over a modest 20½-mile route. The size of the circuit and the international importance of the race grew considerably until the outbreak of World War II. Now the Ulster Grand Prix is one of six races that comprise the world championship series. Five other events at which races in Europe accumulate points in competition for the championship of the world are the Belgian Grand Prix, the Dutch T.T., Italy's Grand Prix of the Nations, the Isle of Man T.T., and the Swiss Grand Prix.

The Scots tend to excel in a variety of athletic contests such as tossing the caber, hammer throw, and shot-put, and those skills are displayed at Highland games. The Highland games, a feature of gatherings that are basically home-coming festivals, have been taking place in Scottish Highland towns and villages during August and September for centuries. They are good examples, too, of how an idea for a specific type of festival can spread from country to country, be enlarged upon, and survive for centuries. For example, the sports programs of the Scottish gatherings offer such well-organized contests in wholesome athletics intended to encourage the development of chivalry, independence, skill, and strength that they have frequently been compared with the ancient Greek games. In turn, the home-coming aspects of the Highland games inspired Governor Frank West Rollins, of New Hampshire, to introduce the famous Old Home Week to his state, and to the rest of America as well, in 1899.

To many Scots the Highland games are the most important festivals of the year. The greatest of them all, the Royal Brae-

mar Gathering in the little village of Braemar during the first
week in September, is practically a national holiday in Scotland. To date Braemar has had the patronage of six reigning
sovereigns, beginning with Queen Victoria. Often the Royal
Family in summer residence at nearby Balmoral on Upper
Deeside enlivens the proceedings by holding court for a few
hours in the presence of thousands of their subjects on the
Braes o' Mar. As a rule the Royal party arrives at Princess
Royal Park at about 3:00 P.M., and the Royal Standard is
hoisted on the Royal Pavilion immediately. That is usually
the sign for the assembled motorists to honk their horns in
greeting. Like the thousands of natives and visitors, the Royal
Family thrills to the three main features of any gathering:
dancing and piping and athletic contests by amateurs and
professionals. The cream of the nation's crop of dancers and
pipers in particular assemble at Braemar for the competitions,
and often a hundred or more pipers serenade members of the
Royal Family in the historic Green Arena. In 1953 orchestral
concerts and art exhibitions were added to the program.

Since 1950 the Isle of Skye, the largest island in the Hebrides, has been welcoming its wandering sons and daughters
with a home-coming week late in May or early in June. The
skirl of the pipes provides the theme music, and leading events
now include Highland games, piping competitions, sheep-dog
trials, a garden party, country dancing, exhibitions of home
weaving, and a *feill,* which is Gaelic for a fair or market.

The Royal Tournament, which is usually staged at Earl's
Court, London, for about three weeks in June, is supposed to
have received its start as a stopgap performance back in 1878
when marksmen from all parts of Britain assembled on Wimbledon to shoot for the Queen's Prize. In order to keep the
contestants occupied and physically fit for the shoot, a group
of officers organized a pageant. It took root almost immediately, grew rapidly, and now draws capacity crowds. The pa-

trons see trick riding; physical training displays; musical rides of the Household Cavalry and the King's Troop, Royal Horse Artillery; pike drill by the Honourable Artillery Company; jumping for the King's and Prince of Wales' Cups; and even demonstration jumps from the roof of the building by Royal Air Force paratroopers!

Interest in firearms and marksmanship might well be second nature with people who love sports as much as the British do. As a rule in mid-July they get an opportunity to show what crack shots they are at the annual meet of the National Rifle Association, Bisley Camp, Brookwood, Woking, Surrey. Shotguns, large- and small-bore pistols, military and sporting rifles are used, and the meet embraces many types of shooting, including military fire with movement, rapid, and snap shooting. Revolver events include contests similar to the Olympic Silhouette Competition. The main rifle event is H.M. the Queen's Prize, open only to subjects of the Queen.

Aviation

The fact that the British Royal Aero Club was founded in 1901, two years before the Americans Orville and Wilbur Wright made the first successful airplane flights at Kill Devil Hill near Kitty Hawk, North Carolina, on December 17, 1903, should be proof enough that the British have a vested interest in aviation. However, the club took its own sweet time about sponsoring air meets, waiting until 1922 to launch the British National Air Races. To show his approval of the project King George V gave the King's Cup from his own silver. That trophy has become the prize most coveted by British sporting and private pilots, and the race for it over a sixty-mile course is the crowning event of the annual National, which usually takes place around June 20 at a different airport each year. The contest is limited to twelve British starters who qualify for the honor by winning one of the first four places in the Grosvenor Challenge Cup Race, the Norton-Griffiths Challenge Trophy Race, or the Kemsley Challenge Trophy Race staged earlier in the meet. Each of the three races is flown over three laps of a ten-mile course, and thus far each has been restricted to machines not exceeding 3,858 pounds in weight at take-off.

In 1916 British aviation enthusiasts and technicians founded the Society of British Aircraft Constructors. Their enterprise resulted in the formation of the Royal Aircraft Establishment at Farnborough, Hampshire, where the annual Flying Display and Exhibition usually takes place during the second week in September. The event was inaugurated in 1932, discontinued during World War II, and revived in 1947. Although the exhibition lasts about a week it is open to the public only during the last two or three days because originally it was intended for buyers only. On a single day during the 1953 show 155,000 visitors went to Farnborough in 20,000 vehicles. The total attendance for the three public days that year was 315,000, a new record. The people went to see about fifty different types of aircraft, two-thirds of which were powered by turbo-jet or air-screw turbine engines. A dramatic example of the great progress that aviation has made in the western world since the first machine took to the air exactly fifty years before was the model of a projected continental jet air liner, the HP97. It will have two decks and will be capable of carrying up to 150 passengers over long distances at almost sonic speed. It could fly from New York to London with 122 passengers in 6½ hours, and from London to New York with 117 passengers in 7½ hours, prevailing winds determining the elapsed time of the flight and number of passengers to be carried. Also there was the Saunders-Roe Princess flying-boat powered by ten prop-jet engines and capable of carrying 250 troops; Britain's first delta-wing bomber, the four-jet Avro 698, and a model of Britain's first gas turbine-powered passenger-carrying helicopter, the forty-seat Fairey Rotodyne, which combined features of the rotary wing and conventional fixed-wing aircraft. It could cruise at almost 200 miles per hour, which is well above the present world record for helicopters. The visitors also watched planes whiz through the sky and dive at speeds greater than the speed of sound. The stars of the show were Britain's intrepid test pilots, among them Squadron Leader Neville Duke, one of the best in the world. Whenever Mr. Duke and his colleagues crashed the sound barrier, their achievement was made known by the now familiar sonic booms that always announce the attainment of supersonic speeds. As one British reporter described the planes that make that noise: "Like gentlemen, they knock before entering!" Actually, the bangs are believed to be caused when the nose, then the wings, then the tail of the plane pierce the barrier. That can happen at speeds between 650 and 760 miles per hour, depending on the altitude, because while sound normally travels 760 miles per hour at sea level, it can slow down to 650 miles per hour at higher altitudes. Throughout the fall of 1953, world speed records for sustained flight in standard planes fell like autumn leaves. Over England a British Hawker Hunter flew 727.6 miles per hour, then a British Supermarine Swift flew 737.3 miles per hour. Next a U.S. Navy Douglas F4D Skyray averaged 753.4 miles per hour on four passes over Southern California, and on November 20, Scott Crossfield, a thirty-two-year-old American research pilot of the National Advisory Committee for Aeronautics, flew 1,327 miles per hour in a Douglas D-558-II Skyrocket over Edwards Air Force Base, Muroc, California. He was the first person to fly twice the speed of sound.

The brightest red-letter days on Britain's aviation calendar are those that designate Battle of Britain Week, the third week in September. The day of days is Battle of Britain Day, September 15, anniversary of that glorious hour in 1940 when British airmen repulsed the hordes of invading German planes in perhaps the most decisive air battle of World War II. The Germans lost fifty-six planes; the British "under forty." In his tribute to the stamina and valor of the fighter pilots who passed that severe test Prime Minister Winston Churchill told the House of Commons: "Never in the field of human conflict was so much owed by so many to so few." In 1953 the occasion was marked by the first all-jet fly-past when 252 jet planes took part. It was all-jet except for the place of honor at the head of the flight, which was reserved for a Hurricane and a Spitfire, symbols of the famous fighters that won the Battle of Britain. Anniversary colour-hoisting and parades at Royal Air Force stations often attract at least a million visitors.

Holidays

It is important that visitors to Great Britain know the Bank Holidays there because on those days everything closes up tighter than the skin on a grape. Lord Avebury's Bank Holidays Act, 1871, established the list of holidays on which banks shall be closed in England and Ireland: Easter Monday; Monday in Whitsun Week, Whit Sunday being the seventh Sunday after Easter; the first Monday in August, and December 26, if it is a weekday, or the twenty-seventh if the twenty-sixth is on a Sunday. Ireland also observes March 17, St. Patrick's Day. In Scotland the official bank holidays are Christmas and New Year's Day, if they fall on a weekday, otherwise in each instance the next following Monday is observed; Good Friday; the first Monday of May, and the first Monday of August.

Traditional Festivals

On Shrove Tuesday, the day before Ash Wednesday and the beginning of Lent, a famous pancake race that is believed to date at least from 1445 gets under way at Olney, Buckinghamshire, when the "pancake bells" of the church warn the contestants, first, that it is time to start frying their pancakes, then to assemble by the pump in the market square for the start of the race. At the sound of the third bell all the competitors start off. They race along a quarter-mile course to the church, flipping pancakes merrily as they run. The cakes must be tossed at least twice while being raced along the street, and once coming up the church path at the end of the 415-yard course. The custom is said to have started more than five hundred years ago when a woman of Olney was so late for church she raced through the streets still carrying a skillet and a sizzling pancake. Today as many as 10,000 spectators watch the feat, while in Liberal, Kansas, another 10,000 persons watch a similar stunt, and the results of the two races are compared. In 1953 Mrs. Isabel Dix, of Olney, England, covered the distance in a record 1 minute, 7.2 seconds, whereas in Liberal, Kansas, Mrs. Walter Dick flipped her pancake over the finish line in 1 minute and 9 seconds. Even though she lost the international contest Mrs. Dick received $350 and a pressure cooker.

Mothers have been remembered on their own special day in Britain for centuries, the very first such festivals being staged in pagan times to honor the Mother of the Gods. As long ago as the seventeenth century Robert Herrick, the English poet, wrote: "I'le to thee a Simnell bring, 'Gainst thou go'st a mothering so that, when she blesseth thee, half that blessing thou'lt give to me." Now Mothering Sunday is the fourth Sunday in Lent, usually in March.

A famous distribution of largess during Lent is known far and wide as the Tichborne Dole. It began in 1150 and takes place annually at Alresford, Hampshire, on Lady Day, March 25. In compliance with the deathbed wish of Lady Mabel in 1150, the head of the Tichborne family still makes a gift of one gallon of flour for each adult and half a gallon for each child to every resident of the village of Alresford. That came about because Lady Mabel's husband agreed to give to the poor each year the value of the acres she could encompass while holding a flaming torch. Despite the fact that she was gravely ill when she extracted this promise from Lord Tichborne, she managed to crawl around twenty-three acres. To ensure that the bargain would be kept after her death she proffered a curse on the house of Tichborne if it was not kept. The curse provided that if the dole were not given seven daughters would be born, and the house of Tichborne would fall. In 1794, after the wish had been fulfilled continuously for 644 years, the dole was stopped. Seven daughters were born and the house fell. The dole was soon reinstated and continues to this day. During the period of bread rationing in World War II special permission for an allocation of flour for this purpose was granted by the Government.

It is quite a coincidence that three anniversaries important in the history of England should fall on April 23. On that date, in 1564, William Shakespeare was born at Stratford-on-Avon, and on the same date in 1616, his fifty-second birthday, he died there. On April 23, 304, St. George, the patron saint of England, is believed to have been martyred during the early stages of the ten-year persecution of Christians by Diocletian, the Roman Emperor. The saint became a favorite with Englishmen who took part in the early Crusades when he is said to have come to their rescue at Antioch near the end of the eleventh century. When Richard I returned home from the Crusades he popularized the cult of St. George, and later the Council of Oxford ordained that the date of his martyrdom and death should be held as a national festival. However, it was not until the middle of the fourteenth century, during the reign of Edward III, that he became the patron saint of England. The anniversary is marked by a memorial and greeting ceremony by the Knights of the Order of St. Michael and

St. George in St. Paul's Cathedral, London. Also, at Windsor Castle the sovereign takes the salute at the annual St. George's Day parade by the King's Scouts and holders of scout gallantry awards, which follows the national scout service in the St. George's Chapel at the castle.

The advent of spring, summer, autumn, and winter probably inspired the very first festivals ever staged by man. One of the ancient observances of such perennial festivities is at Stonehenge, on Salisbury Plain, Wiltshire, in the south of England, where the Druids, a Celtic priesthood, are said to have met in the oak groves some four thousand years before Christ was born. The contemporary group, which follows the Rite of Mount Haemus, "inheritors of the Ancient Faith," was organized in 1245 by Philip Prydod and named after Haymo of Faversham, who did much to preserve the doctrine.

Today the changes of seasons are celebrated at Stonehenge by the General Council of An Druid Uileach Braithreachas (The Druid Universal Bond) with such ceremonies as the lighting of the twin fires of Beltane and Samhain to mark the universal resurrection of spring, the vernal equinox, on March 21; the midsummer ritual of Caevron (Light) on June 24; harvesttime observances around the time of the autumnal equinox on September 22; and the blessing of the mistletoe "and the heralding of the Birth of the Eternal Child (The Word), the Mabin of the Druid System," late in December if not on December 22. But the most elaborate of all is the midsummer fete when an annual pilgrimage is made by the membership "to maintain unbroken, the link with the ancients, and for the special intention of receiving inspiration and guidance from The Great Arch-Druid, God, The Ancient of the Days, from Whom the Blessed Awen (Knowledge of the Life of The Spirit), was received in the Light of the Dawning Creation." An Druid Uilecah Braithreachas is believed to be the only Druid Order that has carried out these rites in Stonehenge in June, within living memory. The ritual begins at sunrise, about 4:30 A.M. The Druid bards, dressed in white and purple robes and carrying hooked staffs as symbols of their faith, file into the circle. As the first rays of the sun shine on the altar the Druid sacrament is administered, and the Chief Druid offers up a solemn prayer of worship and thanksgiving. The ceremony is public. All are invited.

A more modern custom, redolent of the spirit of democracy, is also observed on June 24, Midsummer Day, when the citizens of the old City of London—that square mile which starts at Ludgate Hill and includes St. Paul's Cathedral, the Bank and the business district—assemble in the Guildhall to elect sheriffs and officers for the ensuing civil year. There are two sheriffs of the City of London, and they have been elected for many centuries by members of the livery of the guilds. Such companies derive their name from the assumption of a distinctive dress, or livery, by their members in the fourteenth century. Some ten thousand liverymen who belong to about seventy-nine guilds still in existence are entitled to vote at elections in Common Hall. Extinct now are such once prominent guilds as the combmakers, fishermen, longbow string makers, silk-throwers, starch makers, and woodmongers. A master of prime warden is also elected annually, and on September 29, St. Michael's Day, the Lord Mayor of London is elected by the aldermen.

Another landmark in the history of parliamentary rule in Great Britain is the Tynwald Parliament, which has been the legislature of the Isle of Man for more than a thousand years. It consists of the Governor and Council and the House of Keys. The annual open meeting at St. John's during the first week in July includes a civic and ecclesiastical procession to historic Tynwald Hill, where all sit around in tiers. The bills passed by both bodies are read to the assemblage in English as well as Manx and become the laws of the island.

One of the most memorable, albeit villainous characters in the folklore of England is Guy Fawkes, who played such a big part in the Gunpowder Plot to blow up the House of Lords in 1605. To this day celebrations still take place throughout the country on Guy Fawkes Day, November 5. Typical of the festivities are the torchlight procession and display of horrific guys at Bridgewater, Somerset; the fireworks display and conflagrations at Edenbridge, Kent; a tableau at Lingfield, Sussex, and the traditional burning of boats at Rye, Sussex.

The year in Great Britain, as in other predominantly Christian countries, draws to a close during the happy festival of Christmas. In Britain that means carol singing and burning the yule log.

The exact dates on which festivals will take place in Great Britain, as well as the latest travel information pertaining to that country, may be obtained by writing to the British Travel Centers: 336 Madison Avenue, New York 17, New York; 90 Adelaide Street West, Toronto, Ontario, Canada.

Bank Holidays established by Lord Avebury's Bank Holidays Act, 1871: Easter Monday; Whitmonday, fifty days after Easter; the first Monday in August; December 25; and December 26, if it is a weekday, or December 27 if December 26 is on a Sunday. Northern Ireland also observes March 17, St. Patrick's Day. In Scotland: January 1; Good Friday; the first Monday in May; the first Monday in August; Christmas. If Christmas and New Year's Day fall on Sundays, the following Mondays are observed.

Chronological list of events in Great Britain:

JANUARY. Harrogate: toy, fancy goods fair. London: Bertram Mills Circus, December, January; Changing of the Guard, Buckingham or St. James's Palace, every forty-eight hours throughout the year; folk dance, song festival; mounting of the Guard, at Whitehall daily throughout the year; National Schoolboys' Own Exhibition. Nationwide: Rugby football, to April.

FEBRUARY. Altcar: Waterloo Cup Meeting, the Blue Riband of coursing. King's Lynn: fair. London: British Ciné, Photographic

Show; Cruft's Dog Show. Nationwide: point-to-point horse races, to May.

FEBRUARY or MARCH. Mother's Day: nationwide, fourth Sunday in Lent. Shrove Tuesday Pancake Race: Olney.

MARCH. Aintree, Liverpool: Grand National Steeplechase. Alresford: Tichborne Dole. Banbury: arts, crafts festival. Bournemouth: flower show. Cheltenham: Cheltenham Gold Cup, hunt meeting event; national hunt meeting. Edinburgh: Calcutta Cup, rugby match, at Edinburgh, or Twickenham. Harrogate: music festival. Lincoln: Lincolnshire Handicap, horse race. London: Ideal Home Show. Nationwide: flat racing, to November; Lady Day, March 25. Stonehenge: Druid spring ritual. Stratford: Shakespeare Festival, through October. Twickenham: Calcutta Cup, rugby match, at Twickenham, or Edinburgh.

MARCH or APRIL. Auto-racing season opens Easter Monday: Goodwood. University Boat Race, or the Boat Race, Cambridge vs. Oxford: London.

APRIL. A different place each year: English Amateur Golf Championship. Birmingham: British Industries' Fair, also at London, to mid-May. Blackpool: hockey festival. Bournemouth: British Hard-Court Tennis Championship. Buxton: one-act play festival. Epsom: flat meeting. Folkestone: hockey festival. Glasgow: Scottish Football Cup Final. London: British Industries' Fair, also at Birmingham, to mid-May; British table tennis finals; London-Stratford-Penzance, auto, motorcycle test run. Lowestoft: hockey festival. Morecambe: music festival. Nationwide: cricket, to autumn; St. George's Day, April 23. Newington: blessing cherry orchards in bloom. Newmarket: Craven Meeting, horse racing. Newry: feis, festival. Paignton: hockey festival. Scarborough: hockey festival. Stratford: Shakespeare's birthday festival, April 23; Shakespeare Festival, through October. Wembley: Football Association Amateur Cup Final; Rugby League Cup Final.

MAY. A different place each year: British Amateur Golf Championship. Bath: Bath Assembly, festival of arts. Belfast: feis, festival; Royal Ulster Agricultural Show; Ulster hard-court championship. Birmingham: British Industries' Fair, also at London, April, May. Boreham: auto races. Brands Hatch: auto races. Chester: Chester Cup, horse race, at the Roodee. Dundrod Circuit: Ulster Trophy, auto race. Goodwood: auto races. Hastings: music festival. Helston: Flora Day. Isle of Skye: Skye Week. London: British

Industries' Fair, also at Birmingham, April, May; Cart Horse Parade, Regents Park; Chelsea Flower Show; Chestnut Sunday, when chestnut trees are in full bloom; Fashion Fortnight. Minehead: May Week. Nationwide: croquet, to October. Newmarket: First, Second Spring Meetings, horse racing. Pitlochry: drama festival. Silverstone: auto races. Stratford: Shakespeare Festival, through October; steeplechase. Windsor: Royal Windsor Horse Show. Warwick: music festival. Wembley: Football Association Cup Final.

JUNE. A different place each year: British National Air Races, including the King's Cup Air Race; Royal Counties Agricultural Show; Scottish Professional Golf Championship; Welsh Professional Golf Championship. Aldeburgh: music, arts festival. Alloa: Royal Highland Agricultural Show. Ascot: Royal Ascot Meet, horse racing. Bath: Bath and West and Southern Counties Agricultural Show. Bridport: Royal Charter Pageant. Cheltenham: British Contemporary Music Festival. Douglas, Isle of Man: British Empire Trophy auto race, and Manx Cup auto race. Epsom Downs: The Derby, horse race; The Oaks, horse race. Glasgow: Yachting Fortnight, Firth of Clyde. Glyndebourne: opera festival, through July. Hereford: Three Counties Agricultural Show. Isle of Man: Tourist Trophy motorcycle races. Lisburn: Ulster Derby, horse race. London: Antique Dealers' Fair; Election of sheriffs, officers, for City of London, Guildhall, June 24; Greyhound Derby Finals; Royal Tournament; Trooping the Colour. Pitlochry: drama festival. Richmond: Royal Horse Show. St. Ives: music, drama festival. Scotland: Bo'ness Hill Climb, for autos. Stonehenge: Druid midsummer ritual. Stratford: Shakespeare Festival, through October. Wimbledon: All-England Lawn Tennis Championships, into July.

JULY. A different place each year: British Open Golf Championship; Irish Open Golf Championship; Northern Ireland Open Amateur Golf Championship; Scottish Amateur Golf Championship. Aberdeen: sheep-dog trials. Barnstaple: Taw and Torridge Festival of Arts, also at Bideford. Bideford: Taw and Torridge Festival of Arts, also at Barnstaple. Bisley: National Rifle Association Meeting. Blackpool: Royal Agricultural Society of England Show. Camphill, Great Hucklow: gliding championships. Canterbury: Canterbury Festival, to mid-August. Cardiff: Royal Welsh Agricultural Show. Dunbar: sheep-dog trials. Dunoon: sheep-dog trials. Glyndebourne: opera festival, June, July. Haslemere: Festival of Early Music. Hayfield: sheep-dog trials. Henley-on-Thames: Henley Royal Regatta. Isle of Jersey: Bouley Bay Hill Climb for autos. Isle of Man: sheep-dog trials; Tynwald Parliament. King's Lynn: festival. Llandudno: sheep-dog trials. Llangollen: International Music Eisteddfod. London: American pilgrimage, Boston–London; International Horse Show. Newmarket: First, Second July Meetings, horse races. North Berwick: sheepdog trials. Pitlochry: drama festival. St. Helier: Jersey auto road race. Scarborough: professional lawn-tennis tournament. Scotland: Rest-and-be-thankful Climb for autos. Silverstone: British Grand Prix auto race. Stratford: Shakespeare Festival, through October. Wimbledon: All-England Lawn Tennis Championships, June, July. Windsor: Royal Windsor Rose Show.

AUGUST. A different place each year: British bike championships; English National Sheep-Dog Trials; National Eisteddfod of Wales; Scottish National Sheep-Dog Trials; Welsh National Sheep-Dog Trials. Belfast: Ulster Grand Prix motorcycle race at Clady Circuit. Brands Hatch: auto races. Boreham: auto races. Callandar: sheep-dog trials. Canterbury: Canterbury Festival, July, August. Charterhall: auto races. Denbigh: sheep-dog trials. Edinburgh: Edinburgh Festival, to mid-September. Goodwood: auto races. Hathersage: sheep-dog trials. Helensburgh: sheep-dog trials. Hope: sheep-dog trials. Hythe: Venetian Fete. Isle of Wight: Cowes Week, yachting. London: Model Engineer Exhibition. Oban: regatta. Patterdale: sheep-dog trials. Pitlochry: drama festival. Rydal: sheep-dog trials. Scotland: Highland gatherings, games. Shrewsbury: music, floral festival. Southport: flower show. Stratford: folk-dance festival; Shakespeare Festival, through October. Torbay: yachting fortnight. Wales: United Counties Show.

SEPTEMBER. A different place each year: Curtis Cup, golf match, even years; International Sheep-Dog Trials; Irish Amateur Close Golf Championship; National Brass Bands Championships; Welsh Amateur Golf Championship. Abbotts Bromley: horn dance. Aboyne: Highland gathering. Bala: sheep-dog trials. Birmingham: horse show. Braemar: Royal Braemar Highland Gathering. Brands Hatch: auto races. Brighton: auto races; industries' show. Cardiff: Welsh Industries' Fair. Cheltenham: Chrysanthemum show. Devon: steeplechase. Doncaster: The St. Leger, horse race. Dundrod: Tourist Trophy auto race. Edinburgh: Edinburgh

Festival, August, September; Royal Caledonian Flower Show. Exeter: flower show; steeplechase. Farnborough: Flying Display, Exhibition. Folkestone: steeplechase. Gloucester: Three Choirs Festival, every third year; other years at Worcester, Hereford. Goodwood: auto races. Guernsey: Battle of Flowers, water carnival. Harrogate: flower, horse show. Hastings: cricket festival. Hereford: Three Choirs Festival, every third year; other years at Gloucester, Worcester. Isle of Man: Manx Grand Prix auto race. Leamington Spa: women's open bowls tournament. Lichfield: steeplechase. Llandovery: sheep-dog trials. London: auto show, September or October. Longshaw: sheep-dog trials. Nationwide: Battle of Britain Day, September 15; most impressive celebration in London; Battle of Britain Week, week high-lighted by September 15; soccer or association football, to April. Oban: Argyllshire Highland Gathering. Pitlochry: drama festival. Prescot: auto races. Preston: Royal Lancashire Agricultural Show. Rhayader: sheep-dog trials. Romsey: agricultural, horse show. Ryde: Carnival on Isle of Wight. Scarborough: Angling festival; cricket festival; motorcycle races. Scotland: Highland gatherings, games. Silverstone: motorcycle races. Southwell: steeplechase. Stonehenge: Druid autumn ritual. Stratford: Shakespeare Festival, through October. Wimbledon: Great Britain Junior Tennis Championship. Worcester: Three Choirs Festival, every third year; other years at Hereford, Gloucester.

OCTOBER. A different place each year: *An Comunn Gaidhealach,* or Gaelic Mod; Ryder Cup, golf match, odd years; Walker Cup, golf match, odd years. Ascot: horse races. Birmingham: dog show. Cheltenham: Festival of Contemporary Literature. Edinburgh: Royal Caledonian Chrysanthemum Show. Harrogate: drama festival. Hastings: Open International Angling Festival. Lichfield: music, drama festival. London: antiquities, fine arts fair; dairy show; Horse of the Year Show; international dance festival; auto show, September or October. Morecambe: dance festival. Nationwide: steeplechases, into May. Newmarket: First, Second October Meetings, horse races; Houghton Meeting, horse races. Pitlochry: drama festival. Stratford: Shakespeare Festival. Torquay: British National Covered Courts Tennis Open.

NOVEMBER. A different place each year: national plowing championship. Deal: Sea Anglers' Festival. Great Yarmouth: Open Sea Angling Festival. Hereford: cattle show. London: bike, motorcycle show; Emancipation Day, Veteran Car Run, London-Brighton; Lord Mayor's Show; National Poultry, Cage Birds Show; Shoe, Leather Fair. Manchester: November Handicap, horse race. Nationwide: Guy Fawkes Day, November 5.

DECEMBER. Birmingham: racing pigeon show. London: Bertram Mills Circus, through January; Chelsea Arts Ball; National Cat Club Show; Smithfield Show. Nationwide: Boxing Day, December 26. Stonehenge: Druid Blessing of the Mistletoe.

GREECE

MOST ANNUAL celebrations in modern Greece spring from rites of the Greek Orthodox Church. Second to such religious festivals are the stage dramas, pageants, and folk dances amid the ruins of ancient amphitheaters, in a valiant attempt to keep alive the artistry for which that land has long been famous.

Religious Festivals

The Greek Orthodox Church traces the spread of Christianity throughout Europe and the western world from the time St. Paul landed in Greece in 51 A.D. The evangelistic trail he blazed through the land was recorded in the Acts of the Apostles, and today the faithful may follow the route of St. Paul by going to Neapolis (Cavalla), Philippi, Barroea (Verria), Salonika, Crete, Rhodes, Corinth, and Athens. One of St. Paul's first sermons is believed to have been delivered while he stood on a rock in the shadow of the Acropolis.

Today there are at least a dozen observances throughout the year which are purely religious, or have religious overtones.

To the Greeks Epiphany is Theophania, God's appearance at
the Baptism of Christ. It is celebrated on January 6 in Angli-
can, Eastern Christian, and Roman Catholic churches. To the
ceremony the Greeks have added a water phase that symbolizes
the baptism of Christ by John the Baptist, so in port towns
particularly there are usually processions from the church to
nearby bodies of water where a priest tosses a wooden, silver,
or golden cross into the water and men dive for it. The one
who retrieves the cross receives a special blessing. Many Americans have seen the ritual performed in Tarpon Springs, Flor-
ida, and New York City, where there are many persons of
Greek descent.

On March 25 and again on August 15 there are pilgrimages
to the Tenos Island where a miraculous icon of the Virgin's
Annunciation is believed to heal incurable diseases. Even government officials and other dignitaries make the trip by ships
of the Royal Hellenic Navy. In fact, the trek on August 15,
Feast of the Assumption of the Virgin, is so popular that tourists are urged to obtain berths on the ships on which they are
traveling for the complete duration of the journey, or to book
accommodations on land well in advance of their visit. The
Church of the Virgin is on a hill overlooking Tenos, and its
original sumptuousness has been enhanced by the gifts of
grateful pilgrims. Also, in a special section of the church are
the paintings and sculptures of Tenian artists.

Inasmuch as the Greeks are so mindful of church feast days
it is to be expected that they would mark the Easter holidays
with great solemnity. One especially dramatic observance is
the Good Friday procession. The effigy of the body of Christ
is removed from the crucifix and placed on a bed of flowers,
then borne about the church or through the streets while worshipers chant and bands play funeral marches. In Athens the
Procession of the Epitaphios, the Holy Ceremony of the Burial
of Christ, is particularly noteworthy because the magnificence

of the vestments worn by prelates, priests, and deacons of the cathedral, and the uniforms of Greek and foreign dignitaries, add color to the demonstration. When the ceremony is at night, the marchers usually carry lighted candles.

On Glory Saturday, or Easter Eve, services begin near midnight and continue until early Sunday morning. The climactic point in the ceremony is reached when, to commemorate the risen Christ, the church is darkened, the priest lights a single candle at the altar, and then invites the worshipers to kindle their tapers from it. Soon the church is bright with pin points of lights, which are carried homeward by the worshipers.

Easter Monday is a time for folk dancing and a vivid display of traditional costumes at Megara, a village near Athens, and at Jerisso, near the monasteries of Mount Athos, near Salonika.

St. George's Day, April 23, is also a day for worshiping and feasting since George is one of the popular names among the Greeks. St. George was martyred in 304 A.D.

On August 11 and December 12 the people of Corfu usually salute the memory of St. Spyridon. He was born in Cyprus in the third century, but his remains, however, are said to be preserved in a handsome coffin at Corfu. St. Spyridon's Day is December 12, and the celebration at Corfu includes a procession with the relic of the saint dressed in costly vestments and carried by prelates.

The relic of St. Gherasimos is kept at the monastery named for him at Cephalonia, and on August 16 and October 20 the faithful venerate the relic, which is believed to cure otherwise incurable diseases.

Zante, too, has its patron saint, Dionysios, who was born there in 1547. His relic reposes in an expensive coffin in the church dedicated to his memory. It is paraded on August 24, the anniversary of his death. Fairs, games, regional dances and a parade of illuminated boats also are part of the celebration.

The true cross on which Christ is supposed to have been crucified is said to have been discovered in Jerusalem in 325 by St. Helena, mother of Constantine the Great. It remained there until 614, when the Persians occupied Palestine and the cross was removed to Persia. When Herakleios whipped the Persians in 628 he rescued the Patriarch Zacharia, who had been a prisoner of the Persians, and also brought the cross back to Jerusalem, where it was exhibited by Zacharia at the historic Elevation of the Cross celebration on September 14, 629, to convince the people that it was safe in Jerusalem once more. As a form of penance Herakleios walked barefoot in the procession that was a part of the festivities. Now Greeks everywhere celebrate September 14 as Holy Cross Day, and autumn fairs in Greece usually open about that time. Parts of the cross are still enshrined in three different places. One piece is in Jerusalem, a second piece is at the monastery at Holy Mount of Athos, near Salonika, Greece, and the third is at the Vatican in Rome, Italy. The piece in Rome is said to have been taken from Jerusalem by the Crusaders.

On October 26 Salonika honors St. Demetrios, its patron, who is second only to St. George in popularity among the Greeks. Demetrios' memory is sacred because according to tradition he saved the town so many times from invasions by barbarians that even the invaders began to call on him for help. The annual celebrations started in the Middle Ages. For a long time they were so popular that they were one of the top tourist attractions in Greece, luring people from Spain and Central Europe.

Dances, Drama

On special occasions the Greeks are fond of traipsing out to the ruins of ancient amphitheaters or temples where the tragedies of old and a variety of archaic, medieval, and modern dances are performed. Such a place is the open-air Odeon of Herodes Atticus at the foot of the Acropolis in Athens. Others are at Epidaurus, Delos, Delphi, and Sounion.

Fair

The International Fair at Salonika, which usually lasts for three weeks in September, is the only event of its kind in Greece. Although the current series of annual exhibitions began in 1926, this fair is a lineal descendant of the Demetria Fair, which was a big event in the Middle Ages. Now the wares of many countries displayed on 215,000 square feet of show space attract more than 600,000 visitors.

Independence Day

Military parades on March 25 commemorate the day in 1821 when the Greeks proclaimed their freedom from the Turks.

Sports

International championship tennis matches for the Eastern Mediterranean Challenge Cup are usually held in Athens late in August and early in September.

The exact dates on which festivals will take place in Greece, as well as the latest travel information pertaining to that country, may be obtained by writing to the Royal Greek Consulate General, 30 Rockefeller Plaza, New York 20, New York.

Bank holidays in Greece: January 1; Epiphany, January 6; First Day of Lent, February or March; anniversary of Greek Independence, March 25; Easter holidays, March or April; Ascension Day, forty days after Easter; St. Paul's Day, June 29; Assumption Day, August 15; Christmas, December 25; and December 26.

Chronological list of events in Greece:

JANUARY. Nationwide: Epiphany.

MARCH. Nationwide: Feast of the Annunciation, March 25; Independence Day, March 25. Tenos Island: trek to Tenos Island, March 25.

MARCH or APRIL. Easter Eve midnight church services in Eastern Orthodox Churches: nationwide. Easter Monday festivities: Ierisso, near Salonika; Megara, near Athens. Religious procession, Good Friday: Athens.

APRIL. Nationwide: St. George's Day, April 23.

JUNE. Athens: classic dances, concerts, tragedies in open-air Odeon of Herodes Atticus, June, July; regattas. Nationwide: St. Peter's and St. Paul's Day, June 29.

JULY. Athens: classic dances, concerts, tragedies in open-air Odeon of Herodes Atticus, June, July.

AUGUST. Athens: Eastern Mediterranean Tennis Cup, August or September. Cephalonia: Veneration of St. Gherasimos, August 16. Corfu: Feast of St. Spyridon, August 11. Nationwide: Assumption of the Virgin, August 15. Tenos Island: trek to Tenos Island, August 15. Zante: St. Dionysios' Day, August 24.

SEPTEMBER. Athens: Eastern Mediterranean Tennis Cup, August or September. Nationwide: Holy Cross Day, September 14. Rhodes: regattas. Salonika: fair.

OCTOBER. Cephalonia: Veneration of St. Gherasimos, October 20. Salonika: St. Demetrios' Day, October 26.

DECEMBER. Corfu: St. Spyridon's Day, December 12.

HOLLAND

SOON AFTER World War II ended, the Dutch decided to put an end to the prim practice of insisting that the story about the boy who saved a town by plugging the dike with his finger was just a myth. Instead, they joined in the fun of perpetuating the joke by erecting a statue to commemorate the implausibility and honor the imaginary hero who performed it. The finger-plugging was supposed to have been done near Haarlem by mythical eight-year-old Pieterje (Little Peter) in *Hans Brinker or The Silver Skates,* a story fabricated in 1865 by Mary Mapes Dodge. For many years the tale was a favorite with American and British school-children, but not well known in Holland, so year after year American and British tourists would ask the residents of Haarlem just where the little tyke stuck his finger in the dike to save the city from a flood. Eventually the people of Haarlem grew tired of trying to drown the legend, so they persuaded the Dutch Tourist Association to erect a bronze statue of a boy kneeling before an embankment with his finger in the hole. It was unveiled in June, 1950, by seven-year-old Princess Margriet as her first public function. The dedicatory note in English says: "Dedicated to our youth to honor the boy who symbolizes the perpetual struggle of Holland against the water."

Just how much of a problem the North Sea can be was dramatically demonstrated in 1953 when late winter storms and floods caused millions of dollars of damage. Nevertheless, the tulip and other flower festivals were held on schedule, and so were the Holland Festival of Music and the festivities connected with the nation's three favorite liberation days.

Flowers

The importance of flowers to the ten million Dutch in Holland is shown in the fact that their annual bill for potted plants and cut flowers runs around $40,000,000. That makes the Netherlanders probably the greatest users of horticultural products per resident. Of course, Holland is also one of the world's great exporters of bulbs and flowers. In April and May, 1953, alone, it transported to the United States via just one airline, K.L.M., the Royal Dutch Airlines, fifteen tons of cut flowers, mostly tulips. That was in addition to eleven tons of lilacs and rose plantings shipped via the same air line during 1952 and six tons of fresh lilacs and other flowers sent in that manner between December, 1952, and April, 1953. In 1950 the bulb merchants formed an association, and since then they have been helping to dramatize their product for the benefit of tourists. One spectacular way they do that is by staging a giant Tulip Festival at Hillegom, Lisse, and Sassenheim, usually in the last week in April and the first week in May in order to encompass in it the Sunday that the tulip bloom is usually at its peak.

The time of the peak of the tulip bloom may change fourteen days either way, depending on the weather. The Sunday between the two weeks when the blooms are at their best is called Bulb Sunday, and it is the Sunday when everyone goes to the tulip fields in autos, on bicycles, and on foot. They also buy enormous strings of flowers at roadside stalls for only a few cents. That is the time too when the contests of the flower mosaics are held, and also when the Tulip Rally, an auto race, inaugurated in 1951, takes place. Of course, just about everyone goes to the flower exhibition at the Keukenhof then, and to the Flora, when it is staged, which is about every ten years. The most recent one was in 1953, and it opened right on time in mid-March and remained open until May as an outstanding tourist attraction despite the severe storms that had swept parts of Holland earlier in the year. The Flora is on sixty acres of an old estate that is beautifully planted with millions of bulbs and flowering plants at Heemstede near Haarlem. In 1953 there were five consecutive indoor shows featuring lilacs, carnations, roses, and orchids as well as tulips; Europe's largest rock garden; and half a dozen exhibits stressing fashions in flowers.

From mid-March to mid-May there is a flower exhibition on seventy-five acres of the Keukenhof Estate at Lisse. The first was put on in 1950 in natural surroundings in the magnificent park of the estate where crocuses, bluebells, tulips, narcissuses, and hyacinths bloom in profusion. Sometimes there are flower parades that feature animals and objects made of flowers.

There is also a Flower Parade in Zundert, near the Belgian border on the road from Amsterdam to Brussels, on the first Sunday in September. It is among the more impressive ones in the region.

Another new flower festival, inaugurated in 1951 and usually staged during the first or second week in August, takes place at The Hague. The Hague, also called 's Gravenhage, was founded around 1248 by Count William II because its surroundings were suitable for shooting and hunting. Now it is the seat of the Netherlands Government, of the diplomatic corps, and of the International Court of Justice. The flower festival was organized with the idea of making The Hague known as a sea of flowers. A typical schedule calls for flower floats, flower balls, flowers in the streets and parks, a flower horse show, flower relay race, coronation of a flower queen, sports contests, and fireworks.

Since 1946 both Aalsmeer and Haarlem have been staging flower festivals annually around the first week in September. There are flower parades, stage performances, concerts, and fireworks. The parade from Aalsmeer always goes through a great part of Amsterdam, covering about fifteen miles.

Music, Drama, Art

Next to being famous for tulips and other horticultural products Holland is becoming well known for its music festival, which has been a yearly event only since 1947. The Netherlands Opera Company, as well as orchestras, opera and drama companies, choirs, and soloists from various countries of Europe make up a typical program. For instance, one year the big attraction was the English Opera Group led by Benjamin Britten. The troupe performed Monteverdi's *Combattimento de Tancredi e Clorinda*, Purcell's *Dido and Aeneas*, and chamber music. The Holland Festival usually offers performances in The Hague and Amsterdam, and sometimes in smaller communities like Bloemendaal, Delft, Gouda, Haarlem, and Naarden, where the medieval market places are used as natural settings for open-air performances. The character of the Holland Festival is best described by emphasis on the trend to bring to the fore little-known works that are performed only occasionally during the regular musical season. Although no prizes are given to participants in the Holland Festival, the city of Haarlem does present a silver tulip to the best young organist each year.

At Apeldoorn from about July 16 to August 25 a midsummer evening opera fantasy features various well-known operas. The first series of concerts was held in 1950, and since then at least 90,000 persons have attended each year.

In the summer of 1949 and again in 1952 Arnhem staged the first two of its triennial summertime outdoor sculpture exhibits in Sonsbeek Park and drew at least 100,000 spectators each time.

A once-every-five-years show is the Passion Play at Tegelen, a village in southwest Netherlands. First staged in 1931, the four-hour pageant was put on most recently in a 6,000-capacity open-air theater on Saturday and Sunday afternoons from May to September in 1950. The cast is made up of about 500 villagers who are extremely proud of their impersonations of biblical characters.

Special Days

The Dutch have three distinct anniversaries of liberation that they celebrate with a great deal of fervor. One is Leyden Day, on October 3, which marks the lifting of the Spanish siege of Leyden in 1574. The special dish on Leyden Day is a mixture of mashed potatoes, carrots, and onions boiled together with a piece of meat. It tops the day's menu because it was discovered by an orphan boy, who was the first to venture out from the besieged city. The first of the current series of Leyden Day celebrations took place in 1886. Since then the typical programs have included services at St. Peter's Church, where thanksgiving services took place in 1574, pageants, concerts, parades, and fireworks.

Second of the three liberation days is on August 28 and commemorates the relief of Groningen when it was besieged by troops in 1672. At that time Holland was at war with

France, England, and Munster. The festival is usually centered on the public squares where there are fairs, horse shows, concerts, and fireworks.

Most recent of the big three liberation days is May 5 when the victorious Allied Forces chased the Nazi soldiers out of Holland in 1945. The first of the current series of celebrations began in 1949.

On Flag Day in May the herring fleet of Scheveningen, the resort town of The Hague, puts out to sea. The ships in the harbor and those of the fishing fleet are gaily decorated, and the whole town turns out to wave farewell, since the fishermen will be gone until the autumn.

April 30 is the birthday of Queen Juliana, so it is a national holiday celebrated by a personal appearance of Her Majesty at The Hague, and concerts in the city square. The costume of the day for women consists of white frocks and orange scarves to salute the House of Orange.

The Queen makes another important annual appearance on the third Tuesday of September when she rides in the golden coach drawn by six black horses from her palace to the medieval Knights Hall where the two houses of Parliament are united in a combined session to hear the Queen open the new session with the so-called *troonrede,* her speech giving a brief outline of the plans of the Government for the ensuing year.

Sports

Ice skating is almost as popular as bicycling in Holland, so the Dutch are happy, when a cold winter causes their canals to freeze solid. When the ice is right, one of the big skating events is the Eleven Towns Tour, a 120-mile journey that usually begins and ends in Leeuwarden. It was inaugurated as an experiment in 1890 by W. A. Mulier, a Frisian gentleman, who also introduced football to the Netherlands. However, the Frisian Eleven Towns Association was not formed until 1909, and that year the race was won by a clergyman who sped in ahead of the sixty other contenders. Those taking part in the race skate as fast as possible, of course, while thousands of other persons follow the route at a more leisurely pace. One year as many as five thousand skaters took part. They greatly overtaxed the hotel facilities along the way, so extra beds for the overflow were set up in as many private homes as possible. The eleven towns include Leeuwarden, Dokkum, Franeker, Harlingen, Bokward, Workum, Hindelopen, Stavoren, Stoten, Ijlst, and Sneek.

Unique in the field of sports is the annual great tilting competition, believed by its sponsors to be the largest contest of its kind in northern Europe, usually staged on the last Thursday of August on the island of Walcheren. Festivities connected with this championship display of horsemanship, balance, and marksmanship are staged with all the trappings of the period when knights were in the saddle. Some 1,200 horsemen in traditional Zeeland costume of black cloth with silver buttons and round hats, often made of beaver, ride their work horses at full speed while they aim lances at targets suspended between two poles.

Another important equestrian event is the International Horse Show at Rotterdam, usually during the first week in September.

Since the end of World War II the Dutch have become increasingly automobile-racing-conscious. They launched the first automobile races on the circuit of Zandvoort, where the lap length is 2.6 miles, around the middle of June, 1949, and the track now draws at least 10,000 autos and 3,000 motorcycles a year.

Zandvoort is also the scene of the Royal Netherlands Auto Club's international auto race for the Grand Prix of Holland early in June. It is one of the ten major events that contribute points to the world championship each year. The others are: Argentina, Belgium, France, Germany, Great Britain, Indianapolis Speedway, Italy, Spain, and Switzerland.

Late in April, 1951, the motor-minded Netherlanders staged their first International Tulip Rally, fashioning it after the famous Monte Carlo Rally, to stress endurance, map reading, and speed. Typical routes for participants begin at Brussels, Berne, Copenhagen, Manchester, Milan, Monte Carlo, Rome, and The Hague. The drivers follow the prescribed courses for more than 2,000 miles and are expected to converge at Noordwijk, near the tulip-bulb fields about three days after the race starts.

If you are driving a car in Europe about the middle of September you might like to join the International Torch Rally of Eindhoven. This unique competition was inaugurated in 1949, and its scenic and historic course traces the route followed by the liberating armies of World War II from the beaches of Normandy to Eindhoven. It is definitely not a race for professional daredevil drivers, but a sports event planned for men and women pleasure drivers to test their driving and map-reading abilities. The average speed over the 875-mile course is approximately 25 to 30 miles per hour. The parts of the course that have to be done within that average speed are indicated in the itinerary, and contestants must cover the distance mentioned in the itinerary. For example, if the direct road from one place to another is 20 miles, and the itinerary indicates 25 miles, the contestant must find a combination of roads that will add up to 25 miles. The itinerary is planned so that there is only one combination of 25 miles. Entries can be submitted as individual competitors, club teams of three persons, all of whom are members of the same officially recognized national district or local automobile club, police teams of one person with the approval of his superior, "make" teams of three persons representing the make of a special car, or a journalist team, with one participant in the name of a newspaper or a magazine.

The Dutch have also been motorcycle enthusiasts for at least twenty-five years. Back in 1928 at Valkenburg they put on their first annual road championship for amateurs and newcomers, and now conduct it at the circuit of Zandvoort. In 1928 they also launched the road championships for professionals and independents in Valkenburg in the southern part of the Province of Limburg, and the championship of the Netherlands for amateurs and professionals on the cycle track in Amsterdam.

International T.T. Races, yearly motorcycle contests for the tourist trophy on the circuit of Drente, usually take place around the last week in June. Now considered a classic event, the competition inaugurated in 1927 has four classes: 125, 250, 350, and 500 cubic centimeters. Winners' names are inscribed on a perpetual silver trophy, and they receive silver cups, gold medals, and other objects of silver and gold.

In bicycling, high lights include the Round Holland Race, which starts and finishes in Amsterdam during the second week in May; sprint races for the great prize of Amsterdam, which draws an estimated 150,000 spectators to Olympic Stadium, Amsterdam, in July; and the Netherlands Championship, which attracts a similar crowd to the same place in August. Other bicycle-racing events of particular interest to tourists include: Round North Holland for Amateurs, the Round of Mid-Netherlands for Amateurs, Round of the Netherlands for Professionals, the Benelux Contest for Amateurs, and the race from Amsterdam to Arnhem and return. All have been launched since 1945.

A mixture of gymnastics, athletic games, and cycle racing has been featured during Olympic Day at Amsterdam every June during peacetime since 1933, while in even years at a different city each time some 22,000 gymnasts tumble and perform feats of strength and balance before 50,000 spectators.

Rowing and sailing are naturally popular in a land surrounded by so much water. Rowing contests of the Royal Netherlands Sailing and Rowing Association take place on an artificial canal called the Bosbaan, which was made especially for rowing contests at Amsterdam. The Varsity is rowed on the upper Rhine Canal at Jutphaas in June, the National Youth Championship for the Holland Cup on the Bosbaan in Amsterdam in June. The Varsity was organized in 1878, the Youth Championship in 1886. Since 1946 the Ladies National Championship has been staged on the Bosbaan in Amsterdam in June. The National Championships were held for the first time in 1913, and since 1937 have been rowed on the Bosbaan at Amsterdam in June.

The four important yearly sailing contests in the Netherlands are Kaagweek, the third week in July, on the Kaag Lakes near Leyden; Holland Week, early in August, on the Loosdrecht Lakes and Ijsel Lake; Sneekweek, in mid-August, which dates to about 1800; and the sailing contest on Westeinder Lakes between The Hague and Amsterdam in the middle of June. About four hundred sailors take part in each of these contests.

Sailing contests and competitions for tugs and fisherboats fill the program of the Neptune Festival at Delfzijl in May or June. It dates to 1876.

The Dutch even stage sailing contests for freight ships from time to time. The first race was held in 1840. The current series began around 1920 and usually takes place at one of the ports in the Province of Friesland during June or later in the summer.

The Ilsy, which stands for the Internationale Luchtvaart Show, Ypenburg, near The Hague, is Holland's international air show. Staged regularly in July since 1947 it now attracts about 100,000 visitors.

Fairs

Holland's big semiannual expositions are the International Trade Fairs at Utrecht. Staged for the first time in 1917, the spring show takes place for nine days during the last half of March, and the fall show for nine days during the first half of September. It is closed on Sundays, and the first two days are reserved especially for visitors from abroad. About half a million people look at the latest industrial achievements in forty-eight categories. The spring fair usually emphasizes textiles, medical and pharmaceutical products, and building equipment. The fall fair stresses furniture and agricultural and dairy products.

The world-famous china-making city of Delft has been staging an Art and Antique Dealers' Fair at the Prinsenhof Museum from mid-August through the first week in September every year since 1949. When the fair is on, Delft becomes the European center for antiques and works of art. Among the displays are books, bronzes, ceramics, chinaware, drawings, etchings, furniture, glass, jewelry, paintings, pewter, silver, statuary, and tapestries. The museum, which was a convent in the Middle Ages and later was converted into a royal residence, has several permanent exhibitions of Dutch art, furnishings, and interiors.

Other fairs and exhibitions include the *Nesova,* a Dutch souvenir trade fair organized in 1953 and staged during the second or third weeks in January at Amsterdam; the Furniture and Soft-furnishings Fair inaugurated in 1952 and put on in the Fair Buildings at Utrecht around the second week in February; and the Automobile Show in the R.A.I. Building, Amsterdam, late in February and early in March.

The exact dates on which festivals will take place in Holland, as well as the latest travel information pertaining to that country, may be obtained by writing to the Netherlands National Tourist Office, 10 Rockefeller Plaza, New York 20, New York.

Bank holidays in Holland: January 1; Good Friday; Easter Saturday; Easter Monday; the Queen's birthday, April 30; Liberation Day, May 5; Ascension Day, forty days after Easter; Whitmonday, fifty days after Easter; Christmas, December 25; and December 26.

Chronological list of events in Holland:

JANUARY. Amsterdam: *Nesova,* Dutch souvenir fair; packing fair. Leeuwarden: Eleven Towns ice-skating tour. Lisse: flower show. The Hague: national rabbit, poultry show. Utrecht: leather fair.

FEBRUARY. Amsterdam: motorcycle show. Lisse: flower show. Utrecht: furniture fair.

FEBRUARY or MARCH. Auto show: Amsterdam. Pre-Lenten carnivals: Limburg Province, Noord-Brabant Province.

MARCH. Amsterdam: household fair; long-distance rowing championships. Haarlem: The Flora, about every ten years; most recent in 1953. Hillegom: flower-garden demonstrations, to mid-May. Lisse: national flower show, Keukenhof Estate, to mid-May. Utrecht: industrial fair.

APRIL. Alkmaar: first of traditional weekly cheese markets, to November, usually Fridays, 10:00 A.M. Amsterdam: commercial motor vehicles show. Haarlem: flower mosaics, April, May. Hillegom: flower-garden demonstrations, to mid-May; tulip festival. Leyden: flower mosaics, April, May. Lisse: national flower show, Keukenhof Estate, to mid-May; tulip festival. Nationwide: Birthday of Queen Juliana, April 30; tulip season, April, May. Noordwijk: finish line for international Tulip Auto Rally; flower festival. Sassenheim: tulip festival, April, May. Utrecht: agricultural fair.

MAY. A different place each year: national gymnastic festival, May or June, even years. Amsterdam: Round Holland bike race. Bois le Duc: music festival. Delfzijl: Neptune festival, May or June. Gonda: cheese market once a week, usually Fridays, into October. Haarlem: flower mosaics, April, May. Hillegom: flower-garden demonstrations; tulip festival. Jutphaas: varsity rowing race on the Upper Rhine Canal. Leyden: cheese market once a week, usually Fridays, into October; flower mosaics, April, May.

Lisse: national flower show, Keukenhof Estate; tulip festival.
Nationwide: Liberation Day, May 5; tulip season, April, May.
Sassenheim: tulip festival, April, May. Scheveningen: Flag Day,
the day herring fleet sails, ships and resort bedecked with flags.
Tegelen: Passion Play, May to September, usually in years ending
in zero or five. The Hague: tulip tour.

JUNE. A different place each year: national gymnastic festival,
May or June, even years. Alphen: rowing contest of Rowing and
Sailing Association Hollandia on Rhine, June or July. Amster-
dam: Holland Festival, June, July; also at The Hague, Schevenin-
gen; National Youth Rowing Championship for Holland Cup, on
Bosbaan Canal; rowing contest of Royal Netherlands Sailing,
Rowing Association, on Bosbaan, June or July. Circuit of Drent:
Tourist Trophy motorcycle races. Delfzijl: Neptune festival, May
or June. Friesland: freighter sailing contests. Scheveningen: Holland Festival, June, July; also at Amsterdam, The Hague. Tegelen:
Passion Play, May to September, usually in years ending in zero
or five. The Hague: Holland Festival, June, July; also at Amsterdam, Scheveningen. Zandvoort: Grand Prix of Holland, auto race;
auto races to September.

JULY. Alphen: rowing contest of Rowing and Sailing Association Hollandia on Rhine, June or July. Amsterdam: bike sprint
races; Holland Festival, June, July; also at The Hague, Scheveningen; national rowing championship, on Bosbaan Canal, July or
August; National Youth Rowing Championship for Holland Cup,
on Bosbaan Canal, June or July; rowing contest of Royal Netherlands Sailing Association, on Bosbaan Canal, June or July. Apeldoorn: opera fantasy, through August. Assen: Tourist Trophy
motor races. Nijmegen: endurance march for individuals, marching clubs, military units. Scheveningen: Holland Festival, June,
July; also at Amsterdam, The Hague. Tegelen: Passion Play, May
to September, usually in years ending in zero or five. The Hague:
Holland Festival, June, July; also at Amsterdam, Scheveningen.
Ypenburg, near The Hague: air show.

AUGUST. Amsterdam: women's national rowing championship,
on Bosbaan Canal; national rowing championship, Bosbaan
Canal, July or August; Netherlands' bike championships. Apeldoorn: opera fantasy, July, August. Delft: antique dealers' fair,
into September. Groningen: Relief of Groningen Day, August 28.

Tegelen: Passion Play, May to September, usually in years ending in zero or five. The Hague: flower festival. Walcheren, Zeeland: tilting tournament.

SEPTEMBER. Aalsmeer: floral parade. Amsterdam: film exhibition: floral parade. Delft: antique dealers' fair, August, September. Eindhoven: Torch Rally, auto run over World War II liberation route, Normandy to Eindhoven. Rotterdam: *Femina*, women's fair, to mid-October; horse show. Tegelen: Passion Play, May to September, usually in years ending in zero or five. The Hague: Opening of The States General, Parliament, by Queen Juliana, third Tuesday. Utrecht: cattle, horse show; fair. Zundert: floral parade.

OCTOBER. Leyden: Relief of Leyden Day, October 3. Rotterdam: *Femina*, women's fair, September, October. Zuid-Laren: horse market.

DECEMBER. Nationwide: St. Nicholas festivities, December 5, 6.

ICELAND

ONE OF Iceland's outstanding claims to distinction is the venerable age of its *Althing,* or parliament. The thousandth anniversary of the *Althing* was celebrated in 1930. To commemorate that anniversary the United States of America presented to Iceland a statue of Leif Ericson, "son of Iceland, discoverer of Vinland." The Icelanders, of course, are proud of the fact that parliamentary law has prevailed in their land for so many years; and they are so mindful of their struggle for complete independence they commemorate it twice a year, in June and December.

Special Days

The big annual celebration in Iceland is National Day, June 17, for on that date in 1944 the *Althing,* Iceland's parliament, formally severed its union with Denmark following a vote of 70,536 to 365 by the people of Iceland to complete the re-establishment of an independent republic. Iceland had been an independent republic from 930 to 1262 when it joined with Norway. In 1380 the two came under Danish rule. Norway separated from Denmark in 1814, but Iceland continued in union with Denmark until December 1, 1918. At that time Denmark acknowledged Iceland as a sovereign state, while the Danish King Christian X continued as King of Iceland. It was that link which was broken on June 17, 1944. Icelanders selected June 17 as their latest Independence Day because that was the birthday of Jon Sigurdsson, the man who has been credited with making the greatest contribution to the ultimate freedom of Iceland. He was born in 1811. Now the anniversary is marked by a full day of festivities in Reykjavik. During the morning the President and the entire cabinet place a wreath beneath the statue of Sigurdsson just outside the *Althing*. At 1:00 P.M. there is a parade of students and workers. They march with flags waving and bands playing all along the route from the university to the *Althing,* where the President speaks to the crowd from the balcony. After the speech the parade moves on to the cemetery, where a wreath is placed on Sigurdsson's grave, and then the procession heads for the stadium, where the principal sports contests of the year take place. About nine o'clock that night there is folk singing and dancing on a small hill overlooking the city, and at 11:00 P.M. several public dances begin. The people dance in the streets the whole night through, and since the festival takes place in June the midnight sun shines all the time.

The degree of independence achieved in 1918 is marked on December 1. Since the students of Iceland were very active in the struggle for freedom they play a major part in the celebration. Usually there is a parade from the university to the *Althing* and speeches in the daytime and dances at night.

April 24 is Children's Day in Iceland. During the morning the youngsters march from their school to the *Althing* to hear an address. In the afternoon they are entertained with music and other amusements. On this occasion money for projects from which children will benefit is raised through the sale of badges.

May 1 is Labor Day throughout Iceland. Skilled and unskilled workers parade in the morning, listen to speeches in the main squares or in public parks during the afternoon, and go dancing at night.

The exact dates on which festivals will take place in Iceland, as well as the latest travel information pertaining to that country, may be obtained by writing to the Icelandic Consulate General, 50 Broad Street, New York 4, New York.

Bank holidays in Iceland: January 1; Holy Thursday; Good Friday; Easter Saturday; Easter Monday; Ascension Day, forty days after Easter; Whitmonday, fifty days after Easter; Independence Day, June 17; the first Monday in August; Christmas, December 25; and December 26.

Chronological list of events in Iceland:

JANUARY. Nationwide: winter sports.

FEBRUARY. Nationwide: winter sports.

MARCH. Nationwide: winter sports.

APRIL. Nationwide: Children's Day, April 24.

MAY. Nationwide: Labor Day, May 1.

JUNE. Nationwide: National Day, June 17; most impressive ceremonies at Reykjavik.

JULY. Vestmannaeyjahatid, Westman Island: week-long county fair.

SEPTEMBER. Reykjavik: Iceland Industries' Fair.

DECEMBER. Nationwide: independence celebration, December 1; most impressive ceremonies at Reykjavik.

IRELAND

IRELAND'S record for festivals goes back almost four thousand years to the time about nineteen hundred years before Christ when King Eochaidh Mac Erc, last Firbolg monarch of Erinn, gathered his subjects together and staged the first Tailteann Games as a tribute on the death and burial of his wife, Queen Tailte. Thereafter, the Cuiteach Fuait, as the funeral games were called, were held to honor the great who died. They featured all sorts of athletic, gymnastic, and equestrian contests, such as running, long jumping, high jumping, hurling, quoit throwing, spear casting, sword and shield contests, wrestling, boxing, swimming, horse and chariot racing, spear or pole jumping, sling contests, and bow and arrow marksmanship competition, as well as singing, dancing, spinning, weaving, and dyeing. Transportation and communications being as limited as they were in those times, the ruler always took advantage of the opportunity afforded by such large gatherings to promulgate the new laws of the land and to clear up any other business of government.

The Irish are still sports-loving people, and their love of music is reflected in the comparatively modern feis ceoil.

That they still honor the illustrious dead is shown in the several pilgrimages that take place throughout the year, and in the manner in which Irishmen everywhere salute the memory of St. Patrick on his day.

Special Days

As almost everyone knows, the great day for the Irish in all parts of the world is St. Patrick's Day, March 17, when the sons and daughters of the ol' sod commemorate the death of a man who was not born in Ireland but brought religion to that land and inspired some mighty legends before he died in Saul, County Down, in 493 A.D. It is believed that he was laid to rest in Armagh, Down or Saul. Among his memorable deeds was the conversion of the heathen in Ireland to Christianity, the founding of churches, including the cathedral and monastery of Armagh, healing the sick, and, most famous of all, clearing the snakes out of Ireland. That is supposed to have happened when St. Patrick used the shamrock to illustrate the doctrine of the Trinity. It was generally believed at that time that snakes avoided shamrock, so as the shamrock prospered as a symbol the snakes ran away. Now the biggest of all St. Patrick's Day celebrations is in Dublin, where the Irish mark the day by watching either military or industrial parades along O'Connell Street. The observance begins with high mass at the procathedral, presided over by the Archbishop and attended by civic leaders.

From now on St. Patrick's Day might be a prelude to a very elaborate springtime celebration to be known as *An Tóstal*, or Ireland at Home. The first of the proposed annual homecoming celebrations to be staged in the nation's thirty-two counties went on for three weeks in April, 1953. That inaugural program of cultural, social, and sporting events was so successful it boosted off-season tourism substantially. To enter-

tain the visitors the Irish lined up enough events to fill a
thirty-two-page booklet. There were pageants, parades, Irish
storytelling, art and industrial exhibitions, new plays, operas,
symphonic concerts, ballets, folk dancing, and championship
athletic events. Visitors from America were especially welcome
at the festival. To prove it, the Irish invited one Sam O'Reilly
of New York to carry Ireland's national flag at the head of the
parade, and gave other representatives of Irish organizations
in the United States places of honor in other parades in different counties.

Pilgrimages

Ireland is such a popular place for pilgrimages that often
approximately 35,000 persons make visitations during the
traditional season, June 1 to August 15, to the most popular
shrine of all, the island of Sanctuary, Lough Derg, County
Donegal, on the northwest coast of Ireland, about 175 miles
from Dublin. It is believed to have been St. Patrick's Purgatory. The story goes that Christ revealed it to the saint and
promised him that whoever spent a day and a night in the place
would witness both the torments of hell and the joys of heaven.
On the island, a narrow strip of rock less than a mile from
shore, are the remains of a monastery destroyed in 1632, a
burial ground, and some small mounds, sites of the ancient
penitential cells. The modern buildings on the island consist
of St. Patrick's and St. Mary's Chapels, a bell tower, a presby-
tery, two large hospices with accommodation for pilgrims, and
some boardinghouses where penitents may also stay. St. Patrick's Church, noted for its beautiful stained-glass windows
depicting the stations of the cross, has been raised to the dignity
of a minor basilica. Penitential devotions there begin with a
visit to St. Patrick's Church, around which several circuits are
made, visits being paid to the various penitential beds of earth

and stone that are named in honor of St. Brigid, St. Brendan, St. Catherine, and St. Columba. One all-night vigil has to be kept in the church. "Stations" are performed every day, and the usual religious devotions are also attended. In performing the exercises the pilgrims are barefooted, and a rigorous fast must also be observed. Only one meal a day is allowed. It consists of black tea and dry bread. The only other refreshment is the water of the lake, boiled and sweetened, which the pilgrims call wine. Prospective pilgrims can obtain all necessary information from the Rev. Prior, Lough Derg, Pettigo. Those who do not intend to perform the pilgrimage must seek permission to land on the Station Island.

Just as St. Patrick is the patron saint of Ireland, St. Brigid is its patroness. From time immemorial Faughart has been regarded as her birthplace, so people go there to pray at the stream and holy well around which the saint spent her youth. However, it was not until 1933 that a shrine was erected in her honor. The formal opening took place in July, 1934, and the first Sunday of July each year was appointed as the day of National Pilgrimage to Faughart. His Eminence, Cardinal MacRory, Archbishop of Armagh, in whose diocese the shrine is located, presided. Some 15,000 persons, including church dignitaries and representatives of the state, were present. Now the average attendance on the first Sunday in July is about seven thousand. On other Sundays throughout the summer attendance is smaller, but there usually is a big turnout on the saint's birthday, February 1. On days of national pilgrimage, such as July 1, parochial sodalities, choir, schoolchildren, and many of the faithful assemble at St. Brigid's Church in Kilcurry, about two miles from the shrine. Bands play, hymns are sung, and the relic of St. Brigid—a portion of the skull of the saint kept at the church—is carried in procession to the shrine where it is placed for public veneration by the side of the shrine altar. Prescribed prayers are recited, a sermon is preached on the life of the saint, and benediction is given. The pilgrims then begin private devotions, by going round the grounds and reciting prayers by the stream, the well, and special places marked by tradition as spots where pilgrims of the past knelt and prayed.

The newest of Ireland's popular pilgrimage places is the Shrine of Our Lady of Knock in County Mayo. The treks were inspired by a vision which is said to have been seen by fifteen witnesses between seven thirty and eight o'clock on the evening of August 21, 1879. Our Blessed Lady crowned and clothed in white garments, her hands raised as if in prayer and her eyes turned toward heaven, appeared at the gable wall of the parish church of Knock. On her right hand was St. Joseph, his head inclined toward her, and on her left was St. John the Evangelist, attired as a bishop, his left hand holding a book and his right hand raised as if in preaching. To the left of St. John there appeared an altar on which stood a cross and a lamb about eight weeks old, around which the wings of angels hovered. The wall was bathed in soft light, and the vision is said to have lasted at least two hours despite the fact that rain fell heavily all the time. Now the season for visiting the shrine opens with the Tuam diocesan pilgrimage led by His Grace the Archbishop of Tuam on the first Sunday of May, and closes on the first Sunday of October with a special Rosary Crusade pilgrimage. On every Sunday throughout the season, except the last Sunday in July which is reserved for the national pilgrimage to St. Patrick's Mountain, Croagh Patrick, organized groups visit the shrines and make the traditional Station, a public ceremony there. The faithful usually reach the shrine in time for the last mass at Our Lady's altar at the Oratory, twelve noon. The Station, which includes Stations of the Cross, fifteen mysteries of the Rosary, and the Litany of Our Lady, begins at 3:00 P.M., and closes with the benediction of the Most Blessed Sacrament about 4:30 P.M.

The Shrine of Our Lady of Knock is a favorite of invalids. Often as many as two hundred afflicted, some on stretchers or in invalid chairs, take part. They are attended by five hundred handmaids and stewards, voluntary helpers attached to the shrine. According to records kept by the late Archdeacon Cavanagh, the first cure noted was the instantaneous recovery of a totally deaf girl ten days after the apparition in August, 1879.

In Drogheda, County Louth, on July 1 there is a regular pilgrimage to the shrine of Blessed Oliver Plunkett, who was hanged for treason, drawn and quartered at Tyburn, July 1, 1681, despite his solemn protests of innocence. Some of the remains of the man who was Catholic Primate of Ireland during the reign of Charles II were transferred to the Oliver Plunkett Memorial Church when it was built, and lie in a special shrine where they may be seen. They include his head, his arms, and the breastplate of his coffin.

Another pilgrimage, this one to the summit of Croagh Patrick in County Mayo near the shore of Clew Bay, is held on the final Sunday of July. The strength of the Croagh Patrick tradition may be gauged from the fact that 70,000 persons made the trek on July 29, 1951. Scholars of the Gaelic past are divided in their opinions about the origin of the Croagh Patrick tradition. Since the earliest days of Christianity in Ireland Croagh Patrick has been hallowed as the remote solitude to which the country's apostle climbed to spend weeks in prayer and penance. Other poetic, and perhaps fanciful, traditions point to the plateau above the precipice of Lugnanarrib as the place where the saint rang his bell and banished the serpents from Ireland. The pilgrims begin the ascent of the mountain during the brief summer dusk, and masses are celebrated from 5:00 A.M. onward in the tiny church on the summit.

To the south of Carnsore Point, County Wexford, is the

sea inlet called Lady's Island Lake. Lady's Island, which is connected with the mainland by a causeway, was the site of an ancient monastery dedicated to the Blessed Virgin and was for centuries a celebrated place for pilgrimage. On the island are the ruins of an Augustinian priory and a Norman castle. The age-old pilgrimage to Our Lady's Island, discontinued for a while, was revived by the Rev. Fr. Whitty, the local parish priest, in 1897, and is staged on Assumption Day, August 15.

Another of Ireland's well-known holy places is Clonmacnois, on the banks of the Shannon, four miles north of Shannon-bridge. It was there in 548 that St. Ciaran founded a monastery that subsequently became the most famous of all monastic cities in Ireland. Despoiled centuries ago, the site contains ruins of eight churches, two round towers, three sculptured high crosses and portions of two others, some two hundred monumental slabs, and the remnants of a castle. The Pilgrims' Road, still being used, was the only road to Clonmacnois in ancient times. The present pilgrimages are held each year on September 9, the feast of St. Ciaran, by local residents, and on the following Sunday by outsiders.

Music

In 1897 the Feis Ceoil Association was formed to promote the study and cultivation of Irish and other music in Ireland, to hold an annual musical festival, or feis ceoil, consisting of prize competitions and concerts, and to collect and preserve by publication the old airs of Ireland. The first feis ceoil was held in Dublin, May 18–21, 1897, and is now staged annually during the week of the second Monday in May. About 1,300 entrants compete in more than 100 contests covering all forms of music, including original compositions, for cups, medals, and prizes. In one section contests are in the Irish language and for Irish instruments. Two prize winners' concerts are held on the concluding day of the feis ceoil, one for juniors in the afternoon, and the other for seniors in the evening.

Art Exhibition

Taispeastas Ealaion an Oireachtais, the Oireachtas Art Exhibition, is one of the foremost exhibitions in present-day Ireland. Held annually at the end of October, it attracts work from established Irish artists as well as from those not so well known. It is truly a cross section of Irish art today because all schools are represented there. The entries include oils, black and whites, watercolors, architectural drawings, and sculptures. The exhibition, which takes place in Dublin in October and November, has been popular since it was started in 1907.

Racing

There are at least three important racing dates in Ireland every year—the Irish Grand National, Conynham Cup, and Irish Derby.

The Irish Grand National is run annually over bush fences over a distance of three and one-half miles at the Easter Monday meeting at Fairyhouse for a stake of about $5,600. The course is in a hunting district in County Meath about eleven miles from Dublin. As the race is held on a Bank Holiday, it attracts a large attendance from the city. Prices of admission range from about $2 to $5 for access to the Parade Ring and Hunt Stand. The remaining sections are usually free, and so are the car parks, except for the members' park, which is situated close to the stands. Attendance usually totals about 25,000.

Two days' racing are held annually toward the end of April at the close of the racing season in the center of the hunting district about twenty-three miles from Dublin. A great many hunting people from all parts of Ireland and England attend, since the course, which is mainly banks with two stone walls, is designed to attract hunters. The principal race, over a distance of four miles, is the Conyngham Cup, run on the second day for a stake of about $3,000. There are two races confined to local farmers for about $1,000 in prizes, the entry for runners being free.

The Irish Derby at the Curragh, County Kildare, in mid-June is for three-year-old entire colts and fillies who are entered for the race as yearlings. First run in 1866 for a sweepstakes of twenty-five sovereigns each and a value to the winner of £425 over a distance of one mile and six furlongs, in recent years about $11,200 has been added to a sweepstakes for acceptors of £50, with lesser amounts for those declaring forfeit on given dates. Also, the distance has been changed to one mile and a half. In 1952 the value to the winner was about $21,000. The race now regularly attracts horses from England, France and the United States.

Stock Shows

The Royal Dublin Society sponsors three main events every year. They are the show and sale of pedigree bulls in March, the spring show and industries fair in May, and the Dublin Horse Show in August. The most important of the three, as far as tourists are concerned, is the horse show.

Since 1868 the Dublin Horse Show at Ball's Bridge, Dublin, during the first full week in August, has been gaining steadily as one of the world's important equestrian exhibitions. The approximately 140,000 persons who attend each year see hundreds of stallions, yearlings, brood mares and foals, made and unmade hunters, riding cobs and ponies, children's ponies and harness horses among 58 classes. The majority of the classes are judged on the first day, Tuesday. Hunter cups and riding pony classes are judged on Wednesday, and children's ponies and ladies' hunters ridden sidesaddle by ladies wearing hunting costume on Thursday. Military and civilian jumping contests take place every day. Prize money usually exceeds $18,000, and there are many valuable cups and trophies awarded. Sales of bloodstock average $350,000. Yet apart from the equestrian attractions there are comprehensive displays of Irish industries and the summer show of the Royal Horticultural Society of Ireland.

The Royal Dublin Society's Show and Sale of Pedigree Bulls in March attracts at least 1,000 bulls of the Shorthorn Aberdeen-Angus and Hereford breeds to the Society's showgrounds, Ball's Bridge. Cash prizes total $1,200 in addition to valuable trophies and medals. The event is primarily an auction sale and is considered a clearinghouse for pedigree animals.

The Spring Show and Industries Fair has been running since 1831. Like the Society's other fixtures, it, too, is staged at Ball's Bridge, Dublin, usually during the first week in May for the entertainment and enlightenment of some 160,000 visitors. The show features about 800 poultry and dairy produce exhibits, and at least a thousand animals from all sections of farm stock, such as cattle, sheep, pigs, ponies, and poultry. Prize money totals about $12,000, and sales of cattle, sheep, and pigs average $36,000. At the same time a great educational exhibit is staged by the Department of Agriculture. Special facilities are provided for students to attend the show at reduced prices so that they may see the most up-to-date methods of production demonstrated by experts. Stock-judging competitions for members of young farmers' clubs are arranged, and there are also jumping contests and gymkhana events.

Plowing

The National Plowing Championships of Ireland began in 1930, and since then the farmers of Ireland have been showing off their skills in different sections of the country each year during the first week in October. The site of the contest is changed annually to bring the entrants into different kinds of land. Recently when the championships were held at Slanemore, near Mullingar, County Westmeath, there were seventy-three horse plows and thirty-five tractor plows.

Coursing

Coursing, the pursuit of running game with dogs that follow by sight instead of scent, is in full swing from September to February. It is the winter sport of rural Ireland. During the five-month season nearly two hundred meetings are held, many of them a nursery for the larger county, provincial, or national meets. Of the approximately twenty cup meetings offering prizes totaling $1,000 and up, the Irish Cup run at Clounanna, County Limerick, in November, and the National Meeting held at Clonmel, County Tipperary, in February, are the big events of the season. The Irish Cup is worth $1,500 to the winner. It is a stake race open to greyhounds of any age and of either sex and takes place about the second or third week in November. The first Irish Cup was run at Clounanna in 1906, and since then it has been considered the Irish counterpart of the English Waterloo Cup. It is the most severe test of speed and stamina in Ireland's coursing calendar. Although some meetings were held at Clonmel as long ago as 1914, the National Meeting there dates from 1925. In 1930 a separate stake for dogs and another for bitches were introduced, the Derby and the Oaks were established, and the number of trial stakes increased to 128.

The same meeting stages the International Cup, the main purpose of which was defeated temporarily by World War II when English owners were unable to participate. But the international flavor and the prewar popularity have returned.

While coursing is popular in all parts of Ireland, it is particularly favored in Cork, Kilkenny, Kerry, Limerick, Midland, Tipperary, and Wexford Counties. Open coursing, which is the old style and one of the oldest of field sports, is also popular in many parts of the country. Most organized meetings are mainly social gatherings. There is little or no betting, and the coursers are more interested in the day's sport for its own sake than for the outcome of it.

Hurling

Hurling, which shares with Gaelic football the distinction of being one of Ireland's national sports, has been succinctly described as hockey without skates. Men were hurling in Ireland when ancient Greece was young, and the Irish like to believe that it was invented by the legendary Finn McCool. The game gets its name from the fact that players catch a ball on the flat of a stick, then hurl it. Contests of this sort were played without supervision until about 1884, when the Gaelic Football Association began governing it even though hurling and Gaelic football are entirely different. Now when the All-Ireland finals take place at Croke Park, Dublin, around the fourth week in September some 90,000 spectators crowd into the arena.

The exact dates on which festivals will take place in Ireland, as well as the latest travel information pertaining to that country, may be obtained by writing to the Irish Tourist Bureau, 33 East 50th Street, New York 22, New York.

Bank holidays in Ireland: January 1; St. Patrick's Day, March 17; Good Friday and Easter Monday, March or April; Whitmonday, fifty days after Easter; the first Monday in August; Christmas, December 25; and December 26.

Chronological list of events in Ireland:

JANUARY. Nationwide: Rugby football, into March.

FEBRUARY. Clonmel: national coursing meet. Faughart: pilgrimage to St. Brigid's Shrine.

MARCH. Dublin: hockey championships for men, women; show, sale of pedigree bulls. Nationwide: St. Patrick's Day, March 17; most impressive celebration in Dublin.

MARCH or APRIL. Dublin: Conyngham Cup, horse race, and Irish Grand National Steeplechase, both on Easter Monday.

APRIL. Nationwide: *An Tostal,* Ireland at home, into May.

MAY. A different place each year: Golf Open Challenge Cup; Irish Women's Close Golf Championship; President's Cup, golf match. Clonmel: horse races. Curragh: The Irish 1,000 and 2,000 Guineas, horse races. Dublin: agricultural show; bike race; *Feis Ceoil,* cultural festival; horticultural show, May, June; Spring Show, Industries' Fair. Dun Laoghaire: Irish Sea yacht race. Gleninchiquin Lakes: angling contests. Knock: Our Lady of Knock pilgrimage. Nationwide: *An Tostal,* Ireland at home, April, May.

JUNE. An Uaimh: Tourist Trophy bike race. Cork: livestock show. Curragh: Irish Derby, horse race. Drogheda: feis, festival. Dublin: horticultural show, May, June; Irish Grand Prix, bike race. Lough Derg: pilgrimage to St. Patrick's Purgatory, Island of Sanctuary, June, July, August. West Limerick: historical pageant.

JULY. A different place each year: Irish Close Tennis Championship. Ardmore: pilgrimage honors St. Declan. Cork: agricultural show. Croagh Patrick Mountain: pilgrimage to mountain in County Mayo on last Sunday in July. Drogheda: pilgrimage to Shrine of Blessed Oliver Plunkett, July 1. Dublin: Irish Youths' athletic, bike championships. Faughart: Pilgrimage to St. Brigid's Shrine, first Sunday in July, other Sundays to September. Graiguenamanagh: pilgrimage honors St. Mullins. Lough Derg: pilgrimage to St. Patrick's Purgatory, Island of Sanctuary, June, July, August.

AUGUST. Carnsore Point: pilgrimage to Lady's Island Lake, August 15. Cork: Irish swimming championships. Drumshanbo: Portuncula Indulgence Pilgrimage. Dublin: coast-to-coast bike race, Dublin–Galway–Dublin; Horse Show Week; Irish all-around athletic championships. Galway: coast-to-coast bike race, Dublin–Galway–Dublin. Killarney: agricultural show. Lough Derg: pilgrimage to St. Patrick's Purgatory, Island of Sanctuary, June, July, August. Nenagh: agricultural shows.

SEPTEMBER. Ardbraccan: Pilgrimage to St. Ultan's Well. Clonmacnois: pilgrimage honors Ciaran, September 9. Curragh: Irish St. Leger, horse race; Wakefield Trophy, auto race. Dublin: agricultural show; Irish senior football final; Irish senior hurling final. Rural Ireland: coursing, the pursuit of game with dogs, September to March.

OCTOBER. A different place each year: Irish plowing championships. Dublin: *An tOireachtas,* Gaelic festival of music, literature; Oireachtas hurling final. Loughrea: Connacht Cup Meeting, coursing, at Mason Brook Meadows. Wexford: music, arts festival, October or November.

NOVEMBER. Clounanna: Irish Cup, coursing event. Dublin: bloodstock sales. Galway: *Feis Ceoil an Iarthair,* western music festival. Wexford: music, arts festival, October or November.

DECEMBER. Dublin: dog show.

ITALY

MUSIC IS the all-pervading force at festivals in Italy. It ripples delicately over provincial fairs and *festas* like water in a shallow brook and rolls magnificently in mighty waves against the stone walls of innumerable cathedrals and opera houses. You will hear it not only in obvious places like the May Musicale in Florence, the Festival of Piedegrotta in Naples, and the dozens of other festivals where music is the mainstay, but also at community celebrations that are not primarily musical, such as the Palio in Siena, and the regattas on the Grand Canal at Venice.

Religious Festivals

Since the Roman Catholic Church plays such an important part in the lives of Italians, festivals that have a religious connotation dominate the yearly calendar of events. When Holy Year occurs events in Italy as well as in other countries of Europe are arranged to take advantage of the great influx of pilgrims who flock to Vatican City, the nerve center of the Roman Catholic Church in the heart of Rome. The first Holy

Year was proclaimed in 1299 by Pope Boniface VIII, who was impressed by the multitude of pilgrims who traveled to Rome in order to receive his blessing and indulgence for their sins as a new century was about to begin. Boniface also decreed that Holy Year be celebrated every hundred years, but that was altered by later popes to give all Roman Catholics an opportunity "to share in the rich graces of the jubilee." In 1343 Pope Clement VI declared that Holy Year should be held every fifty years. He also ordained that daily visits to the Church of St. John Lateran, the Basilica of St. Peter, and the Basilica of St. Paul's Outside-the-Walls must be made in order to receive the Jubilee Indulgence. In 1373 Pope Gregory XI named Santa Maria Maggiore as the fourth basilica to be visited daily by the faithful during Holy Year. The length of time between Holy Years was reduced to thirty-three years by Pope Urban VI in 1389, to commemorate the number of years Jesus Christ is believed to have lived on earth. In 1470 Pope Paul II further reduced the interval to twenty-five years beginning in 1475, and that rule has prevailed ever since. The most recent Holy Year was observed in 1950. It began on Christmas Eve, 1949, when Pope Pius XII opened the Holy Door at St. Peter's, and ended on Christmas Eve, 1950, when he sealed it shut. A similar ceremony is performed simultaneously at the other three basilicas. Beatification and canonization ceremonies and receptions for special groups of pilgrims at the Vatican are the important activities of Holy Year.

Among the hundreds of religious festivals that enliven the daily lives of Italians are a few that have long had special appeal for visitors. January is just six days old when the people of Rome top off their Christmas celebration with the Feast of Epiphany by holding a traditional fair in Piazza Navona, which was once a racecourse for chariots and occasionally, in the old days, was converted into a lake for miniature naval battles. At the same time, in Rivisondoli, an

Abruzzi maiden is chosen to impersonate the Virgin in the living *presepe*, a representation of the Nativity staged there every year.

The Feast of St. Agatha at Catania, Sicily, usually lasts for five days around the first week in February. In 251 the saint is supposed to have been tortured because she would not yield to her father, who was Quintianus, King of Sicily. Now the saint's urn is carried through the streets in a procession, and often several men carry huge candles decorated with scenes of her life.

On Ash Wednesday in Rome hooded and robed penitents march to Santa Sabina Church as a mark of repentance for their sins at the beginning of Lent. The participants are members of the fading aristocracy of Rome, and their pageant dates back to the Middle Ages when the Pope led the parade.

Holy Week starts with the blessing of palms on Palm Sunday and is climaxed on Easter Sunday in Rome when the Pope usually addresses a crowd gathered in St. Peter's Square. Throughout the week in various communities there are pageants that have a strong appeal for visitors. At the "Deposition" in Assisi after sunset on Holy Thursday a fourteenth-century statue of Christ is taken from the wooden cross and lowered upon a bier draped with black velvet in the middle of the cathedral. Worshipers then file past to kiss the pierced feet of the statue. It is removed on Good Friday and not brought back until Holy Saturday after an impressive procession in which the Virgin is borne through the streets "looking for her son."

A painfully realistic dramatization of the final episodes of the Passion is re-enacted at Grassina, near Florence. There the person representing Jesus toils up a steep slope, weighed down by a cross, and lashed by Roman legionaries. On the hilltop three men are hung on three crosses to reproduce the scene of the crucifixion.

Living groups also take part in the Golgotha Celebration at Francavilla di Sicilia in the province of Messina. They ride on floats that are paraded through the town, each float carrying a scene from the original Passion Week: the episode in the Garden of Gethsemane, Peter's betrayal, Judas receiving the thirty pieces of silver and later hanging himself, and Golgotha. Some six hundred persons take part in the pageant, and since Christ figures in thirteen episodes He is impersonated that many times. The largest float of all is the last one, which carries a reproduction of the crucifixion.

At Trapani, Sicily, the Procession of the Mysteries is a tableaux of figures carved by local artists of the Renaissance. Christs, madonnas, anxious apostles, and leering mercenaries and scourgers are represented. Participants represent the city trades and guilds. Bands provide funeral marches.

The Passion play at Sezze, near Rome, is a sacred drama in the traditional pattern, and so is the drama called *"Mortorio"* at Garessio.

A more jovial note to the Easter celebration is struck at Florence on Holy Saturday when the Scoppio del Carro, explosion of the cart, takes place in front of the cathedral. As a rule a lavishly carved cart is drawn through the streets by two white oxen. The cart is festooned with fireworks that are ignited before the cathedral by a dove-shaped firecracker that travels along a wire connecting the cart with the altar. As the powder explodes the "dove" attempts to make the return trip to the church. If he succeeds, the countryfolk consider that a good omen for the year's crops. The celebration is believed to date to the Crusades. At that time members of the Pazzi family who had gone to Jerusalem brought back to Florence several chips of the Holy Sepulchre to be used in lighting the blessed fire. Today a procession that includes city officials in period costume goes to the very old church of the SS. Apostoli on the Saturday before Easter "to get the fire and bring it to the Duomo." The gay celebration at the cathedral follows.

In 1462, the year after St. Catherine was canonized, a solemn feast was held in her honor in Siena. Since 1630, the annual celebration has taken place on April 29, the anniversary of her death, and April 30, the National Liturgical Holiday. The two-day festival is inaugurated with a procession of votive candles on the night of April 28, at which time one candle is placed in the former home of the saint, and another in front of the *Santa Testa,* the Holy Head of the saint, which rests in the Basilica Cateriniana of St. Domenico. Characteristics of the festival include the exposition of the Holy Head in its shrine, distribution of bread to the poor, and blessing of the armed forces. Santa Caterina was proclaimed patron saint of Italy in 1939. She shares the honor with St. Francis of Assisi.

The Feast of Corpus Christi or Corpus Domini, sixty days after Easter, has been timed just right to take advantage of the flowers that bloom in the spring. A familiar sight in every Corpus Christi procession are the lines of young girls who scatter flowers in the path of the blessed sacrament. That is done in Italy as it is elsewhere. But at least two towns in Italy carry the use of flowers to a beautiful extreme on this festival and carpet streets with mosaics of varicolored blossoms to honor the institution of the Eucharist. One of the towns is Genzano, near Rome, and the other is Ravello, not far from Naples. Often the floral tapestries extend for blocks. The blossoms for them, of course, are gathered days in advance of the actual start of the project. Then the artisans begin to weave the patterns with white acacia, golden broom, red roses, poppies, and violets, following designs outlined in chalk by the senior artist.

The floral mosaic is said to have been invented by Benedetto Drei, head gardener at the Vatican more than three hundred years ago. He made one each year for the Confession of St.

Peter on June 29. The first *infiorata* at Genzano is believed to have been built by Leofreddi in front of his own home to honor Pope Pius VI, 1775–1800, who passed through town. The Feast of Corpus Christi, itself, is of Italian origin. It was instituted in 1264 by Pope Urban IV, who had been in Orvieto in 1263 taking refuge from a threatened invasion of Rome from Sicily. A Bohemian priest named Peter of Prague, en route to see the Pope, was tortured by doubts whether the wafers consecrated by priests really became Christ's body, in accordance with church doctrine. While at Bolsena, a town near Orvieto, the Host began to bleed in Peter's hand. At mass spots of blood fell from the wafer onto the corporal, a white linen cloth on which the chalice rests while it is on the altar. The Pope is supposed to have ordered that the blood-spotted corporal be brought to Orvieto for safekeeping, and to commemorate the miracle he instituted the feast of Corpus Christi. Orvietans commissioned Ugolino di Vieri, a Sienese artist, to make a silver and enamel reliquary to hold the corporal, and later built a cathedral to house the reliquary. To emphasize Pope Urban IV's directive that the corporal belongs to the people of Orvieto ownership is symbolized by the distribution of four keys to the reliquary. One is held by the artist who tends to it, and one each is possessed by the Mayor, the Town Council, and the Bishop.

On the first Thursday in May in the village of Cocullo the townsfolk honor their patron St. Dominic by draping his statue with live snakes and parading it through the streets. The reptiles are nonpoisonous, and when they have served their purpose at the festival they usually are sold to laboratories in the big cities where the snake oil is used for serums. St. Dominic da Sora, who lived between 951 and 1031 and whose saint's day is January 22, is saluted with snakes because he is supposed to have cured a Cocullo woman of snake bite.

At Gubbio on or about May 15 the elevation and procession of the Ceri, three colossal wooden tapers about seventeen feet high and weighing about eight hundred pounds each, attracts a good crowd. The Ceri represent the real wax tapers presumably offered after Bishop Ubaldo, the patron saint of Gubbio, triumphed over twelve enemy towns in 1251. One is dedicated to him, and the other two to SS. Anthony and George. The bearers of the Ceri, called *ceraioli,* wear white trousers, red or white shirts, a colored sash, and the Neapolitan fez on their heads. The masons carry St. Ubaldo, the traders take St. George, and the rural people parade St. Anthony. Not only are they content to march their burdens calmly through the streets, the bearers race them, often covering as much as a mile in fifteen minutes. The race begins in the afternoon when the bell of Palazzo dei Consoli rings out, following a benediction by the bishop. The Ceri bearers pause in Piazza della Signoria, circle the square three times, then continue at a trot up to Monte Ingino.

A celebration similar to the elevation of the Ceri at Gubbio is the Dance of the Lilies at Nola in the Province of Naples. It commemorates the return of St. Paulinus to his native town following his release by Genseric, King of the Vandals. Now on the third Sunday in June the statue of the saint is placed on a boat-shaped platform and carried to the people, who offer him their lilies. In this instance the "lilies" are extremely high steeples made of papier-mâché, wood, and cloth, adorned with holy statues and even having a platform for musicians. The hundred-foot tall ornaments are called lilies because the people greeted the Bishop Paolino with lilies in 400. Each of the eight modern lilies is distinguished by the symbol of the ancient corporation and is supported by a group of fifty young men who are trained for their tasks. When the lilies and the boat of St. Paulinus meet, the bearers begin to dance slowly, causing the lilies to roll and rock. In that way they escort the statue back to the church.

The Feast of the Vow at Assisi on June 25 marks the time around 1240 when St. Chiara seized the monstrance and placed it on top of the walls of the cloister when the Saracens attacked. The gleam of light from the monstrance is supposed to have frightened the invaders, and they fled. Traditional observances at the Church of St. Damian include the curfew, procession of the defenders, and the vow of the tabernacle.

From July 5 to 15 the people of Palermo honor their patron saint, Santa Rosalia, who is believed to have saved the city from the ravages of the Black Death around 1625 at the same time her reputed relics were found in a cave on Mount Pellegrino, where she lived as a recluse. The relics, now encased in an elaborately carved silver urn, are paraded through the streets of Palermo at the climax of the feast on July 15. A second festival honoring Santa Rosalia takes place on September 4. There is usually a grand procession, and often the urn with the relics of the saint is again the center of attraction in the parade.

Deliverance from the plague in 1577 is also celebrated by the Venetians on the third Sunday in July. The festival is called the Feast of the Redeemer and consists of a procession of notables, clergy, and citizens across a bridge of boats to the Giudecca to give thanks in the Church of the Redeemer. After the church service there is a grand parade of gondolas festooned with lanterns and loaded with string bands and people who enjoy themselves by eating, drinking, and just drifting.

There is only one portable tower carried through the streets of Viterbo to honor Santa Rosa on her feast day, September 4, but it is a sixty-foot-tall wooden belfry copiously decorated and illuminated. It takes more than sixty men to race it through the streets, which they do in honor of St. Rose, who roused the people of Viterbo to resist invasion and later delivered them from a plague. There is also much eating and drinking while the illuminated *macchina* wobbles through the streets.

In Naples on the first Saturday in May and again on September 19 the devout gather at the cathedral to witness the liquefaction of the blood of their patron saint, the martyr San Gennaro, or St. Januarius. According to church history the saint, who was the Bishop of Benevento in the fourth century, was martyred in Pozzuoli. Some of his blood was gathered in two glass phials by a faithful nurse. The blood is supposed to have coagulated normally, but liquefied later when the phials were brought to Naples. Some Neapolitans believe that if the blood liquefies all will go well with Naples during the ensuing year. When it doesn't liquefy, the faithful rail and call the saint hard names.

The good St. Nicholas, whose tomb is in the Basilica of St. Nicholas, which was built in Bari in 1087, is honored in that city for three days during the second week in May and on his day, December 6. Often at the Maytime celebration there is a parade of sailors who carry an image of the saint through the streets, put it on a vessel bedecked with flowers and banners, and take it for a ride on the sea. That night it is returned, there are bonfires, fireworks, and the typical carnival type of celebration.

The processions of the *giganti*, effigies of two giants named Mata and Grifone who are credited with having founded Messina, and the *vara*, a huge car carrying a pyramid of rotating angels with the Madonna triumphant, are the big attractions of *Mezzagosto*, the mid-August festival in Messina. Ordinarily the thirty-five-foot giants are paraded through the streets on August 13 by hundreds of young men wearing white trousers and shirts and red caps. The procession ends in Piazza del Duomo, where the statues remain for two days. The feast is climaxed on August 15 by the procession of the *vara*. Until 1860 the numerous saintly figures on the *vara* were live, but now they are statues. At least 300,000 persons take part in the festival.

The Italian *presepio*, a representation of the Nativity that can be found in homes, churches, and cathedrals throughout Italy at Christmastime, is believed to have been introduced by St. Francis of Assisi in 1223 when he celebrated Christmas Mass in a stable in the Bosco di Greccio. He merely reproduced the storied scene in its simplest, most natural way, even to the point of leaving the cradle bare so that worshipers could see the infant with the inner eye of faith. Since then, however, others have filled the cribs with all sorts of dolls. Communities well known for their displays of Christmas cribs and scenes include Acireale, Amalfi, Caprio, Caserta, Cosenza, Loreto, Naples, Norcia, Rome, Scicli, Torre Annunziata, Vico Equense, and Volterra. Particularly famous *presepi* are at San Giovanni a Carbonara, Naples; Santa Maria Maggiore, Rome; Church of San Bartolomeo, Scicli, Sicily; and in the Duomo, Volterra.

Carnival

Once upon a time Italy was fairly jumping with pre-Lenten carnivals, but now the celebrations are staged by just a few communities. Probably only one of them, the carnival at Viareggio, compares with the world-famous festivals at New Orleans, Nice, Rio de Janeiro, and Trinidad. In Viareggio, as in most carnival capitals, the spirit of fun is rampant for several days before the climax on Shrove Tuesday, the day before Ash Wednesday, when Lent begins, in February or March. The big attractions are huge allegorical floats that require dozens of maskers and operators, historical processions, masquerades, flower displays, contests, and dancing in the streets. Smaller celebrations might be found at Acireale, Alassio, Arco, Fano, Foggia, Frascati, Grosseto, Ivrea, Limone

Piemonte, Mondovi, Palermo, Peveragno, Putignano, Saluzzo, and Termini Imerese.

A genuine carnival spirit also prevails in the Trastevere District of Rome at the *Festa de Noantri,* Our Festival, the fourth week of July. Focal points are the church and the Piazza Santa Maria in Trastevere and restaurants. Often restaurateurs compete with one another for the reputation of having the tastiest food in the Quarter, at least for various specialties, so during the festa they invite celebrities and journalists to judge their fare in a series of progressive dinners. The judges try appetizers in one place, soups and main courses at others, and so on until a seven- or eight-course meal, complete with fine wines, has been consumed. At the feasts prepared soon after World War II the judges sometimes lost their appetites because often they were watched by audiences of good-natured but obviously underfed Italians. Happily, by 1953 the fun- and food-loving people of Trastevere were noticeably well fed, so the festival was fun for everyone.

Sports

The Palio at Siena on July 2 and August 16 might be classed as a carnival by some people, but it is primarily a sports event inasmuch as the horse race around the Piazza del Campo is the main attraction. The Palio is a banner adorned with historical figures, a symbol and remembrance of the victory obtained, and in this instance it is the prize for which jockeys from various sections of town compete. Some historians say that the first Palio took place in 1482 after a popular insurrection against the tyranny of the Nine who had imprisoned the Governor of the Republic. After religious services of thanksgiving there were festas of all sorts, and a contest in which the participants competed for a banner adorned with historical figures, the Palio. In those days the competition took the form of jousts, tournaments, and wrestling matches, and during the Spanish period the inevitable bullfight was staged. In the sixteenth century there were buffalo races, and in the seventeenth century the race of the Barbary horses was introduced. In fact, the current series of Palii was inaugurated in 1656 to pay homage to the Madonna of Provenzano, whose feast occurs on July 2; on August 16, 1701, the second Palio was added for the Feast of Our Lady of the Assumption, patroness of Siena. The horse races are still in vogue, with the jockeys sometimes acting much more barbaric than the horses they ride. The main idea is to win, and what is normally regarded as fair play is often considered an encumbrance in this contest. On the morning of the race the captains, pages, standard-bearers, and drummers who represent the seventeen *contrade,* or quarters, parade to Piazza del Campo arrayed in the brilliant costumes of their communes. The standard-bearers give demonstrations of tossing the flag, and there is much beating of drums and blowing of trumpets. As a rule when the race is over, representatives of the victorious *contrada* run to the steeple of their church to ring the bell in celebration, and the party shifts from the Piazza del Campo to the neighborhood of the victors. Throughout the festival Siena's great musical tradition shines through, particularly in the playing of the Palio march, which is based on ancient airs. The trumpeters sound the march when the procession is about to begin, and those who are familiar with old Italian music might recognize the tunes that were inspired by songs sung in the various *contrade* represented at the festival. In July, 1953, Siena copyrighted the name Palio, so now no other town can use the word to describe its festivals.

In Pisa, usually on May 1, much is made of the Battle of the Bridge, a re-enactment of an encounter in the sixteenth century when men of the town's two factions, the Mezzogiorno and Tramontana, met. In the modern battle, which was dreamed up around 1935 as a tourist attraction, the combatants wear medieval armor and push against a contraption that resembles a blocking dummy used by American football teams in practice sessions. The team that pushes its opponents off the bridge wins, of course.

During the last week in May the people of Gubbio usually revive the ancient pastime of arbalest shooting. The arbalest is a medieval sort of iron bow and arrow, used for assault purposes. Sometimes, as in 1952 when the Italians invited the Swiss to an international contest, more modern weapons are introduced. The Swiss brought along a modern arbalest, believed to be not older than fifty years, which was so precision-perfect it could pick off a five-lire coin at a hundred feet.

The *Gioco del Calcio,* a football game in which players wear flamboyant sixteenth-century costumes, takes place annually on the first Sunday in May and on June 24, St. John's Day, in the Piazza della Signoria, Florence. It was first played in 1530 in Piazza Santa Croce during the siege of the French troops of Charles V. The city was under enemy fire, so the Florentines devised the game as a challenge and to indicate their low regard for the invaders. The old-time contest was revived in 1930 to celebrate the four-hundredth anniversary of its inauguration as well as the anniversary of the death in 1530 of Francesco Ferrucci, a Florentine patriot who played a prominent part in the struggle to oust the French and regain independence for the Republic of Florence. At the twentieth-century revival the ancient costumes made such a big hit with the spectators it was decided to make them a permanent part of the two yearly presentations. The game is played by the Greens and the Whites, two teams representing the sections of the city divided by the Arno. Before it begins there is a procession of foot soldiers, mace bearers, trumpeters, flag bearers, and heralds.

Il Torneo dei Butteri, the horsemen's tournament, in

Grosseto sometime in May, dates to medieval times when knights used to prove their skills on horseback. Now at the Campo Sportivo it represents the folkloric event in the Maremma region that best depicts the activities of the past and present. It has three parts: Joust of the Saracen; gymkhana, a series of athletic contests, especially in racing; and the Rodeo of the Roses. The horsemen of the Maremma region are the cowboys of Italy, and their actions at the tournament are an extension of their workaday activities. In the Joust of the Saracen the horsemen gallop toward a wooden Saracen holding an iron ring at the end of his outstretched arm. The rider whose lance pierces the ring wins, total prizes being worth about twenty dollars. The gymkhana in this instance is a display of fancy horsemanship. The Rodeo of the Roses is played by two teams. Each participant has a red or white rose pinned on his left arm. The object of the game is to capture the most roses from the opposing team. Total value of prizes in the rodeo is about fifty dollars.

Still another medieval show is the Giostra del Saracino which usually takes place in Arezzo during the first week in June and the first week in September. It is a tournament game played as long ago as the thirteenth century. Now a large retinue of knights in armor parade, and some ride against the dummy dressed in breastplate and having a whip in one hand and a shield in the other. The dummy is called Buratto, King of the Saracens. At the whip's end are three wooden balls. The knight rides his horse at top speed, lance extended, toward the "King," aiming his lance at the shield. He must also be adept enough to avoid being hit by the three balls, which swing around in his direction as the dummy is spun around. Each of the city's four quarters sends two knights to the tournament. Each quarter also has its own captain, standard-bearers, jousters, riders, drums, buglers, macers, foot soldiers, and bowmen. The musicians come from all quarters, and their program usually consists of warrior tunes or the Saracino hymn.

The first regatta of the season in Venice is the *Festa del Gondoliere,* usually on St. Mark's Day, April 25. Two-oared gondolas are used in this race, which was started in 1949 to encourage young gondoliers to participate in a contest that does not include competition by experts. The prizes include money and flags, but the main trophy is the *Trofeo Marciano.* It becomes the permanent possession of a three-time winner.

Venice uses its famous Grand Canal for a number of fetes and sports events, and one of the most exciting of all is the one staged on the first Sunday in September. The regatta dates back to 1300 when the crossbowmen with their boats went to the Lido for target practice. A race among the boats developed naturally and eventually became more important than the archery contests. Boats with as many as fifty oars, and some with women rowers, took part. Today the rowers and their boats are dressed up as though for a royal wedding. As a rule the course is from the Bacino on to the Grand Canal. At the end of the canal the contestants turn around and head for the floating pavilion where the judges award the winners the flag of victory.

The historic Regatta of St. Ranieri at Pisa, dedicated to the patron saint of the city and customarily staged on June 17, is said to date to the sixteenth century. Originally the men who rowed the boats representing the four sections of Pisa named Sant' Antonio, San Francesco, S. Maria, and S. Martino were prisoners. Now contestants are citizens who dress in striped costumes. Each crew has eight rowers and one steersman, and they race toward a *navicello,* small boat. On the bow of each racing craft is the *montatore,* the climber, who jumps from his boat to the smaller one in order to climb up its ropes and retrieve a flag flying atop the mast.

Another festival dedicated to the memory of the Saracens

is the traditional *Sbarco dei Saraceni,* landing of the Saracens, at Positano around August 14. Originated in 1949, the festival is based on two legends. One relates how a pirate ship was caught in a hurricane when the hopeless crew heard a voice say, *"Posa! Posa!"* Stop! The pirates headed their ship in the direction of the voice, landed at a small beach, and were saved. They called the beach Positano. The voice was attributed to a Byzantine portrait of the Madonna that was on board as part of the pirates' loot. To show their gratitude the pirates erected a church to the Madonna. The second story describes how a fleet of Saracens neared the coast of Positano bent on pillaging the town. They engaged in a terrific battle, and after plundering the place stole a miraculous painting of the Madonna. Both legends are fused in the modern celebration. The landing of the Saracens is re-created, fireworks simulate the burning of the town, and the pirates return carrying the painting of the Madonna.

Back on land the same high pitch of excitement that attends the regatta at Venice is evident at the *Mille Miglia,* the thousand-mile automobile race that begins and ends in Brescia, usually late in April or early in May. The first *Mille Miglia* was staged in 1927. Since then it has become one of the outstanding road races in the world, because it is a race rich in technical problems and sporting thrills. The route, which goes as far south as Rome, is through such ancient cities as Ancona, Aquila, Bologna, Ferrara, Padua, and Siena.

Second in interest only to the *Mille Miglia* among auto-racing enthusiasts in Italy is the *Gran Premio d'Italia,* which took place for the first time in Montichiari (Brescia), September 4, 1921. Now in mid-September it attracts more than 80,000 spectators to the track of Monza, northwest of Milan. The course is almost four miles long and is considered one of the fastest in Europe. The *Gran Premio d'Italia* is one of the ten classic events that contribute points to the world championship each year. The others are: Argentina, Belgium, France, Germany, Great Britain, Holland, Indianapolis Speedway, Spain, and Switzerland. Alberto Ascari, of Italy, who won the *Gran Premio* in 1952 with an average speed of 109.74 miles per hour, then went on to cop the world championship that year by winning six of the Big Ten, clinched the title again in 1953 when he won five of the classic events. He was the first person to win the championship two years in a row.

More than twenty other outstanding auto races take place in Italy between March and October. The list includes: Gran Prix of Syracuse, Sicily, March; Tour of Sicily, and *Mille Miglia* at Brescia, April; Gran Prix of Naples, Targa Florio in Sicily, Inter-Europe Cup and Gran Prix Autodromo of Monza, Sardinian Trophy, and Tour of Tuscany, May; uphill race Parma–Poggio–Berceto, Gran Prix of Rome, and the Perugina Cup, June; uphill race Bolzano–Mendola, Dolomiti Cup, uphill race Susa–Moncenisio, uphill race Aosta–Great St. Bernard, and Circuit of Senigaglia, July; Tour of Calabria and twelve-hour circuit of Pescara, August; Gran Prix Cortemaggiore at Merano, Gran Prix d'Italia at Monza, uphill race Catania–Etna, and Gran Prix of Bari, September; Golden Cup of Sicily, October.

The *Coppa Automobilistica della Toscana*, an increasingly popular auto race in Tuscany, was inaugurated in 1949 and is limited to Italian cars and drivers. A typical route approximately 425 miles long follows a circle from Florence to Siena, Radiocofani, Viterbo, Vetralla, Tarquinia, Grosseto, Livorno, Pisa, Pietrasanto, Lucca, and Florence.

Hunting wild doves in the medieval manner is still practiced in the vicinity of Cava dei Tierreni between September and November. At that time of year wild doves desert Central Europe for the Mediterranean Coast. Hunters take their stand on the ancient towers not far from Salerno, and as the birds fly past, the hunters toss white-painted rocks. More often than not the doves follow the white objects, and thus descend into nets set to trap them.

Music

In Italy music of the finest quality seems to be everywhere throughout the year. During the traditional opera season, from December to May, Italians and their guests fill four of the world's foremost opera houses: Massimo, at Palermo, a national monument; San Carlo in Naples; the Rome Opera in Rome; and La Scala in Milan. Sometimes in the summer and autumn those halls are open for concerts and special performances, but usually during the so-called off seasons music-lovers are entertained elsewhere.

High on the growing list of spring and summer music festivals in Europe is the May Musicale, a festival of concerts, ballet, and opera at Florence, first held in 1933 and usually staged there annually from early in May until mid-June. One season a typical program of opera included Robert Schumann's only opera, *Genoveva,* Haydn's *Orfeo ed Euridice,* Ildebrando Pizzetti's *Ifigenia,* Weber's *Oberon,* and two works by Verdi, *Macbeth* and *I Vespri Siciliani.* That season Herbert Graf, of the Metropolitan Opera in New York City, was given permission to stage Weber's *Oberon* on an island in the lovely Boboli Gardens so that the surrounding water could be used as a convincing prop for the mermaids of the libretto. Since the war an international music conference has been held in conjunction with the festival. Attendance at the six-week music festival often totals 80,000 persons.

To attract visitors to their city in May the people of Bari began staging their *Maggio di Bari* in 1951. Typical festival programs include international athletic tournaments, exhibitions of contemporary Italian paintings, ballet, drama and opera, folkloric costume displays, flower shows, aquatic events, and fireworks.

Opera singers manage to work a good part of the year in Italy, because most cities have discovered that old castles and ancient ruins that used to attract visitors only by day can do double duty by serving as theaters at night during the warm seasons of the year. A fine sample of what is to be found at these gala off-season shows is offered regularly in the Court-yard of the Arms in the Castle of Lombardia, at Enna. The castle is a great medieval stronghold of irregular form, flanked by six towers. Every year during the last three weeks in July some 10,000 spectators go there to hear the brightest stars of Italian opera sing *Aïda, Norma, La Favorita, Manon, André Chenier,* and *Stabat.* The long list of improvised theaters includes such notable show places as the Villa Floridiana near Naples and the Baths of Caracalla in Rome. Between June 28 and August 30, 1953, thirty-eight operatic performances were sung at the Baths of Caracalla. An average of 7,888 spectators attended each program, and of the approximately 300,000 who went there, at least 90,000 sat in Section C, the hundred-lire (sixteen American cents) section.

As long ago as 1930 the people who organized the Biennial Art Show of Venice decided that it might be well to exhibit contemporary music as well. So now in Venice each September the International Festival of Contemporary Music is a fixture. It has become a testing ground for the world's foremost composers, many of whom conduct their own works at the festival. Among the composers whose work has been performed there are Franco Alfano, Manual de Falla, Ottorino Respighi, Arnold Schönberg, Dimitri Shostakovich, and Igor Stravinsky. Ballet, too, is usually included. Three famous troupes that have appeared there are the American Ballet Theatre, Champs Élysées Company, and Grand Ballet du Marquis de Cuevas. The Venetian Autumn Musicale, devoted entirely to classical music, runs concurrently with the Contemporary Music Festival.

In the churches of Assisi, Cittá de Castello, Perugia and Spoleto the two-week *Sagra Musicale Umbra,* or Umbrian Festival of Church and Religious Music, which dates to 1937, is usually timed to end on October 4, the day of St. Francis of Assisi. Spiritual music-drama is the aim of the sponsors, who have presented Carissimi's *Jonah,* Respighi's *Maria Egiziaca,* Pizzetti's *Abraham and Isaac,* Berlioz' *Childhood of Christ,* and Stradella's *St. John the Baptist Oratorio.* The Sistine Chapel Choir has been heard in classical and modern polyphonic music, and choirs have been imported from Vienna and Salzburg. In 1953 seven concerts were given in Perugia alone. Visitors heard the choruses of the *Wiener Singakademie* and the *Maggio Musicale Fiorentino,* and the Vienna Symphony and Florentine orchestras. The conductors were Franco Capuana, Karl Elmendorff, Paul Hindemith, and Emidio Tieri. The programs included Pfitzner's *Palestrina,* Mendelssohn's *Paulus,* Schumann's C-minor mass, Schubert's *Lazarus,* Hugo Wolf's *Christnacht* and *Feuerreiter,* and Hindemith's *Cantique de l'Espérance.*

Definitely on the lighter side among music festivals is the ancient Festival of Piedigrotta in Naples around the first week in September. The high point is a competition among poets and composers for the honor of writing the hit song of the year. Although primarily a pagan religious celebration, Piedigrotta is truly a festival of Neapolitan songs, for one hears the new tunes played by the young men and women who ride about the streets on gaily decorated floats in a parade that wanders as aimlessly as the famous Zulu Parade at the Mardi Gras in New Orleans. Singing, shouting, dancing in the streets, making as much noise as possible, and eating and drinking go on through the night. The Feast of Piedigrotta has its roots deep in the past. In pagan times the grotto is supposed to have

been the site of the Temple of Lampasco, and was the scene
of erotic rites by pagan priestesses. In their war on paganism
early Christians are said to have torn down the temple and
built a chapel. On September 8, 1356, the Madonna is reported to have appeared to a hermit, a priest, and a nun, and
told them to replace the chapel with a church. When the build-
ers went to work some five hundred years ago to build the
present Church of Santa Maria di Piedigrotta they are supposed to have found a statue of St. Mary holding a baby. The
statue is still a treasured possession of the church, and is ven-
erated by thousands of the faithful, especially at the time of
the festival.

Drama

Thespians as well as vocalists use the old ruins of ancient amphitheaters and palaces in all sections of Italy in an admirable
attempt to recapture an aura of authenticity. Sometimes the
charm of the surroundings contributes real magic to the performance, particularly at places like D'Annunzio's estate at
the Vittoriale in Gardone on the shore of Lake Garda, which
was conceived by the Italian poet and playwright before his
death and designed for the production of his own plays; the
arena at Verona, the Roman theater at Pompeii, and the Olympic Theatre in Vicenza. The ancient Arena at Verona has
been the scene of drama and opera since 1913. That year
Giovanni Zenatello and Ester Mazzoleni starred there in *Aïda*.
Since then each summer, save during the war years, capacity
audiences have cheered such classics as *Carmen, Mephistophe-
les, The Prodigal Son, The King of Lahore,* and *Turandot.*
Also, each year the program includes at least one play by
Shakespeare, usually *Romeo and Juliet* or *Two Gentlemen
of Verona.* Nearby, of course, is one of the most romantic spots
in Italy, the tomb of Juliet, heroine of Shakespeare's *Romeo*

and Juliet, near the Campo della Fiera where Friar Laurence's convent is supposed to have stood. Now lovers may be married in a lovely little chapel built in those sentimental surroundings. Not far from Verona are the castles of the Montecchi and Capuleti, where the families of the ill-starred lovers are supposed to have lived.

The Greek Theatre at Syracuse, considered by some authorities to be the greatest Hellenic arena extant, is a natural for the tragedies of Aeschylus, Euripides, and Sophocles, so the Italians have been presenting the plays there regularly since 1914, usually for about ten days in May during even years.

At Taormina the Greek theater, one of the most impressive to be found anywhere, is used for several days during the last week in August. The current series of plays was inaugurated in 1947. Ancient Greek plays are customarily staged during even years, and plays and operas of a later vintage are put on during odd years. For example, in 1953 the attraction was Molière's *Don Juan.*

Vicenza's Olympic Theatre is said to date to 1585. The inaugural performance that year was Sophocles' *King Oedipus.* During the seventeenth and eighteenth centuries the theater was used for receptions and tournaments as well as for dramatic and musical performances, but in the nineteenth century it reverted to the classical tradition. Now in September visitors might see Sophocles' *Electra* or *Love's Intrigues,* a comedy by Torquato Tasso.

Sacred drama, too, has its place in the Italian repertoire. Two noteworthy ones are *Miracolo del Corporale,* author unknown, which is staged in Orvieto usually around the Feast of Corpus Christi in May or June, and the Passion play at Sezze, near Rome, which is a stand-by of Holy Week and is often repeated in the spring and summer. *Miracolo del Corporale* is enacted on the steps of the cathedral at Orvieto where the original corporal, or altar cloth, which inspired the Feast of Corpus Christi, is enshrined. The Passion play at Sezze is presented in the open in a valley flanking Monte del Gallo, which dominates the Pontine plain from Terracina to Anzio. There are olive groves, the mountain is remindful of Golgotha, and the Pontine plain might be likened to the plain of Jerusalem.

The Venice Film Festival, which was inaugurated in 1932 and lasts from about the second week in August to the second week in September, is one of the longest and most firmly established of all the film festivals in Europe. At least a dozen countries send their finest motion pictures to the international contest because an award there can have a salutary effect on box-office receipts when the picture is released at home and in other countries. The festival offers feature-length films, scientific movies and art documentaries, movies for children, a fashion show and displays of movie costumes, and an exhibition of books about the movies.

In 1934 the Italians inaugurated the International Theater Festival and since then have staged it annually during peacetime in Venice each September. Its aim is the presentation of the great works of the theater.

Since 1947 Taormina has been sponsoring an international contest for short movies on travel. The exhibition usually takes place around the second week in October. Its aim is to give public recognition to effort put forth by the makers of thirty-five-millimeter movies to publicize the natural and artistic features of each country. The contest is open to anyone who makes travel shorts, whether they have been shown to the public or not, but entries are confined to those movies made during the year of the show. Travel movies taken before the year of the current show are sometimes shown but are not entered in the competition. Prizes are awarded to the directors of the best short on any country, best foreign short, best

Italian short, and best short on Sicily; to the best cameraman, for the best musical comment, and to the Italian producer who has produced the greatest number of shorts dealing with travel since the beginning of the year.

Il Festa del Passo Ridotto, dedicated to sixteen-millimeter film, takes place regularly in the Salone de Cemmo of the cinema Aquilletta at Brescia during the second and third weeks in September. The festival was launched at Gardone Riviera in 1948 and was staged there for three years before being transferred to Brescia in 1951.

Art Exhibits

Every other year since 1895 peace permitting, of course, the world-famous Biennale of Art has been the big attraction in Venice from mid-June to mid-October, usually during even years. The works of art are from all over the world, and the show is so firmly established that most countries have their own permanent pavilions. Prizes distributed to painters, sculptors, and engravers total almost $15,000, and recently sales of some 350 works of art out of 1,386 entered in the show exceeded $85,000. Sometimes in the Pavilion of Decorative Art there is an exhibit of exquisite Murano glassware, lace, mosaics, lacquer, and enamel.

Fairs

The big International Samples Fair staged at Milan for about three weeks in April was organized in 1920 to revive interest in trade following the devastation of World War I. It began with 1,233 exhibitors. That number was increased steadily until World War II. The fair was reorganized in 1946, and by 1951 there were 8,428 exhibitors who showed their wares to almost 4,000,000 visitors along an estimated 28 miles of displays. The exhibits include everything from autos to yachts. In 1954, the last two days were set aside for foreign visitors and customers expressly invited by exhibitors. Visitors cards entitled foreigners to twelve free admissions and other privileges.

The International Agricultural and Horse Fair at Verona, which usually begins on the second Monday in March and lasts three days, stems from the famous fairs of the seventeenth century. The modern version was introduced in 1898, and now about six thousand horses are exhibited and sold every year.

Italy's National Handicraft Show usually takes place in the Piazza Liberta, Florence, and is visited by 250,000 persons during May. The first fair was staged in 1931 to select the best artisans and to encourage exportation of their products. Prizes are valued at about $2,500.

Another exhibition of particular interest to visitors is the Levant Fair at Bari, usually staged for about three weeks in September, because it is a clearinghouse for Near Eastern as well as Italian wares. Organized in 1930, it now has 160 permanent pavilions that are visited by almost 2,000,000 persons from 52 countries every year.

Food

Many experts in the art of cooking consider Bologna the gastronomic capital of Italy. The Bolognese encourage that opinion by staging a gastronomic festival in the Parco della Montagnola during May and June, as they have been doing in peaceful years since 1935. About 150,000 persons go to the *festa* to admire the work of some of Italy's best chefs. Among the specialties of Bologna are *lasagnette, maccheroni alla Bolognese, mortadella, tagliatelle*, and *tortellini*.

Flowers

In 1935 the Tuscan Horticultural Society staged its first flower show in collaboration with the Office of Gardens and Public Parks of the City of Florence in Piazza della Signoria and around the *piazzale* of the Uffizi Gallery. Now each year early in May about fifty exhibitors convert the areaway into a rippling river of multicolored blossoms, for which Italy is famous in the spring.

Palermo's *Festa del Fiore*, festival of the flowers, was launched only in 1949. Now late in May and early in June it attracts about 300,000 spectators, who watch a flower show that offers $2,000 in prizes, a national exhibit of floral paintings with $500 in prizes, a national poetry contest dedicated to flowers, for which prizes total $250, a floricultural competition with $3,500 in prizes, a $350 contest for floral displays in the railroad station of Palermo and the surrounding area, and a $700 contest to find the best decorated parks, balconies, and private villas.

Grape Festivals

Whenever someone makes the mistake of suggesting that practically all Italian wine is Chianti, the people of Tuscany are quick to correct him. For the genuine, classic Chianti comes from a small, rocky section of Tuscany, between Siena and Florence, which covers not more than 700 kilometers, or about 450 miles. Four-fifths of the wine it produces is placed on the market. Representative of the Chiantian celebrations that honor the grape is the *Festa dell "Uva"* at Impruneta. The town is a favorite haunt of Florentines who wish to venerate the Madonna of Impruneta, or rest in the pine forests nearby. The festival was inaugurated in 1928 and now takes place regularly in the main square on the last Sunday in September. It features a parade of allegorical carts representing the districts of Fornaci, Sant' Antonio, Santa Maria, and Pallo, and exhibitions of pottery, ceramics, lace, leather goods, wood work, and articles of straw. During September and October in other grape and wine districts of Italy festivals are usually staged at Acireale, Bagni di Casciana, Capri, Castiglion De Lago, Dogliani E Carru, Frascati, Marino, Masserano, Ravello, Soave, and Sorrento.

The exact dates on which festivals will take place in Italy, as well as the latest travel information pertaining to that country, may be obtained by writing to the Italian State Tourist Office, 51 East 51st Street, New York 22, New York; Room 131, International Trade Mart, 124 Camp Street, New Orleans 12, Louisiana; International Aviation Building, 1080 University Street, Montreal, Canada.

Bank holidays in Italy: January 1; Epiphany, January 6; St. Joseph's Day, March 19; Easter Monday, March or April; World War II Liberation Day, April 25; May 1; Ascension Day, forty days after Easter; Corpus Christi, May or June; Anniversary of the Proclamation of the Republic, June 2 (1946); St. Peter's Day, June 29; Assumption Day, August 15; Victory Day in World War I, November 4 (1918); Feast of the Immaculate Conception, December 8; Christmas, December 25; and December 26.

Chronological list of events in Italy:

JANUARY. Altipiano: winter sports contests, to April. Comigliatello Silano: winter sports contests, to April. Cortina d'Ampezzo: winter sports contests, to April. Di Lavarone: winter sports contests, to April. Florence: trotting races. Limone Piemonte: winter sports contests, to April. Madonna di Campiglio: winter sports contests, to April. Piana Degli Albanesi: Epiphany, according to Greek rites. Rivisindoli: Epiphany, the living *presepe,* re-enactment of the Nativity. Rome: Epiphany, Piazza Navona. San Remo: festival of songs. Sestriere: winter sports contests, to April. Tortona: Epiphany.

FEBRUARY. Agrigento: almond-blossom festival. Catania: Feast of St. Agatha, and Dance of the Candles. Rome: trotting, horse races. San Remo: auto race for women, Paris–St. Raphaël–San Remo; floricultural show.

FEBRUARY or MARCH. Agnelli Cup, auto rally: Sestriere. March
of the Penitents, Ash Wednesday, first day of Lent: Rome. Pre-
Lenten carnivals: Acireale, Alassio, Arco, Fano, Foggia, Frascati,
Grosseto, Ivrea, Limone Piemonte, Mondovi, Palermo, Peveragno,
Putignano, Saluzzo, Termini Imerese, Viareggio.

MARCH. Casal Fiumanese: Feast of the Ravioli. Milan: bike race,
Milan–San Remo. Nationwide: Mid-Lent festivals, feasts for the
poor, usually on St. Joseph's Day, March 19. Palermo: orange-
blossom festival. Pistoia: *La Giostra dell 'Orso,* joust of the bear.
San Remo: bike race, Milan–San Remo. Syracuse: Grand Prix auto
race. Verona: agricultural fair, horse show.

MARCH or APRIL. Holy Week: nationwide; more spectacular ob-
servances at Acireale, Assisi, Caltanissetta, Florence (*Scoppio del
Carro,* blowing up of the chariot, Holy Saturday), Francavilla di
Sicilia, Genoa, Grassina, Isnello, Parma, Piana Degli Albanesi
(Greek rites), Rome, Sezze, Trapani (Procession of Mysteries).

APRIL. Brescia: *Mille Miglia,* thousand-mile auto race, begins,
ends at Brescia, April or May. Florence: handicrafts fair. Milan:
fair. Naples: bike race, Rome–Naples–Rome. Palermo: tennis
tournament; Tour of Sicily, auto race. Rome: bike race, Rome–
Naples–Rome; horse show. Siena: Feast of St. Catherine, patroness
of Italy, April 28–30. Stromboli: religious festival. Turin: auto
show, into May. Veni:e: *Regata dei Traghetti,* regatta for all
types of rowing craft.

MAY. Agrigento: classical drama. Bari: Feast of St. Nicholas;
Maggio di Bari, cultural, sports events. Bologna: fair; gastronomic
festival. Bolzano: costume festival. Brescia: *Mille Miglia,* thousand-mile auto race, begins, ends at Brescia, April or May. Cagliari:
Feast of St. Efisio. Catania: Sicilian song festival, flower corso.
Cocullo: Feast of St. Domenico da Sora, in which snakes play a
prominent part. Florence: *Festa del Grillo,* Feast of the Cricket;
Gioco del Calcio, football game in sixteenth-century costumes,
first Sunday in May and June 24; handicraft show; *Maggio Musicale,* May music festival, May, June; *Mostra dei Fiori,* flower show.
Grosetto: *Torneo dei Butteri,* medieval jousting tournament in
region famous for horsemanship; Joust of the Saracens; Rodeo of
the Rose. Gubbio: Arbalest-shooting contests; *Festa dei Ceri,* or
race of the candles. Milan: bike tour of Italy, usually starts in
Milan; Inter-Europe Cup, Grand Prix Autodromo, auto races at
Monza Circuit. Naples: Feast of San Gennaro, or St. Januarius,

first Saturday in May, September 19; Grand Prix of Naples, auto race. Palermo: fair, May, June. Pesaro: drama festival, May, June. Pisa: Battle of the Bridge. Rome: concerts at Basilica of Maxentius, often to September. Sardinia: Sardinian Trophy, auto race. Sassari: cavalcade in costume. Sorrento: feast of the oranges. Syracuse: chamber music, classical dances, opera at the Greek theater, usually to July. Tremezzo: art, ballet festival. Turin: auto show, April, May; photography show.

MAY or JUNE. Corpus Christi: nationwide; more spectacular observances at Brindisi, Genoa, Genzano (streets carpeted with fresh flowers), Orvieto (*Miracolo del Corporale,* sacred drama), Ravello (streets carpeted with fresh flowers). Flower festivals: Palermo, Ventimiglia. Four Altars Festival: Torre el Greco. Tour of Tuscany, auto race: Florence.

JUNE. Amalfi: religious festival. Arezzo: *Giostra del Saracino,* Joust of the Saracen. Assisi: Feast of the Vow. Bologna: *Festa Gastronomico.* Como: thousand-mile motorboat race. Florence: *Coppa Automobilistica della Toscana; Gioco del Calcio,* football game in sixteenth-century costumes, first Sunday in May, June 24; *Maggio Musicale,* May music festival, May, June. Genoa: motorboat regatta. Palermo: air tour of Sicily. Montecatini Terme: flower competition. Nationwide: Feast of St. John, June 24; most important observance at Rome; Feast of St. Peter; most spectacular celebration at Rome when dome of St. Peter's is lighted by thousands of torches, June 29. Nemi: strawberry festival. Nola: Dance of the Lilies. Padua: fair; Feast of St. Anthony, who is buried in the Basilica at Padua, June 13. Palermo: fair, May, June. Parma: uphill auto race. Perugia: Perugia Cup, auto race. Pesaro: drama festival, May, June. Pisa: historic regatta of San Ranieri. Ravello: Wagner concerts, Villa Rufolo, to August. Rome: Grand Prix auto race. Syracuse: chamber music, classical dances, opera at the Greek theater, usually into July. Trieste: fair. Turin: popular dance, costume festival. Venice: Biennial of Art, to October in even years; water-skiing contests.

JULY. Acireale: Feast of St. Venera. Ancona: fishing fair. Aosta: uphill auto race, Aosta–Great St. Bernard. Assisi: Feast of Pardon. Bolzano: uphill auto race. Como: ballet festival, into August. Cortina d'Ampezzo: Dolomiti Gold Cup, auto race; fashions festival. Enna: opera at the Castello di Lombardia, into August. Gardone: D'Annunzio's plays in theater he designed for them at

Vittoriale, his estate. Naples: Feast of the Madonna del Carmine; opera at Villa Floridiana, into August. Nervi: Open-air theater. Palermo: Feast of Santa Rosalia. Pistoia: *Giostra dell'Orso,* Joust of the Bear. Pompeii: drama in ancient open-air theater, into September. Ravello: Wagner concerts, Villa Rufolo, to August. Rome: *Festa de Noantri,* Our Feast, centers in piazza, restaurants of Trastevere; opera at Baths of Caracalla, through August. Senigaglia: auto race. Sezze: *Passion of Christ,* sacred drama, near Rome. Siena: Palio, July 2, August 16. Solda: giant *slalom* competition. Susa: uphill auto race, Susa–Moncenisio. Syracuse: chamber music, classical dances, opera at the Greek theater. Trieste: opera in Castle of San Giusto, into August. Venice: Biennial of Art, to October in even years; *La Veglia del Redentore,* Feast of the Redeemer, third week end. Verona: drama, opera in ancient Roman arena, into August.

JULY or AUGUST. *Miracle of Bolsena,* other sacred plays: Orvieto. Song, dance festival: Perugia.

AUGUST. Camogli: *Stella Maris,* Star of the Sea Festival. Castel Gandolfo: peach festival near the Pope's summer home. Como: ballet festival. Cortina d'Ampezzo: golf, tennis championships. Enna: opera at the Castello di Lombardia. Gardone: D'Annunzio's plays in theater he designed for them at *Vittoriale,* his estate. Messina: Procession of the *Vara,* decorated boat, and *Giganti,* giants, August 15. Naples: opera at Villa Floridiana. Pescara: folklore festival; Twelve-hour Circuit of Pescara, auto race. Pompeii: drama in ancient open-air theater. Positano: *Lo Sbarco dei Saraceni,* Landing of the Saracens. Ravello: Wagner concerts, Villa Rufolo. Reggio: Tour of Calabria, auto race. Rome: opera at Baths of Caracalla. San Gimignano: operatic performances in Cathedral Square. Siena: Palio, August 16; Procession of the Wax Candle. Taormina: play festival, with ancient Greek plays in even years, more modern plays, operas in odd years; religious festival. Tivoli: *L'Inchinata,* Feast of Obedience, in beautiful gardens near Rome, usually on Assumption Day, August 15. Trieste: opera in Castle of San Giusto. Varese: *Tre Valli Varesine,* three valleys of Varesine, bike race. Venice: Biennial of Art, to October in even years; Film Festival, into September; *Il Fresco,* nocturnal festival on the Grand Canal. Verona: drama, opera in ancient Roman arena. Vicenza: fair.

SEPTEMBER. Ancona: accordion festival. Altavilla Milicia: religious pilgrimage, folk dancing. Arezzo: *Giostra del Saracino,* Joust of the Saracen. Assisi: Satriano cavalcade. Bari: Grand Prix, auto race; Levant Fair; thousand-mile air race. Bergamo: dog show; motorcycle regularity race. Bolzano: costume festival, parade; fair; piano contest for Busoni Prize. Brescia: *Festa del Passo Ridotto,* festival of reduced or 16-mm. film. Cagliari: Sardinian Region Trophy, national auto race. Candia: Feast of St. Michele. Catania: uphill auto race, Catania–Etna. Cefalú: religious feast. Como: auto gymkhana; floriculture show; musical Saturdays, Villa Carlotta; parade of flower-decked boats. Cremona: Bike touring rally. Florence: *Rificolone,* festival of the lanterns. Foligno: Joust of the *Quintana,* medieval contest in the square. Gardone: D'Annunzio's plays in theater he designed for them at *Vittoriale,* his estate. Impruneta: *Festa dell'Uva,* grape harvest festival. Mandello Lario: Italian rowing championships. Merano: Miss Cinema, Miss Italy, contests. Milan: air show; amateur bike race, Milan–Rapallo, near Genoa; *Gran Premio Automobilistico d'Italia,* auto race at Monza Circuit; leather show; motorcycle Grand Prix at Monza Circuit. Modena: Gran Premio, auto race. Naples: Feast of San Gennaro, or St. Januarius, September 19; Piedigrotta. Palermo: Favorita Circuit, auto race; festival of art, grace. Parma: food fair. Pegli: concerts, drama in Arena Estiva at Villa Doria. Perugia: *Sagra Musicale Umbria,* Umbrian festival of sacred music, to October 4. Petralia Sottana: Crossing of the Madonie, auto race. Pisa: auto gymkhana. Pistoia: Joust of the Bear. Pompeii: drama in ancient open-air theater. Pontedera: contests for contemporary artists. Prato: fair. Rapallo: amateur bike race, Milan–Rapallo, near Genoa. Rima San Giuseppe: Festival of the Chamois. Rome: cat show; model aircraft races. San Gimignano: classical music festival, Church of St. Augustine. Sant' Andrea Bagni: accordion festival. Siena: Musical Week. Sorrento: folk-dance, costume festival. Spoleto: festival of experimental opera. Taormina: religious festival. Terni: Silver Wheel auto race up the Nera Valley. Tirrenia: contests for contemporary artists. Trento: jazz festival. Turin: contests for contemporary artists. Venice: Biennial of Art, to October in even years; contemporary music festival; Film Festival; historical regatta on the Grand Canal, usually the first Sunday; pigeon shoot, $15,000 prizes; tennis tournament for Volpi medals; theater festival, into October. Vicenza: national wool show, fair. Viterbo: Feast of Santa Rosa.

SEPTEMBER or OCTOBER. Grape, wine festivals: Acireale, Bagni di Casciana, Capri, Castiglion de Lago, Dogliani e Carru, Frascati, Marino, Masserano, Soave, Sorrento. Horse shows: Abano Terme, Bergamo, Bologna, Merano, Perugia, Salsomaggiore.

OCTOBER. Alba: *Fiera del Tartufo,* truffles fair, gourmet festival. Bari: Feast of the Virgins. Cava dei Tirreni: medieval-type pigeon shoot. Foggia: fair. Ischia: sports, folk festival. Merano: Grand Prix of the Nations, horse race. Nationwide: Feast of St. Francis, patron saint of Italy, with most impressive observances at Assisi, La Verna, October 3, 4. Palermo: Golden Cup of Sicily, auto race. Perugia: *Sagra Musicale Umbria,* Umbrian festival of sacred music. Taormina: travel films festival. Torre Annunziata: festival. Treviso: chrysanthemum show, into November; fair. Turin: fair. Vercelli: music, song contests. Verona: horse, cattle fair. Venice: Biennial of Art, in even years; Feast of Our Lady of the Salutation; theater festival.

NOVEMBER. Amalfi: Feast of Sant' Andrea, who is buried in the Duomo at Amalfi, November 30. Genoa: Riviera Cup, auto race, Genoa–San Remo. Milan: bike, motorcycle show; Leather Fair. Nationwide: All Saints' Day, November 1; All Souls' Day, November 2. Palermo: *Giro Ciclistico della Sicilia,* Sicilian bike race. San Remo: Riviera Cup, auto race, Genoa–San Remo. Treviso: chrysanthemum show. Venice: Feast of Our Lady of the Salutation.

DECEMBER. Limone Piemonte: *La Fiaccola d'Oro,* little golden flame. Nationwide: opera season, December to May, with outstanding performances at Florence, Milan, Naples, Palermo, Parma, Rome, Venice; *presepi,* reproductions of the Nativity, with most impressive displays at Acireale, Amalfi, Caprio, Caserta, Corsenza, Loreto, Naples, Norcia, Rome, Torre Annunziata, Vico Equense. Norcia: festival of the black truffles. Syracuse: *La Santuzza,* the little saint. Worldwide: Holy Year, usually every twenty-five years (most recent celebration in 1950) begins and ends in Rome on Christmas Eve.

LUXEMBOURG

IT IS a mere sixty-two miles from the north of Luxembourg to the south, and just thirty-seven miles across at the widest point. The very beautiful, rolling terrain in that small area is heavily wooded, and the one large city, with a population of just about 65,000, is a study in contrasts between the old and new. Most of the few annual festivals in Luxembourg are old, and invariably reflect Roman Catholicism, which prevails in that country.

Processions

Among the few festivals staged annually in Luxembourg the most unusual is probably the Dancing Procession at Echternach on the Tuesday of Pentecost, seven weeks after Easter. It is a religious feast and considered by some to be among the more impressive in Europe. Surely it is among the more unusual celebrations because of the strange antics of the participants as they follow in the wake of priests and church banners. The simple routine performed to an old tune has the dancers go three steps forward, two steps back, until they reach the basilica. As a rule each row has eight or ten dancers abreast, holding hands or handkerchiefs and performing the ritual all the way, even into and out of the nine-hundred-year-old parish church of SS. Peter and Paul. The festival dates to the Middle Ages and is all done in honor of St. Willibrord, the patron of Echternach. He was a holy missionary from Northumberland, England, who brought Christianity to Luxembourg in 698 and is supposed to have worked miracles among epileptics. A picture painted early in the seventeenth century by Antoine Stevens, of Malines, Belgium, shows the saint pronouncing a benediction on the dancers. Apparently it is a benediction that has withstood formidable opposition through the centuries, for even Napoleon is supposed to have tried to put a stop to the ceremony.

Another religious march, called the Procession of the Octave, usually takes place in Luxembourg City on the fifth Sunday after Easter. The celebration dates to 1677 when the civilian authorities proclaimed the Virgin Mary the protector of the country. The high point of the annual observance is the veneration of the Virgin Mary. A statue of the Virgin was found in the hollow of a tree in 1625. Now some 25,000 spectators watch as many as 10,000 marchers surge through flower-festooned streets to the cathedral with the statue up front.

Fairs

Although Luxembourg has few fairs they are geared to appeal to a wide range of tastes. For example, in Luxembourg City on the Monday after Easter is usually a market day featuring toys and pottery. In Grevenmacher on the Thursday after Easter and in Wormeldange on the Thursday after Pentecost the famous wines of the Moselle region have their day. As a rule there are free samples, so the wine fairs are special favorites of amateur wine-lovers.

La Fête des Genets, or poster festival, was launched in Wiltz only in 1949, yet it has gained a large measure of popularity since then. *Genets* are drawings and sketches. The subjects of the posters are products of established industries, history, and literature, past and present. It is staged regularly on Whitmonday, fifty days after Easter.

Another comparative newcomer to Luxembourg City is the annual Days of the Rose, which was inaugurated in 1950. Luxembourg considers itself a country of roses, so they are put on display usually during the fourth week in June. Special activities are arranged to entertain visitors and make the event a true festival of flowers.

The exact dates on which festivals will take place in Luxembourg, as well as the latest travel information pertaining to that country, may be obtained by writing to the Consulate General of the Grand Duchy of Luxembourg, 441 Lexington Avenue, New York 17, New York.

Bank holidays in Luxembourg: January 1; Birthday of the Grand Duchess Charlotte of Luxembourg, January 23; Carnival on Monday before Ash Wednesday, February or March; Easter Saturday and Monday, March or April; May 1; Ascension Day, forty days after Easter; Whitsun Eve, forty-eight days after Easter; Whitmonday, fifty days after Easter; Assumption Day, August 15; first Monday of Luxembourg Kermesse, or fair, late August; All Saints' Day, November 1; Christmas, December 25; and December 26.

Chronological list of events in Luxembourg:

JANUARY. Nationwide: Birthday of the Grand Duchess Charlotte, January 23.

MARCH or APRIL. Fair, Easter Monday: Luxembourg City.

APRIL or MAY. Procession of *l'Octave:* Luxembourg City.

MAY. Dudelange: fair. Esch-sur-Alzette: fair. Luxembourg City: fair; pilgrimage to Our Lady of Luxembourg.

MAY or JUNE. Pentecost: nationwide, most spectacular observance is the dancing procession at Echternach. Wine festival, Thursday after Pentecost: Wormeldange.

JUNE or JULY. Rose festivals: nationwide, with Day of the Rose in Luxembourg City the most important festival of this type.

JULY. Luxembourg City: Grand Prix auto race. Mondorf-les-Bains: blessing of autos on St. Christopher's Day, July 25.

AUGUST or SEPTEMBER. Fair: Luxembourg City.

SEPTEMBER or OCTOBER. Grape, wine fairs: towns along the Moselle River.

DECEMBER. Vianden: Nut Fair.

MONACO

TOURISM is the principal industry in Monaco, so the majority of the festivals on the principality's calendar of annual events are intended primarily to appeal to visitors.

Sports

The year 1911 was notable for two events of lasting importance to the automobile age. In that year the now famous five-hundred-mile Memorial Day Speed Classic was inaugurated in Indianapolis, and the celebrated Rally Automobile Monte Carlo was launched in Monte Carlo. Ever since then the Rally has been staged regularly, except during the two World Wars, and has become so popular with international auto racing enthusiasts that more than three hundred of them take part each year. Although the comparatively primitive plans of 1911 have been revised to meet changing conditions pertaining to travel by automobile, the Monte Carlo Rally remains one of the more popular and strenuous motoring contests in Europe.

It usually takes place in January when, in addition to the

customary hardships of racing some 2,000 miles over mountains and plains, competitors are exposed also to the snow and sleet of the peak of winter as they speed toward the golden sunshine of the Monacan Riviera. In a typical year the starting points might be Glasgow, Lisbon, Monte Carlo, Oslo, Palermo, and Stockholm. But regardless of the starting point, the route of the race from each place is always figured so that all contestants cover the same amount of mileage before they cross the finish line in Monte Carlo. Cash prizes are worth about $10,000, and there are numerous cups and other awards. The winner receives about $2,500 and the Prince of Monaco Cup. Each car is put into one of four categories, depending on its horsepower, and there is a special category for the women competitors who race without masculine passengers in their cars. When the contestants cross the finish line in Monte Carlo they submit to an acceleration-braking test, and, after a day of complete rest, a regularity-speed test. Both are elimination tests reserved for those who covered the route without incurring penalties. After that, the fun of being feted begins and lasts for several days. The parade of cars and distribution of prizes are of particular interest to visitors.

Since 1898 Monte Carlo has sponsored the Automobile Elegance Competition and the Feminine Elegance Competition, two contests spawned by the wealthy who once made Monaco their own playground. Since only the wealthy could afford automobiles around the turn of the century Monte Carlo was an ideal spot to launch a program of automobile events. The two festivals used to take place in March, but recently have been held in September. The cars are exhibited on the Casino terrace in the afternoon. Prizes for the most beautiful current models are distributed that night, then the exquisitely groomed contestants compete for prizes in their own little battle of elegance. Most of the women are dressed in the latest fashions from Paris.

The Grand Prix of Monaco, founded in 1929 and since then dubbed the race around the street corners because the two-mile circuit winds through the tiny town, is one of the official motor races in the international calendar of racing. It usually takes place at the end of May, and is one of the most spectacular events of its kind in the world. More often than not crowds estimated at 100,000 persons line the route.

Since 1870 pigeon shooting has been a particular favorite of regular visitors to Monte Carlo during January, February, and March, the high season on the Riviera, because the sport appeals to gamblers. They can bet on either the pigeon or the shooter and also lay odds when picking the one box out of five from which the bird will be released. The contest is also inexpensive for the promoters, too, because the marksmen pay for each bird at which they are going to shoot. Although pigeon shooting is very popular in Italy, and the Zuritos pigeons from Spain are said to be the best birds for this type of sport, Monte Carlo's contests probably top the list of international events because prizes at the Monte Carlo Grand Prix, which usually takes place the first two weeks in March, often amount to $50,000. Additional money can be won by gambling.

Important international golf tournaments take place at Monte Carlo during the first week in January, the first week in March, and around Easter.

International tennis matches are staged during the week before and the week after Easter, and during the last week in December. The tournament at Eastertime is staged just before the French International Championships at Paris. It is famous for its Butler Cup. Among the tennis greats who have won it are Bergelin, Borotra, Budge, Cochet, Drobny, Patty, Savitt, Tilden, and Von Cramm.

In September, 1953, Prince Rainier III launched a motor

yacht race on the course Monaco–Saint-Tropez, Corsida–San Remo–Monaco. Ocean-going yachts, motor cruisers, and motor sailers entered the first race, and called at Calvi, Saint-Tropez, Voile, Moteur, Portofino, Monaco-Le Port, and San Remo. The race will be held annually.

Galas

The long-established Bal de l'Or, or Golden Ball, is a gala, gilded affair that takes place at the International Sporting Club in mid-Lent at the end of the winter season. Everyone at the ball is dressed in his best bib and tucker, and the women invariably wear their most fabulous jewels. Yet only those dressed in white or gold may take part in a grand tombola, the grand prize of which is another piece of jewelry by a master craftsman. Other notable balls take place at Monte Carlo at Christmas, New Year's Eve, January 6, and Easter. The big night of the week during the high season is Friday night when there are special celebrations.

Battle of Flowers

Battles of Flowers have been a fixture in Monaco since about 1920 when foreigners began to patronize the Riviera in great numbers. During the winter season the de luxe hotels and some civic organizations invite attractive young girls to represent them on flower-bedecked floats and throw flowers at spectators along the route. It is a gay but somewhat subdued affair, compared with the ones staged during the summer season when Monacans and French on vacation join in the fun and toss the flowers right back at the princesses as they ride by on the floats.

Religious Feast Days

The Feast of St. Devote, the young martyr chosen by the House of Grimaldi, the family of the Princes of Monaco, as its patron saint, is celebrated January 27. On the evening before the twenty-seventh crowds gather in front of the saint's sanctuary to watch the symbolic burning of the bark, which is staged to recall the landing of the ship that, according to the legend, carried the body of the martyred saint when it was returned from Corsica. On the saint's day there are services in the cathedral, followed by a procession of the relics through the Rampe-Major to the sanctuary hidden in the Ravine of the Gaumattes.

A religious tradition dear to the hearts of Monacans is the Good Friday Procession called *Christ Mort*, which dates to 1646 when the Chapel of the Penitents was built. Drummers beating a funeral march on drums veiled in black and surrounded by torch-carriers lead the parade, which consists of the Black Cross, the angel with the chalice, the disciples of Christ, Veronica carrying a reproduction of the Holy Face, Mary Magdalene, the Twelve Apostles, Christ dead on the cross, penitents carrying the various attributes of the Passion, the clergy of the principal religious orders, and religious associations.

National Fete

The National Fete on November 19 is actually the official birthday of Prince Rainier III, who ascended the throne in 1949. The occasion also serves as a prelude to the high season at Monte Carlo and is marked by reviews, courtesy calls by warships of friendly foreign powers, elaborate public dances, and magnificent fireworks displays.

Ballet

Thousands of Americans who enjoy ballet today date their interest in this fine art to the first time they saw the world-famous Monte Carlo Ballet Company on one of its extensive tours of the United States during the 1930's. America has become increasingly ballet-conscious since then, and now many Americans visiting Europe make a pilgrimage to one of the more important shrines of Terpsichore, the magnificent Opera of Monte Carlo. That building has been called "the cradle of ballet" because it was there in 1911 that Serge Diaghileff launched his renowned *les Ballets Russes* starring Karsavina and Nijinsky. The annual seasons of ballet were discontinued from 1914 to 1920 because of World War I. When they were resumed in 1920, one of the big attractions was the debut of sixteen-year-old Serge Lifar. Throughout the 1920's Diaghileff presented such extraordinary dancers as Dolin, Vladimir Dukelsky, Markova, Massine, Nemchinova, Nikitina, Sokolova, Tchernicheva, and Nicolas Zvereff, and he always referred to the season at Monte Carlo as the dress rehearsal for Paris. After Diaghileff's death in 1929 René Blum and Colonel de Basil organized the first Compagnie des Ballets de Monte Carlo, and almost immediately began their great campaign to popularize ballet in the U.S.A. When Blum and de Basil dissolved their partnership in 1935, each organized his own troupe and continued to woo American audiences. In 1947 Serge Lifar took charge of the ballet in Monte Carlo and under his leadership were created such new works as *Chota Rostavelli, Nanthéos, Blanc et Noir,* and *Dramma per Musica.* The company of Marquis de Cuevas was featured at Monte Carlo from 1948 through 1950, and some of the now well-known dancers who were acclaimed during that period were Rosella Hightower, Ethery Pagava, and Tallchief. London's Festival

Ballet performed regularly at Monte Carlo in 1951 and 1952. The first season of ballet there is in December just before the grand-opera season begins. The second season follows the opera in March and April.

The exact dates on which festivals will take place in Monaco, as well as the latest travel information pertaining to that country, may be obtained by writing to the Monaco Information Center, Suite 3362, International Building, 630 Fifth Avenue, New York 20, New York.

Bank holidays in Monaco: January 1; Easter Monday, March or April; May 1; Ascension Day, forty days after Easter; Whitmonday, fifty days after Easter; All Saints' Day, November 1; Feast of the Immaculate Conception, December 8; Christmas, December 25.

Chronological list of events in Monaco:

JANUARY. Monte Carlo: auto rally; gala, January 6; golf tournament; opera, to March or April.

FEBRUARY. Monte Carlo: Battle of Flowers.

MARCH. Monte Carlo: Grand Prix pigeon shoot.

MARCH or APRIL. Monte Carlo: *Bal de l'Or,* golden dance; ballet season; *Christ Mort* Procession on Good Friday; Easter golf, tennis tournaments.

MAY or JUNE. Grand Prix of Monaco, auto race; Pentecost.

JUNE. Monte Carlo: Battle of Flowers; Feast of St. John, June 24.

JULY. Monte Carlo: Battle of Flowers; *Tour de France,* bike race, passes through Monte Carlo.

AUGUST. Monte Carlo: Battle of Flowers.

SEPTEMBER. Automobile elegance competition; feminine elegance competition; Prince of Monaco yacht race to coastal towns on the Riviera.

NOVEMBER. National Fete, official birthday of Prince Rainier III, November 19.

DECEMBER. Monte Carlo: ballet season; Christmas tennis tournaments; galas on Christmas, New Year's Eve, Friday nights to April.

NORWAY

NORWEGIANS point with pride to their far-famed Holmenkollen Hill and its attraction for skiers when the winter-sports season is in full swing. Yet they also are quick to remind one that the major festivals in Norway are summertime events. The most impressive of all Norwegian celebrations is the recently inaugurated music festival in Bergen, birthplace of Edvard Grieg.

Winter Sports

Norwegians are proud of the fact that their native land is the cradle of skiing, and the home of *slalom*—the art of dodging around obstacles while on skis—and Telemark, the place where bindings of withes in addition to toe straps were first put on pine skis. As a matter of fact, in the old days the Norwegians were practically forced by nature to take to skis, because before railroads and automobiles were invented skis were the only practical means of locomotion during the winter in many parts of the country. Yet competitive skiing as we know it today did not get going around Christiania, the present city of Oslo, until the 1860's. Since then it has become one

of Norway's big attractions for tourists, and in 1952 it gave
that nation the distinction of playing host to the sixth Olympic
winter games, curtain raiser of the quadrennial international
sports contests, which were centered in Finland that year. The
events at Oslo attracted at least 1,500 from 30 countries. At
Frognersaeteren, near Oslo, they competed in bobsledding on
a twisting, mile-long course with a descent of 410 feet. Skating
and ice-hockey matches were held at Jordal Amphi skating
rink, and the wide range of traditional skiing tests were staged
at Holmenkollen Hill, one of the most famous ski sites in the
world, where the take-off platform is 140 feet high. The record
jump made there thus far is 237 feet. Holmenkollen gives
its name to Holmenkollen Week, which usually takes place
during the fourth week in February, and is one of the top-
flight annual ski meets of the world. European and American
aces vie with one another to capture such trophies as the Norwegian Kandahar, taking part in long-run, *slalom,* and downhill competitions.

But the greatest prize of the meet is the King's Cup, given
to the winner of combined jumping and the 17-kilometer run.
As a rule the meet builds to a slam-bang climax on the last
day, appropriately called "The Holmenkollen Day." Ordinarily on that day the special jumping competition and the
jumping in the combined class take place, and the contestants
soar 220 feet or more through space before landing. Only experts are allowed to compete, so the crowd of approximately
100,000 frequently get thrills aplenty from the "real birds."
The Holmenkollen Day is always a national holiday in Oslo.
The Royal Family usually attends the meet. In fact, Crown
Prince Olaf, himself, used to jump in Holmenkollen.

More often than not the big skating events in Norway begin in mid-January, a month before the international skiing
competitions start.

Even though there are *slalom* ski races at Stryn in July, the last of the big international skiing events is "The Galdhøpiggen Race," which takes place on the slopes of Galdhøpiggen, Norway's highest mountain, at Eastertime. The Galdhøpiggen Cup, put up by Oxford and Cambridge Skiing Clubs, is presented to the winner of the combined downhill and *slalom* races for men on the very fast mile-and-a-half track that has a fall of 3,000 feet.

Music

In 1953 Bergen joined the list of cities that honor their native artists by featuring their works in a festival. Bergen, of course, has a natural for such a celebration because Edvard Grieg was born there in 1843 and stayed right there to write most of his songs, short piano pieces, sonatas, and various orchestral numbers. The Bergen Music Festival was staged during the first two weeks in June of 1953 and probably will be repeated every year for a similar period in June. Among the artists who took part in seven orchestral concerts were Kirsten Flagstad, Adrian Aeschbacher, Yehudi Menuhin, Ricardo Odnoposoff, Leopold Stokowski, Carl Garaguly, Odd Gruner-Hegge, and Oivin Fjeldstad. In addition to compositions by Grieg the program also included a number of classical works by other composers and modern Norwegian music. A play based on the return of the Norwegian Paul Bunyan, Ole Bull, included old folk melodies and dances. It was presented in the courtyard of the medieval fortress, Bergenshus. Participants wore regional costumes, and the country's top-flight fiddlers and dancers joined in the fun.

Independence Day

May 17 is celebrated throughout Norway as Constitution Day because on that date in 1814 the Norwegian Storting, or parliament, assembled at Eidsvold, forty miles north of Oslo, to protest the transfer of its country from Denmark to Sweden, and declared Norway an independent kingdom. That resulted in a short war between Norway and Sweden, which Norway won, because the two countries agreed to a union in which Norway remained "a free, independent and indivisible kingdom united with Sweden under one King." Each country had its own parliament, but its foreign policy was controlled from Stockholm. The Norwegians, of course, didn't like that, so for almost a hundred years they worked to dissolve the union. Finally, on June 7, 1905, the Norwegian Storting declared Norway a sovereign, independent state, and Sweden had to agree. Today the Norwegians celebrate the Maytime Independence Day with processions of children and adults singing, dancing, and speechmaking.

Midsummer

The Arctic zone of Norway is the Land of the Midnight Sun. Norway's North Cape, the northern tip of Europe's mainland, basks in the sunshine day and night for seventy-six days during summer. Even as far south as Oslo the summer night lasts only for an hour or two. So Midsummer Evening, June 23, has real significance for Norwegians. They celebrate it by building bonfires made from logs and tar-soaked barrels, crowning young girls with flowers or veils, and staging folk dances in regional costumes. The historical significance of the festival is shown in open-air museums at Maihaugen, near Lillehammer, and at the Norwegian Folk Museum in Bygdöy, near Oslo. The museum is really a two-fold attraction inasmuch as it shows the development of Norwegian culture through the centuries, and sponsors such divertisements as the New Norwegian Ballet, whose dances are based on Norwegian fairytales and folklore. Often on Sundays it features folk dances in the old farmhouses of the exhibit, or bicycle races in which the riders use only old models.

Olsok Festival

On July 29 Norwegians salute the memory of King Olaf the Holy, who fell in the Battle of Stiklestad in 1030. As a rule the solemn ceremonies include singing, recitations, and speeches.

Emigrant Festivals

From time to time during the summer months different towns in Norway conduct a kind of Old Home Day in the hope of receiving visits from their sons and daughters who have made their homes abroad, many of them in America. On such occasions all the old sentiments are paraded, and there is much wholesome jollification.

Peace Prize

When Alfred B. Nobel, inventor of dynamite, who died December 10, 1896, willed that the interest from a $9,000,000 fund be distributed yearly to those who had contributed most to the benefit of mankind during the preceding year, he ordered that the award for peace be made by a committee of five persons elected by the Norwegian Storting, or parliament. That has been done regularly. When a person is so honored the award is presented in Oslo on December 10. Awards for chemistry, literature, medicine and physiology, and physics are made on that date in Stockholm, Sweden. Admission to the award ceremony is by invitation only, but Norwegians and their guests can watch the laureates and dignitaries enter and leave the hall, and also attend any public lectures that the laureates give.

The exact dates on which festivals will take place in Norway, as well as the latest travel information pertaining to that country, may be obtained by writing to the Norwegian National Travel Office, Norway House, 290 Madison Avenue, New York 17, New York.

Bank holidays in Norway: January 1; Holy Thursday; Good Friday; Easter Eve; Easter Monday; May 1; Independence Day, May 17; Ascension Day, forty days after Easter; Whitmonday, fifty days after Easter; Christmas, December 25; and December 26.

Chronological list of events in Norway:

JANUARY. Oslo: speed skating championships.

FEBRUARY. Norefjell: downhill skiing races, giant *slalom*. Oslo: cross-country skiing race, *slalom;* Holmenkollen Week, skiing meet.

MARCH or APRIL. Galdhøpiggen Cup, skiing race at Easter.

APRIL. Karasjok, Norwegian Lapland: mass weddings. Oslo: trotting.

MAY. Nationwide: Independence Day, May 17. Oslo: dog show; trotting. Oslofjord: yachting.

JUNE. Bergen: Bergen Music, Folk Festival. Gjovik: Norwegian boys' brass bands contests. Hanko: Dragon Gold Cup, regatta. Nationwide: midsummer festivals, June 23, 24. Oslo: Oslo Day, June 14.

JULY. Gjovik: Nordic water-polo championships. Hanko: regatta. Nationwide: St. Olav's Day, July 29. Sarpsborg: regatta. Steinkjer: Norwegian shooting championships.

AUGUST. Oslo: handicrafts show. Oslofjord: Oslo Cup, yachting regatta. Skien: dog show.

SEPTEMBER. Oslo: industrial art, handicraft show. Oslofjord: regatta. Roros: fur market.

DECEMBER. Alta: Lapp market. Oslo: Nobel Peace Prize Award, December 10.

PORTUGAL

PORTUGAL, the southwest-ernmost nation in Europe, draws its festival fare from two main reservoirs. One is the calendar of saints of the Roman Catholic Church and the other the fairs that glorify such important sources of livelihood as livestock, fishing, and agriculture. The outstanding religious pilgrimages in the land are made to Fátima between May and October. They are not only the best attended pilgrimages in Portugal, they are also probably the most popular in the world even though the revelations that inspire them occurred only as recently as 1917.

Religious Festivals

At Fátima on May 13, 1917, three children named Francisco, Jacinta, and Lucia reported that they saw an image of Our Lady of the Rosary appear among the branches of an oak tree. Our Lady is supposed to have suggested prayers and penitence as the best means of combating the misfortunes that had befallen the world. The children described their vision to their elders and aroused so much curiosity that a large crowd was on the spot to welcome the sainted visitor as she made subsequent appearances until October, always on the thirteenth of the month. Among the predictions of the Virgin Mary were the end of World War I and the coming of a second. She also promised that if Russia were consecrated to the Immaculate Heart of Mary, "Russia will be converted and there will be peace."

Still another prophecy given to the children by the Virgin, now resting within a sealed envelope, will not be revealed to the public until 1960. The final appearance of the vision is said to have been punctuated by strange movements of the sun in the sky, visible not only to the young mediators, but also to thousands of spectators. Since 1917 Fátima has become so popular as a shrine among Roman Catholics that it has replaced Lourdes as the favorite place of pilgrimage in Christian countries. Recently when the anniversary of the final appearance of Our Lady was observed, a million persons crowded the village of Fátima. They went in autos, wagons, bicycles, and on foot. Among them were many sick and crippled who hoped for miraculous cures, and together the ailing and the robust took part in masses sung before more than fifty altars. An estimated 200,000 received communion, and all listened attentively to a prayer for universal peace broadcast in Portuguese by Pope Pius XII.

A high light of some observances is a candlelight procession on the first evening of the two-day observance on the twelfth and thirteenth of the month. In it a small, unpretentious image of Our Lady of Fátima is carried from its original niche to a place of prominence in the ensuing ceremonies. On such occasions almost everyone present lights a candle and holds it aloft to light the way. The next day when the statue is returned to its customary niche the crowd waves good-by with fluttering handkerchiefs. Dignitaries of the Catholic Church invariably take part, with as many as five cardinals, including the papal delegate, having been present at one time. Despite the popularity of the pilgrimages almost from the start the cautious churchmen waited from 1917 until 1929 before publishing a pastoral that declared the occurrence worthy of belief.

In 1942 Pope Pius XII spoke to the assemblage on the twenty-fifth anniversary of the apparitions, and in May, 1946, he sent Cardinal Aloisio Masella as his delegate *a latere* to place on Our Lady's statue a beautiful golden crown covered with jewels contributed by Portuguese women to the Mother of Heaven, and to consecrate the world to the Immaculate Heart of Mary. In recent years the statue has traveled through at least seventeen countries—Africa, Argentina, Belgium, the British Isles, Brazil, Canada, Colombia, France, Holland, India, Italy, Luxembourg, Malta, Mexico, Portugal, Spain, and the United States. Typical of the reception the statue receives away from its homeland was the welcome it was given in Rio de Janiero, Brazil, in May, 1953. As the white and gold image, which is just forty-four inches tall and weighs only thirty-three pounds, was carried through the streets in a gilded carriage, the way was lined with thousands of faithful, among them little girls dressed either as angels or as the Virgin herself. Worshipers jammed Rio's Municipal Stadium for a midnight mass and prayed for miraculous cures.

A pilgrimage, which antedates the one at Fátima by several hundred years, is celebrated on September 8 at Nazaré, because on September 8, 1182, Don Fuas Roupinho, Mayor of Porto de Mos and the first Portuguese Admiral of the small fleet of Don Afonso Henriques, first King of Portugal, almost rode his horse over a cliff while hunting deer. On the brink he remembered an image of the Virgin found by some shepherds in a grotto near the city of Nazaré that year, so he prayed to Our Lady of Nazaré to save him from death. He stopped short, and on regaining firm ground promised to build a chapel there in honor of the Virgin to commemorate the miracle. In addition to religious services there is usually a fair that lasts for about a week.

Another important religious celebration honors one of the most popular saints of the Roman Catholic Church, St. Anthony of Padua, who was born in Lisbon in 1195. The celebration centers around the Sé, the church which stands next to the site where the saint was born. Processions, mass, dancing around bonfires, and jumping over the flames are standard events. Also, children erect small altars and ask for contributions for work in the name of the saint, just as they did when they raised funds to reconstruct the original cathedral, which was destroyed by an earthquake in the sixteenth century. St. Anthony of Padua was christened Ferdinand, but changed his name when he entered the Franciscan Order. He died near Padua, Italy, on June 13, 1231.

On the first Sunday of July there is a pilgrimage to Guimaraes in honor of St. Torguatus. At the conclusion of the church service at 10:00 A.M. a band concert begins, there is a parade of decorated carts to honor the memory of the saint, dancing in patios, and fireworks at night.

The *Colete Encarnado,* or Red Waistcoat Festival in Vila Franca de Xira on the first Sunday in July features folk dances, regional dishes, and a bullfight in which the bull is not killed, a Portuguese provision.

The *Festa Gualteriana,* in honor of St. Gualter, lasts for four days during the first week in August at Guimaraes. There are processions, in which a statue of the saint figures prominently, fireworks, and the sale of farm animals.

At Viana do Castelo for eight days beginning around August 18 Our Lady of Agony is honored at bullfights, pageants, serenades, processions, and displays of fireworks.

The most important of the livestock fairs is the one dedicated to St. Martin at Golegã around November 10. The great horse breeders of Portugal offer their animals for sale to military horsemen, cavalieros who perform in the bull ring, and members of international jumping teams. This is a splendid opportunity to see the finest horseflesh in Portugal parade before the grandstand in which sit the elite of high society, representatives of the diplomatic corps, and even visiting royalty.

The year is brought to a bombastic climax on December 31 when one of the most spectacular eruptions of fireworks seen anywhere at any time brightens the streets and the sky over Funchal, the capital of Madeira. It is called the Feast of St. Silvester.

The exact dates on which festivals will take place in Portugal, as well as the latest travel information pertaining to that country, may be obtained by writing to Casa De Portugal, 630 Fifth Avenue, New York 20, New York.

Bank holidays in Portugal: January 1; Corpus Christi, May or June; Camoens Day, honoring Portugal's most famous poet, June 10; Assumption Day, August 15; Portuguese Republic Day, October 5 (1910); All Saints' Day, November 1; Restoration of Independence Day, December 1 (1640); Feast of the Immaculate Conception, December 8; Christmas, December 25.

Chronological list of events in Portugal:

JANUARY. Chamusca: fair. Évora: Feast of St. Sebastian. Fiera: Feast of the Fogaveiras. Obidos: Feast of St. Anthon. Vila Nova de Gaia: Feasts of SS. Gonçalo and Christopher.

FEBRUARY. De Saude: skiing contests. Évora: Feast of Our Lady of the Lamps, or Fair of the Little Earthenware Jars. Festivals of St. Braz at Barcelos, Évora, Lourinhaa, Terras do Bouro, Vila Real. Mourao: Candles Festival of Our Lady. Penhas: skiing contests.

FEBRUARY or MARCH. Pre-Lenten carnival: Loulé, and in restaurants of Lisbon.

MARCH. Povoa de Lanhoso: fair. Santo Tirso: fair. Terras de Bouro: Feast of São Bento da Porta Aberta. Torres Novas: fair.

MARCH or APRIL. Almond trees in bloom: Algarve. Feast of Senhora do Padrão: Viseu. Holy Week: Braga.

APRIL. Alter do Chão: fair. Entroncamento: fair.

MAY. Barcelos: Fair of the Crosses. Fátima: major pilgrimages on May 12, 13, and October 12, 13; others on thirteenth of each month. Matosinhos: Feast of Senhor da Matosinhos; Feast of Senhora da Hora. Vila Nova de Gaia: Feast of Senhor da Pedra.

JUNE. Amarante: Feast of St. Gonçalo. Braga: Feast of St. John. Évora: Feast of St. John. Lisbon: Feast of St. Anthony, who was born in Lisbon. Oporto: Feast of St. John. Vila Real: Feast of St. Anthony; Feast of St. Peter.

JULY. Guimarãis: Feast of St. Torquatus. Lisbon: Circuit of Lisbon, and Portuguese Grand Prix auto race. Santo Tirso: fair. Vila Franca de Xira: *Colete Encarnado,* or Red Waistcoats Festival.

AUGUST. Amares: Feast of Our Lady of the Abbey. Guimarãis: Feast of St. Gualterianas. Terras de Bouro: pilgrimage, Feast of São Bento da Porta Aberta. Viana do Castelo: Feast of Our Lady of Agony.

SEPTEMBER. Lamego: Feast of Our Lady of *Remédios.* Murtosa: Feast of St. Paio da Torreira. Nazaré: Feast of Our Lady of Nazaré. Sintra: Feast of Our Lady of Cabo. Viseu: fair.

OCTOBER. Cascais: tennis championships. Fatima: second of two major annual pilgrimages, October 12, 13; first important one on May 12, 13. Nationwide: Portuguese Republic Day, October 5 (1910); most important celebrations in Lisbon. Vila Franca de Xira: fair.

NOVEMBER. Golegã: fair.

DECEMBER. Funchal (Madeira): Feast of St. Silvester features tremendous fireworks display. Nationwide: Commemoration of National Restoration, December 1 (1640).

SPAIN

WHEN ONE flies across the Atlantic Ocean, he invariably compares his swift flight with the tedious crossing made by Christopher Columbus in 1492. On August 3, 1951, the 459th anniversary of Columbus' historic departure from the Spanish seaport of Palos in command of the *Niña, Pinta,* and *Santa Maria,* Trans World Airlines marked the occasion with a comparison flight by the Constellation "Star of Christopher Columbus" to dramatize the tremendous advance in transportation since the fifteenth century. The study in contrasts was fascinating! For instance, the *Niña* was 60 tons and had an over-all length of 70 feet, whereas the Constellation weighed 45 tons fully loaded and was 90 feet long. The *Santa Maria,* largest of the three vessels, carried 40 men. The Constellation had 47 passengers and a crew of 9. The ships' speed was 4 knots, or about 4.6 miles per hour, while the plane's speed was 300 miles per hour. Columbus' voyage was financed by Queen Isabella for $14,000, an amount that would keep a TWA Constellation in the air a scant 31 hours. As every schoolboy knows, Columbus took 70 days to cross from Palos to San Salvador in the Bahamas, having stopped at the Canary Islands. The "Star of Christopher Columbus" took 20 hours, 55 minutes, to get from Madrid to New York, with stops at Lisbon, Azores, Gander, and Boston.

Now every year thousands of Americans fly to festivals in Spain, particularly to the big three: Holy Week, the Fair at Seville, and the Fallas of Valencia.

Religious Festivals

The high point of the year in Spain for Spaniards as well as for foreigners is Holy Week, the week before Easter Sunday, in March or April. Almost every city and village has its own way of commemorating the most dramatic period of the Christian calendar, and their observances can range from a continual, discordant crashing of drums by hooded penitents to tremendous parades of holy images decked in costly brocades, velvet, cloth of gold, and jewels worth a fortune. The cities that stage the most spectacular demonstrations are Cordova, Granada, Malaga, Madrid, Murcia, Salamanca, Seville, and Valladolid, with the most elaborate celebrations of all being staged in Malaga, Seville, and Valladolid. Seville, like many other cities, climaxes its *Semana Santa* with a procession of *pasos,* elaborately carved, sometimes extravagantly decorated groups of sacred figures mounted on platforms. Many of the *pasos* were carved some five hundred years ago, yet the standards they set still prevail. The gaunt figure of Christ on the way to Calvary or hanging on the cross is the soul of suffering and simplicity, while other characters are regally robed, their garments and headdresses brightened by jewels that glitter in the sun by day and reflect the light of candles and torches at night as the *pasos* wind through the twisting, narrow streets past Roman churches, arches of Gothic or baroque cathedrals, and walls of palaces and stately houses. Murcia parades the famous Salzillo figures, and in Andalusia when Holy Week parades pass by you frequently hear a *saeta,* or sob of lament, which a gypsy or any devout spectator might utter as he expresses his sympathy. It is strange to hear those moans above the silence of the crowd. Salamanca proudly parades the works of Luis Salvador Carmona, Felipe del Corral, and Becerra, while in the chapel of the university there the traditional communion of the professors is celebrated. The most famous Holy Week celebration in Castille is at Valladolid, where the stern, dignified, and artistic General Procession of the Holy Passion of the Saviour is composed of a series of *pasos* by Gregorio Fernandez, Juan de Juni, and other artists of what some critics call the greatest Castilian period. There the *pasos* are led by a hooded penitent carrying a severely plain cross, accompanied by torchbearers. In their wake are the priceless carvings such as "Our Lady of Pain," "Jesus Christ Tied to a Column," and a tortured figure of Christ on the cross. In Valladolid, unlike some other communities, silence is emphasized. The hush is most pronounced when the multitude gathers in the main plaza to hear the Sermon of the Seven Words. Some other cities known for their Holy Week observances are Alcaniz, Alhaurin el Grande, Almeria, Arcos de la Frontera, Baena, Burgos, Cabra, Cadiz, Cartagena, Comillas, Crevillente, Cuenca, El Escorial, Gerona, Hellin, Hijar, Huelva, Huesca, Jaca, Jaen, Jerez de la Frontera, Jumilla Las Palmas de Gran Canaria, Lorca, Medina de Rioseco, Monasterios de Guadalupe, Monserrat, Murcia, Orihuela, Palencia, Puente Genil, Rota, Salamanca, Saragossa, Tarragona, Toledo, Toro, Ubeda, Valencia, Valmaseda, and Zamora.

A fitting prologue to the Holy Week festival is the Lenten performances of the drama of the Passion of Christ in the Catalonian cities of Olesa de Monserrat, near Barcelona; Esparraguera; Molins de Rey; and Cervera. Some critics consider the performances at Olesa, which began in 1642, the best of the lot. However, in each locality a faithful, pious interpretation is given by the townspeople, who begin rehearsals immediately after Christmas and play the roles year after year. Performances are given every Sunday of Lent and often during Holy Week.

Centuries ago churchmen who were masters of psychology realized that it would be smart to temper the forty days of Lenten fasting with a bit of frivolity in midseason. So, St. Joseph's Day, March 19, which ordinarily comes pretty close to the middle of Lent, was selected as a time to relax some of the Lenten restrictions. In Valencia the people decided to make the most of the holiday and welcome spring at the same time by staging the most unusual bonfires in the world. The Carpenters' Guild in particular wanted to do something special for the occasion inasmuch as St. Joseph is their patron, so they created the *fallas,* huge effigies in pasteboard and wood. Then, to dramatize the sacrifice of beauty to fire, they decided to burn the effigies at the climax of the festival. The *fallas* are generally grotesque images of animals and caricatures of persons prominent in national, regional, or local activities. Sometimes they are strongly critical and even sarcastic. Yet often they are veritable works of art. In fact, when the *fallas* achieved an enviable degree of perfection a contest was launched to select the finest each year and save it for posterity in a local museum. Every district builds its own effigy, laboring in secret on its special project until the work is ready to be set up in a public square or important intersection. The first ones appear on or about March 12, and during the next week they crop up all over town. The favorite pastime then is to tour the town comparing one masterpiece with another. Throughout the week the bands play, and there are comparatively minor fireworks displays, which seem very tame alongside the explosion of a string of fireworks several miles long that winds through the streets and ends in the Plaza de Emilio Castelar on March

19. That is also the night of the *cremá,* when the town is brightened by the blazes of the burning effigies.

Hard in the wake of the Easter observances in Spain is the Spring Fiesta at Murcia, which usually begins promptly on Easter Monday in March or April and lasts for about five days. There are lively parades like the *Bando de la Huerta,* a battle of flowers, and the Burial of the Sardine. As a rule every Murcian community is represented in the big parades through the principal streets filled with people in regional costumes. Girls sport frilly dresses and brilliant shawls, while boys show off their favorite *zaraquelles,* white trousers. Flowers are used profusely along the route of the parade on the day of the battle of flowers and embellish many of the ornate coaches that take part in it. The *Entierro de la Sardina,* or Burial of the Sardine, is performed in the glow of torches one midnight toward the close of the fiesta. No one seems to know precisely what it signifies, but some folklorists believe that it represents the burial of Old Man Winter at the rebirth of Adonis, spirit and personification of spring.

The Feast of Corpus Christi sixty days after Easter is another time of pomp and pageantry in Spain. The favorite gesture of veneration, carting enormous *pasos* through narrow, winding streets and along broad avenues, is indulged to an extravagant degree in many places. The cities known for the splendor and color of their Corpus Christi festivals are Barcelona, Burgos, Cadiz, Cordoba, Gerona, Grenada, Pollensa, Toledo, and Seville. In Toledo and Seville, for example, the *pasos* are accompanied by the *seises,* six youngsters dressed in medieval ceremonial robes, who have the age-old privilege of spreading flower petals before the sacred Host during the procession. Cathedral walls are covered with priceless tapestries and garlanded with flowers. The towering, exquisitely wrought shrines of brightly polished metal often are protected from the sun by canopies stretched across the streets, while in some places, such as La Orotava, in the Canary Islands, and Sitges, near Barcelona, streets are carpeted with flowers for the processions. With infinite care and artistic taste, the narrow streets lined with white houses are transformed into beautifully colored patterns, and the cobblestones magically turn into carpets of gorgeous golds, scarlets, and blues. The exquisite designs remain untouched until about 7:00 P.M. on the day of Corpus Christi, when the Holy Eucharist procession treads its way to the parish church that overlooks the sea. For several days after that the air is filled with the heady aroma of carnations. In Granada the festival lasts eight days, and during that time various cultural attractions are presented. Among them are the classical *Autos Sacramentales*, acted on a stage in the courtyard of the cathedral, symphony concerts in the patio of the Palace of Charles V amid the gardens of the Alhambra. In practically all communities the Corpus Christi Festival concludes with a program of regional folk dancing, bullfights, and fireworks displays.

On Pentecost, forty-nine days after Easter, two outstanding celebrations are in the village of El Rocio, near Huelva, and at Roncevalles, Navarre. The observance at El Rocio is in the form of a pilgrimage to the shrine of the Virgin of Rocio. The procession is headed by a caravan of ox-drawn covered wagons similar to the prairie schooners of the American pioneer days, but with this outstanding difference: the Spanish wagons sport coarse, white sheets trimmed in lace and blankets of hemp, fresh garlands, and paper chains. In the first wagon is the silk, velvet, and gold standard of the Immaculate Conception, and horsemen carrying standards and insignia ride alongside it as a guard of honor. Religious services are conducted before the shrine in the morning, and in the afternoon there are songs and dances. At Roncevalles a procession of black-clad penitents wearing hoods with only slits for eyes and burdened with crosses tied to their backs struggle for about two miles up a hillside to attend mass at the Monastery of Roncevalles. The march is said to have been instituted many years ago by members of twenty-three families as an act of penance to atone for sins committed during the year. With their arms outstretched to support the heavy crosses they chant a solemn Miserere and trudge along.

Gunpowder, light and fire, and *hogueras*, patterned after the *fallas* that have made the St. Joseph Day celebration at Valencia world-famous, are used to celebrate the Feast of St. John at Alicante during the last week in June. On the final night of the festival the *Palmera del Fuego*, a fireworks display touched off on the peak of Benacautel Hill, brings the party to a close with a shower of reds, yellows, and orange. Flageolets, timbrels, and large-headed dwarfs are very much in evidence at this particular Fire Fiesta of San Juan.

Another outstanding celebration of the Feast of St. John takes place in Valls on June 24. It features the *Xiquets de Valls*, literally the human towers of Valls. The building of pyramids and other formations is a gymnastic specialty of this region, and at various times throughout the year tower-building may be witnessed at Montblanch, Reus, Tarragona, Vendrell, and Villafranca del Panades, as well as at Valls. The stunt is believed to have been performed for the first time in 1633 at some festival put on for the entertainment of Philip IV and his queen. One of the favorite patterns that has survived through the centuries is the *pila de sis*, a tower that has a base of six men and is six men high. Rhythm for the performances is established by music from a clarinet called the *gralla*, and a small drum, or *tamboril*.

July's big religious fete is the celebration in honor of Santiago de Compostela, which is believed to date at least to the time of Pope Calixto II. Many churches are dedicated to Santiago de Compostela, but the one which is believed to have been opened during the first half of the ninth century in the Galician town named for him ranks with the important ones at Bilbao, Lérida, and Valencia. In small towns the holiday is marked only by mass, impersonations of saints, music, and dancing. But in the cities there are fireworks, a carnival, clowns, Galician bagpiping, religious dramas, popular songs, and regional dances. Sometimes there are prizes for livestock, and bagpipers who take part in *charangas,* a kind of Spanish jam session.

The Feast of the Assumption, which commemorates the miraculous ascent of the Virgin Mary to heaven, is one of the important festivals of the Catholic Church, so it is marked with great solemnity throughout Spain on August 15. One of the unique observances takes place in the Church of Santa Maria, in the town of Elche, where a very traditional popular liturgical drama that dates to the thirteenth century is sung in the Lemosine dialect. It is called the *Mystery of Elche,* and since every part is sung, it is considered by some authorities to be the forerunner of opera, which did not appear in Italy until the sixteenth century. Many of those who take part in the play know little about music. They learn their roles by ear, listening to the conductor, the producer, or to their colleagues in the familiar pattern of folklore tradition. What is more, all roles are interpreted by men. "Female" voices are supplied by adolescent youths. The *Mystery of Elche* is a labor of love for a few families, and they work constantly to maintain high standards.

Also on Assumption Day at La Alberca, a small town in the Province of Salamanca that is so picturesque it has been declared a national monument, the *Ofrenda a la Virgen,* gift of the Virgin, is made every year. The *Ofrenda,* a symbolic offering that takes place in the main plaza, is presided over by a major-domo in a great coat with silver brooches, a cape with tippet, and a huge sombrero with tassels. The next day, August 16, the *Loa,* a dramatic poem, is presented.

Assumption Day is the big feast around which *Semana Grande,* or big week, in San Sebastian, is built. The generous program of events includes bullfights, skeet shooting, golf, horse races, dancing, yachting, and tennis.

The final important link in the chain of Spanish religious festivals that stretch from spring to autumn is the festival of Our Lady of the Pillar, in Saragossa, during the third week in October. There the sacred tradition of the Virgin Mary, who is said to have appeared in person to the Apostle Santiago in 40 A.D., is commemorated. According to the legend the Virgin appeared atop a column of marble and left her image as a souvenir of her visit. The apostle was the one who decided to build a chapel at the place where she appeared in order to glorify the occasion, and that is how the worship of Our Lady of the Pillar began. Modern observances of the festival last for about a week in October. They include religious services in the churches of Saragossa, and in the streets is a general rosary in which richly decorated carriages from all parts of Spain take part, a fair, bullfights, a parade of giants and bigheads, fireworks, and a contest for jota dances, the typical Aragonese folk dance.

Another saint's day celebration noted for its individuality is St. Anthony's Day, January 17. On that occasion animals decorated with ribbons or flowers are taken to church to be blessed, and farmers in the Province of Cataluna ride their horses three times around a different church each year to receive a blessing. They call their observance the Feast of the Three Turns.

The unique *La Tamborrada,* which dates to 1836, is a very important part of the *Fiesta de San Sebastian* at San Sebastian on January 20. For many years a particular fountain in San

Sebastian had been the meeting place for bakers, who used to go there to collect water in barrels shaped like hourglasses. On the feast day in 1836 someone began tapping his fingers on a barrel, and the other bakers picked up the rhythm. Later that simple tapping set the pattern for several tunes, among them *"El Iriyarena,"* and Sarriegui's "March of San Sebastian." Descendants of the original musicmakers are called *tamborradas,* because the barrels they play on are known as *tamborras.* Regional dance and sports contests, including lassoing the bull, complete the program at the *Fiesta de San Sebastian.*

A very popular pilgrimage on May 15 is the one to the hermitage of San Isidro, twelfth-century patron saint of farmers and of Madrid, who lived near that city.

St. Peter's Day ceremonies on June 29 at Lequeitio feature the *kasharanra,* a symbolic dance performed by a man on the ancient coffer of the Fishermen's Confraternity while it rests on the shoulders of four sailors. St. Peter is the patron saint of fishermen everywhere.

At the Fiesta de Santa Tecla in Tarragona on September 23 the *collas,* a group of amateur gymnasts, form human towers in front of the City Hall and on the steps of the Cathedral between performances of *sardanas* dances.

Music Festival

Spain's International Music and Dance Festival inaugurated in 1952 is usually celebrated in Granada during the last ten days in June. The festival site is the Patio of the Lions in the Arab Palace of the Alhambra, the Imperial Palace of Charles V, and an open-air theater especially set up in the gardens of the Generalife. Artists who took part in the festival in 1953 included Andres Segovia, Aldo Ciccolini, Veyron-Lacroix, Jean Pierre Rampal, and Nicanor Zabaleta. There were also two

Spanish ballets by Antonio, two by the classical ballet company of Covent Garden, London, and songs and dances of Spain.

The last week in May and the first week in June are ordinarily the time of the International Folklore Rally at a different Spanish town each year. As the title suggests, songs and dances of many nations are presented. However, most of the participants are from European countries fairly close to Spain, such as Austria, Belgium, Denmark, France, Great Britain, Holland, Italy, and Portugal.

Book Fair

A well-established annual cultural event is the Book Fair, a veritable paradise of books, which usually takes place in Madrid from about mid-April to mid-May. At that time at least a hundred gaily painted stalls filled with more than 150,000 volumes line both sides of the avenue beyond the Paseo del Prado. The displays are open day and night, so at all hours one can mingle with students, connoisseurs, and thousands of just typical, curious people who thumb some of the most unusual books to be found in Spain. The volumes cover all subjects, from art to zoology, with children's books and tomes on architecture, cooking, painting, and poetry usually receiving a lot of attention.

Anniversaries

Several anniversaries of important conquests or victories during the long history of Spain are still vigorously celebrated in many communities. Some of them are linked to amusing legends, such as the one which inspired the play *Las Monidas*, the virgins, at San Pedro Manrique on June 23, 24. According to an oft-told tale many years ago when the town was about to be destroyed by Moors the leader of the invaders offered to spare the town if the inhabitants promised to deliver one hundred *monidas*—virgins—to the chief on the eve of St. John each year. They agreed and followed the practice for several years. Then one day when it was the turn of the mayor's daughter to be among the hundred she appeared stark naked before the City Hall. Other girls in her party also disrobed, and when they were nude they picked up their clothing and began to walk toward the place where they were to be turned over to the hostile Moors. As they saw the enemy soldiers, they donned their cloaks, and when the Spanish soldiers who were accompanying the girls asked them why they acted in this strange fashion, the ringleader spoke up for them. "When women are among women," she said, "they do not mind being nude, but when in the presence of men they prefer to don their clothing. We don't mind being nude before you because for many years the men of the town have been acting like women. The captors who are making the demands are acting like men." That remark is supposed to have infuriated the menfolk of the town, who took up arms and drove the occupation forces from the place forever.

Now on the eve of St. John, June 23, a bonfire is lit before the door of the church, La Virgen de la Peña. At ten that night all the inhabitants gather around the fire, and those who have promised the saints they would do so walk over the fire. It is called the ceremony of the purification by fire. Early in the morning of June 24 the mayor and his officers ride on richly decorated horses to the doors of the city walls. Three beautiful girls dressed in white skirts and red Spanish shawls wait at the house of the superintendent of City Hall until the mayor and his companions call for them. They go to church, and after mass they lead a procession to the town square, where it is customary to read news of the expulsion of the occupation forces, freeing the girls from the demands of the Moors.

The bravery and patriotism of women also figure prominently in the celebration called *Es Firó* staged in the town of Sóller on the second Monday of May. It commemorates the victory of the town's women over Moorish troops that landed on the beaches. According to the legend the women locked up the mayor and the men of the town and went to face the Moors alone. The Moors pretended they would not fight women, but in reality they did not have enough soldiers to bring off the invasion, so they withdrew. The women released the men. All that is re-enacted in the annual celebration.

Fiesta de la Toma is the name given to the symbolic reproduction of the conquest of Granada, celebrated regularly on January 2 since 1492. The observance starts with mass at the Cathedral Real, where Fernando and Isabella are buried. After mass a young officer carries the Pendon de Castilla—perhaps the same one Columbus took on his voyage to America—and waves it as he strolls down the street shouting, *"Viva España, viva Franco, viva Granada."* In the afternoon there is a comedy concerning the conquest of Granada titled *El Triunfo del Ave Maria o la Toma de Granada* (The Triumph of the Virgin Mary or the Conquest of Granada).

The incorporation of Grand Canary with the crown of Castile is marked at Las Palmas, Canary Islands, during the last week in April and the first week in May. Celebrated for the first time on April 29, 1483, it is known as the Feast of San Pedro de Verona, the date on which the people surrendered to General Don Pedro de Vera. The program includes singing, dancing, costume displays, swimming, dog races, cockfighting, football, tennis, a regatta, and exhibitions of flowers, fruits, and animals.

As a rule high mass and patriotic parades mark the anniversary of the Battle of Madrid (the Prado), May 2, 1808. That was when the people of Madrid started their war of independence by revolting against the French General Morat.

Fairs

The world-renowned Fair of Seville usually takes place during the third week in April except when that period coincides with Holy Week. At such times the fair is held later. It started as a regional cattle show more than a hundred years ago, and now it seems less like the typical livestock exhibition than almost anything else. It is a stupendous carnival with gaiety as its trade-mark, so thousands of Spaniards and foreigners travel many miles to attend it. There is much to see and do, but the three things that seem to stand out are the exceptionally fine bullfights, the frilly costumes worn by the Andalusian women, and the *casetas,* small houses set up every year by clubs, organizations, and civic groups for sheer fun. The streets of *casetas* are just about the most popular thoroughfares in Seville. There are so many huts crowded one against the other that it is possible to pass glasses of manzanilla, an Andalusian white wine, from one hut to the other. There are also exhibitions of horsemanship at the fair, colorful parades, championship pigeon-shooting contests, and huge folk-dancing sessions.

Valencia staged its first International Sample Fair in 1917 in honor of its patron Virgin, and continues to salute her in this fashion every year around May 10–25. Displays include agricultural products, livestock, leather goods, furniture, and machinery from Spain and foreign countries.

Barcelona's International Industrial Fair is held in the park of the former World's Exhibition, usually around June 10–25.

The Fair of Segovia, which generally takes place in July or August, is only one reason for journeying to Segovia at that time. The other is a chance to join in the fun at the Fiesta de San Luis, patron saint of the town. The fiesta is celebrated in the gardens of the Palacio de La Granja, which is famous for its fountains. The fountains are turned on just four times a year: May 30, the Feast of San Fernando; late in June on Segovia Day; July 25, Santiago Apostol; and the Feast of San Luis. The fiesta has been going on for more than two hundred years. The main events there now are a horse show, horse races, athletic contests, and fireworks.

The *Romeria de Peña de Francia* in Salamanca during the first week in September dates to 1436. It features a cattle show, craftsmanship contests, a parade of decorated carts, and a series of championship bullfights of which Salamancans are particularly proud.

"Sherry," the people of Jerez say, is an English corruption of the word Xerez which, in turn, was derived from "Sheres," the name given by the Moors to Jerez de la Frontera. Today Jerez publicizes its famous wines with a vintage fair during the second week of September.

Sports

Association football is played throughout Spain from September to June. Ordinarily the season builds to an exciting climax in Madrid around the fourth week in June, when title contenders play the final match to determine the winner of the Generalissimo's Cup.

The Grand Prix of Penya Rhin, an auto race in Barcelona around the last week in October, is the last of the ten major events that contribute points to the world championship. The other nine are: Argentina, Belgium, France, Germany, Great Britain, Holland, Indianapolis Speedway, Italy, and Switzerland.

Pelota, a fast, thrilling Basque game resembling handball played with graceful wicker scoops and baseballs, is played by expert professionals on courts at Barcelona, Bilbao, Madrid, Palma de Mallorca, Pamplona, and San Sebastian from

October to June. In the northern towns the game is played throughout the summer as well. World-championship contests usually take place in or near the Basque country around the end of August.

The *zuritos* pigeons, which thrive in Spain, are said to be the best birds in Europe to use in pigeon-shooting. Competitions are held from time to time between January and June at Alicante, Badajoz, Bilbao, Cáceres, Cadiz, Jerez, Madrid, Malaga, Pamplona, Puerto de Santa Maria, San Sebastian, Valencia, and Zarauz.

Bullfights

Since bullfighting, the national sport of Spain, is an important attraction at most festivals there, the Spanish State Tourist Department has wisely issued a handsome, highly informative booklet entitled *Toros,* compiled by Julián Juárez Ugena. It goes into detail about the art of delivering death in the afternoon from the time it acquired the status of a spectacle around the thirteenth century to the present time. For at least four hundred years bullfighting was considered a nobleman's sport, just as jousting was the sport of knights. About two hundred years ago it became a profession. Today the day's program begins with the appearance of two horsemen dressed as constables of the reign of Philip IV, 1621–65. They pay their respects to the presiding official, then lead the procession of matadors, *banderilleros,* picadors, servants, muleteers, and even the mules that will drag out the bulls to be killed that day. As a rule each matador fights two bulls in an afternoon. After the parade the bull is ushered into the ring to start the prologue and three acts. The prologue is called the "running" of the bull, and is handled by the matador's assistants on foot who wave pink and yellow capes to attract the bull's attention. They are testing to see how the bull charges, which horn it prefers, and whether it hooks or not.

After a while the matador steps in to size up the bull with a few flourishes, and he is followed by two picadors who enter to start Act I. The first picador taunts the bull. It charges, usually aiming for the right shoulder of the horse on which the picador is riding, and just before it connects, the picador jabs the tip of his eight-foot pole into the top of the bull's withers just behind the big hump of neck muscle. After each *pic* thrust a matador draws the bull away with flaps of his cape. That is called a *quite*—pronounced kee-teh. Each bull must receive a minimum of four normal *pics,* but the official can vary the number at his discretion. When the official shows a handkerchief, a trumpet blows, the picadors ride out and the *banderilleros* begin Act II. They plant their *banderillas,* which are eighteen-inch thin, wooden sticks decorated with colored paper and having a two-inch point, into the bull's hide. That makes the bull toss, and weakens its neck muscle, thus lowering its head more for the kill. At last the trumpet sounds for the final act, and almost inevitably, death for the bull. The matador and the bull have the huge arena to themselves, and each tries to outsmart the other. The matador cannot kill the bull at once. He must tire it out as much as possible so that its head is lowered properly, and he can deliver the sword thrust. When that has been done he carries out the final *suerte,* the kill. He can do that by provoking a charge, then standing fast, and putting the thrust into the charging bull, going in on a run at the stationary bull, or meeting the bull halfway as they charge toward each other. That drama is enacted time after time in the approximately 350 bull rings in Spain. The rings with the largest capacity, about 23,000, are at Barcelona and Madrid. The high season is from about mid-March to mid-October.

Of all the Spanish festivals in which bulls are the star performers the most unusual is the Run of the Bulls at the *Fiesta de San Fermin* in Pamplona on July 7–14. For there the beasts perform not only in the arena, but also on the streets. They become the center of attention earlier than usual because they are turned loose in the plaza and chased and tormented all the way to the bull ring in another part of town. Some exhibitionists tempting fate run so close to the bull they are gored by the swaying horns or trampled under the flying hoofs as the frightened, belligerent animal tears through the crowded thoroughfare. The origin of the fiesta is unknown, but records show that a celebration was staged as long ago as 1591. Then, as now, the festival featured bullfights, performances by the best dancers in Navarra, clowns, fireworks, folkloric contests, fencing, and, occasionally, *anillos,* the Spanish joust, thrusting the point of a lance through a ring suspended from a beam while riding on horseback.

As a rule, extraordinary *corridas* in Madrid, which are not fixtures, take place on Thursdays in spring and autumn. Such special programs are usually benefit affairs in behalf of the Bullfighters' Benevolent Societies, the General Hospital, the press, and the Red Cross. The fights invariably feature the best bulls and first-class bullfighters. Similar charity *corridas* also take place toward the beginning or the end of the regular season at Barcelona, Bilbao, San Sebastian, Seville, and Valencia. The places and months in which some fifty fiestas that normally attract prime bulls and matadors are staged are: Castellón de la Plana and Valencia, March; Alcoy, Andújar, Barcelona, Cartagena, Jerez de la Frontera, Madrid, Malaga, Murcia, Saragossa, and Toledo, April; Aranjuez, Cáceres, Cordova, Figueras, Madrid, Ronda, and Talavera de la Reina, May; Algesiras, Alicante, Badajoz, Burgos, Cádiz, Madrid, Málaga, Plasencia, Seville, Toledo, and Valencia, June; Pamplona, Santander, Tudela, and Valencia, July; Albacete, Almería, Bilbao, Cáceres, Corunna, Gijón, Hellín, Huelva, Huesca, Jerez de los Caballeros, Linares, Logroño, Málaga,

Murcia, Oviedo, Pontevedra, Salamanca, San Sebastian, Seville, Toledo, and Vitoria, August; Cuenca, Mérida, and Palencia, September; Jaén, Saragossa, Soria, and Zafra, October.

The exact dates on which festivals will take place in Spain, as well as the latest travel information pertaining to that country, may be obtained by writing to one of the following Spanish State Tourist Offices: 485 Madison Avenue, New York 22, New York; Room 613, 39 South La Salle Street, Chicago 3, Illinois; 68 Post Street, San Francisco 4, California.

Bank holidays in Spain: January 1; Epiphany Day, January 6; St. Joseph's Day, March 19; Victory Day, April 1, end of war in 1939; Holy Thursday to Easter Monday, March or April; anniversary of uprising against Napoleonic troops, May 2; Ascension Day, forty days after Easter; Whitmonday, fifty days after Easter; Corpus Christi, sixty days after Easter; St. John's Day, June 24; St. Peter's Day, June 29; Labor Day, July 18, anniversary of the beginning of the Revolution in 1936; St. James's Day, July 25, honors the patron saint of Spain; Assumption Day, August 15; Our Lady of Mercy, September 24; Day of the Hispanic Race, October 12; All Saints' Day, November 1; Immaculate Conception, December 8; Christmas, December 25; and December 26.

Chronological list of events in Spain:

JANUARY. Aledo: Cavalcade of Three Wise Men. Granada: Fiesta de la Toma. Jaén: *Fiesta de Las Lumbres,* feast of the fires. Las Palmas: Cavalcade of Three Wise Men. Malaga: winter sports contests, to March. Nationwide: Festival of St. Anthony Abbot, with more impressive ceremonies at Barcelona, Benicasim, Gallegon Del Pan, Manacor, Orellana, Puebla de Hijar; at many places animals are blessed; pigeon-shooting, to June, with most meets centered at Alicante, Badajoz, Bilbao, Cáceres, Cadiz, Jerez, Madrid, Malaga, Pamplona, Puerto de Santa Maria, San Sebastian, Valencia, Zarauz. Province of Cataluna: Feast of Three Turns, January 17. Saragossa: religious festival.

FEBRUARY. Cervera: *The Holy Mystery.* Don Benito: fair. Granada: Feast of St. Cecilio. Nationwide: Feast of St. Blaise; more impressive ceremonies at Bocairente, Burriana, Cáceres, Carboneras de Guadazon, Idiazabal, Peralta, Reillo. Tafalla: cattle market. Villarin de los Aires: Feast of St. Agatha. Zamora: Feast of St. Agatha.

FEBRUARY or MARCH. Feast of St. Mary Magdalen, where first-class bullfight often inaugurates bullfighting season, third Sunday in Lent: Castellon de la Plana.

FEBRUARY, MARCH, or APRIL. *La Passio,* sacred drama, performed every Sunday in Lent and during Holy Week at Cervera, Esparraguera, Molins de Rey, Olesa de Montserrat.

MARCH. Fuentepelayo: Feast of El Angel. Illescas: Feast of the Miracle of Our Lady of Charity. Valencia: *Fallas* of St. Joseph, where first-class bullfights often inaugurate bullfighting season, week of March 19.

MARCH or APRIL. Easter Sunday; first-class bullfights at Barcelona, Cartagena, Madrid, Malaga, Murcia, Saragossa, Seville, Toledo. Feast of *Cabezadas:* Leon. Fiesta, begins Easter Monday: Murcia. Holy Week, one of Spain's most spectacular, solemn religious celebrations, observed with special ceremonies at Alcaniz, Alhaurin el Grande, Almeria, Arcos de la Frontera, Baena, Burgos, Cabra, Cadiz, Cartagena, Comillas, Cordova, Crevillente, Cuenca, El Escorial, Gerona, Granada, Hellín, Hijar, Huelva, Huesca, Jaca, Jaén, Jerez de la Frontera, Jumilla, Las Palmas de Gran Canaria, Lorca, Málaga, Medina de Rioseco, Monasterios de Guadalupe, Montserrat, Murcia, Orihuela, Palencia, Puente Genil, Rota, Salamanca, Saragossa, Seville, Tarragona, Toledo, Toro, Ubeda, Valencia, Valmaseda, Valladolid, Zamora.

APRIL. Alcoy: Battle of Moors and Christians; first-class bullfights, honor St. George. Andújar: pilgrimage to shrine of the *Virgen de la Cabeza,* first-class bullfights. Badajoz: fair. Campanario: Feast of Our Lady of *Piedra Escrita.* Cuellar: fair. Cullera: Procession of *La Baixa,* the descending. Jerez de la Frontera: important cattle market, fair, first-class bullfights. La Alberca: riding tournament. Las Palmas: Feast of San Pedro de Verona. Madrid: book fair. Mairena del Alcor: fair. Palencia: pilgrimage honors St. Toribio. Puerto de Santa Maria: cattle fair. San Vicente de la Barquera: *Las Folias,* procession of the boats. Seville: fair, first-class bullfights. Tafalla: Pilgrimage of the Penitents. Tuy: Feast of St. Peter Gonzalez features Gallegan bagpipe contest. Valencia: scenes from life of St. Vincent Ferrer performed for children. Zamora: pilgrimage honors St. Mark.

MAY. Aranjuez: Feast of San Fernando, first-class bullfights.

Cáceres: fair, first-class bullfights. Cordova: Feast of the Virgin of Salud, first-class bullfights. Figueras: first-class bullfights. La Granja: fountain displays. Madrid: Battle of Madrid anniversary; book fair; Fiesta of San Isidro, first-class bullfights. Palma: fiesta. Ronda: fair, first-class bullfights. Santa Cruz de Tenerife: Fiesta of Santa Cruz. Segovia: Feast of San Fernando, fountain displays, May 30. Selva: Fiesta of Santa Cruz. Soller: *Es Firo,* anniversary of a military victory. Talavera de la Reina: Feast of the *Mondas,* pruning of the trees, and first-class bullfights. Valencia: fair. A different place each year: International Folklore Rally.

MAY or JUNE. Corpus Christi: nationwide, with more spectacular celebrations at Barcelona, Burgos, Cadiz, Cordova, Gerona, Granada, Pollensa, Toledo, Seville. National Carnation Show, officially declared of national artistic interest because streets are carpeted with blossoms worked into exquisite designs: Sitges.

JUNE. Algesiras: fiesta, first-class bullfights. Alicante: Feast of St. John, first-class bullfights. Barcelona: Feast of St. John, fair, first-class bullfights. Burgos: Feast of St. Peter, first-class bullfights. Irun: Feast of San Marcial. Lequeitio: St. Peter's Day, June 29. Madrid: Feast of St. Anthony; Generalissimo's Cup, association football. Plasencia: fair, first-class bullfights. San Pedro Manrique: *Las Mondidas,* the damsels, a play. Segovia: Segovia Day, fountain displays. Valls: Feast of St. John features *Xiquet de Valls,* human towers. A different place each year: International Folklore Rally.

JULY. Burgos: folklore contests. La Granja: fountain displays. Pamplona: Fiesta of San Fermin has unique run-of-the-bulls in the streets, and first-class bullfights. Santa Cruz de Tenerife (Canary Islands): Feast of Our Lady of Mount Carmel specializes in local style of wrestling. Santander: fair, first-class bullfights. Santiago de Compostela: fair, *La Fachada,* fireworks display in front of the cathedral, elaborate procession. Tudela: Feast of St. James, first-class bullfights. Valdemosa: folklore contests. Valencia: fair, first-class bullfights.

AUGUST. Albacete: fair, first-class bullfights. Bilbao: *Semana Grande,* first-class bullfights. Cáceres: fair, first-class bullfights. Corunna: *Semana Grande,* Spanish bagpipe contests, first-class bullfights. Elche: *The Mystery of Elche,* famous lyrical-liturgical drama. El Escorial: Feast of San Lorenzo. Gijón: *Semana Grande,* first-class bullfights. Hellín: fair, first-class bullfights. Huelva: fair, first-class bullfights. Huesca: fair, first-class bullfights. Jerez de los

Caballeros: fair, first-class bullfights. La Alberca: Assumption Day celebration, August 15, features *Ofrenda a la Virgen;* "Loa," a dramatic poem, on August 16. Laredo: fair, battle of flowers; fiesta, first-class bullfights. Logroño: fair, first-class bullfights. Málaga: fair, first-class bullfights. Murcia: fair, first-class bullfights. Oviedo: fair, first-class bullfights. Pontevedra: fiesta, first-class bullfights. Salamanca: fair, first-class bullfights. Santander: motor races. San Sebastián: *Semana Grande,* first-class bullfights. Seville: Fiesta of Our Lady of the Kings, first-class bullfights, Assumption Day, August 15. Sitges: Fiesta of San Bartolomé. Toledo: fiesta, first-class bullfights. Valladolid: fair, first-class bullfights. Vitoria: Festival of the White Virgin, first-class bullfights. Zamora: fair, first-class bullfights.

SEPTEMBER. Aranjuez: fountain displays. Barcelona: religious fiesta, folklore competitions. Cordova: fair, parades. Covarrubias: *Rueda Chospona, Rueda Rachela,* dances. Cuenca: commemorate reconquest of the city from the Moors, first-class bullfights. El Escorial: pilgrimage. Granada: fair. Guadalupe: fair. Huelva: Feast of *La Virgen de la Cinta.* Jerez de la Frontera: grape harvest festival. Leon: *Aluches,* distinctive type of wrestling, championships. Logroño: Feast of St. Matthew. Madrid: horse-racing season, into November. Merida: fair, first-class bullfights. Nationwide: association football, to June. Ochagavia: pilgrimage. Oviedo: America in Asturias Day, tribute to American-Spanish relations. Palencia: fair, first-class bullfights. Reinosa: important horse show, fair. Salamanca: pilgrimage. San Sebastian: musical fortnight; tennis championships. Seville: fair, parade. Tarragona: *Fiesta de Santa Tecla, Sardanas* dances, *xiquets,* human towers. Tordesillas: cape-fighting bulls. Valencia de Don Juan: pelota championship. Valladolid: fair, folklore rally.

OCTOBER. Arenas de San Pedro: religious feast. Avila: Feast of St. Theresa; *Juego de Bandera,* or flag play. Barcelona: Grand Prix of Penya Rhin, Barcelona Cup, auto races. Cangas de Onis: cattle, cheese show. Corunna: pilgrimage. Don Benito: pilgrimage. Guadalajara: fair. Jaén: fair, first-class bullfights. Las Palmas: procession of boats at religious fiesta. Madrid: Spanish open golf championship. Melaga: Iberia Cup, golf championship. Nationwide: pelota, Basque type of handball played with scoops and hard balls, attracts better players to Barcelona, Bilbao, Madrid, Palma de Mallorca, Pamplona, and San Sebastian from October to June. Saragossa: Feast of Our Lady of the Pillar, first-class bull-fights. Soria: Feast of St. Francis, first-class bullfights. Valencia: reconquest of the city celebrated. Zafra: livestock fair, first-class bullfights.

NOVEMBER. Huesca: livestock fair. Jaén: pilgrimage to Shrine of St. Catharine. Leon: livestock fair. Saragossa: Procession of the Holy Masses.

DECEMBER. Guadalupe: Christmas Eve service; Feast of Our Lady of Guadalupe. Montserrat: Christmas Eve service. Palma de Mallorca: celebrate reconquest of the city. Torrejoncillo: *La Encamisada,* religious procession.

SWEDEN

THE SPIRIT of festivals has had a happy home in Sweden at least since the days of the Vikings, for then as now men and women under the spell of Walpurgis Night danced and sang hosannas to the returning spring. Through the years the Swedes have added other noteworthy celebrations to their calendar of events, such as the Stockholm Festival, which reflects their interest in music, the Vasa Ski Race, which emphasizes their enthusiasm for winter sports, and the Nobel Prize ceremonies, which are annual reminders of one man's attempt to reap a harvest of happiness from a fortune made in explosives.

Nobel Prize

The most coveted awards in the world today are the Nobel prizes, which, as a rule, are presented annually for superior achievements in chemistry, literature, medicine, peace, and physics. All prizes, except the peace prize, which is presented in Oslo, Norway, are presented at ceremonies in Stockholm.

The winners are invited to be in Stockholm for the presentation, which takes place at 5:00 P.M., December 10, in the Stockholm Concert House in the presence of the King and members of the Royal Family, court officials, members of the diplomatic corps, and prominent private citizens. The laureates, both old and new, wait in an anteroom with the awarding faculty until the King appears at the large concert hall. His entrance is announced by a loud fanfare and the playing of "The King's Anthem." Another loud blast on the trumpets signals the laureates to enter and march to the stage. The King does not sit on the stage, but in the audience. That is a traditional gesture on the part of the Royal Family to honor the laureates by turning the stage and the spotlight over to them. Each presentation of a gold medal, certificate, and bank draft worth between $30,000 and $40,000 is preceded by an address by the sponsor, explaining why the honor is being bestowed. Then the recipient descends the stairs to receive the award from the King, who arises and leads the applause as the first of the people to honor each prize winner. After receiving the prize and congratulations from the King, the recipient must walk backward fifteen or twenty feet, keeping his face turned toward the Royal Family, until he reaches the steps that lead to the stage. The presentation ceremonies are followed by a banquet.

Swedes and visitors to Sweden who are not fortunate enough to attend the festival in the Concert House usually have an opportunity to share in the celebration by attending lectures given by the laureates. On every occasion tribute is paid to the memory of Alfred Nobel, the donor of the prizes, who was born in Stockholm on October 21, 1833. He received little formal education, yet invented dynamite and smokeless powder, and a number of other things. He died at San Remo, Italy, on December 10, 1896, and left this will, which resulted in the formation of the Nobel Foundation:

The whole of my remaining realizable estate shall be dealt with in the following way: The capital shall be invested by my executors in safe securities and shall constitute a fund, the interest on which shall be annually distributed in the form of prizes to those who, during the preceding year, shall have conferred the greatest benefit on mankind.

The said interest shall be divided into five equal parts, which shall be apportioned as follows: one part to the person who shall have made the most important discovery or invention within the field of physics; one part to the person who shall have made the most important chemical discovery or improvement; one part to the person who shall have made the most important discovery within the domain of physiology or medicine; one part to the person who shall have produced in the field of literature the most outstanding work of an idealistic tendency; and one part to the person who shall have done the most or the best work for fraternity among nations, for the abolition or reduction of standing armies and for the holding and promotion of peace congresses.

The prizes for physics and chemistry shall be awarded by the Swedish Academy of Science; that for physiological or medical works by the Caroline Institute in Stockholm; that for literature by the Swedish Academy in Stockholm; and that for champions of peace by a committee of five persons to be elected by the Norwegian Storting (Parliament). It is my express wish that in awarding the prizes no consideration whatever shall be given to the nationality of the candidates, so that the most worthy shall receive the prize, whether he be a Scandinavian or not.

In 1950 when the Foundation celebrated its fiftieth anniversary there were at least two innovations. It marked the first time that the festival was televised, and the first time that King Gustaf VI Adolf, as reigning monarch, presented the prizes to the winners. He had previously made the presentations while Crown Prince when his father King Gustaf V Adolf was too ill to attend the celebration. That year, too, the 264th Nobel Prize was awarded. The only person whose name appears twice on the list is Marie Curie, of France, who was honored in 1903 and 1911 for pioneering research in radioactive elements. Although attendance at the Nobel award ceremonies is by invitation only, the general public can get a glimpse of the laureates and other notables in formal attire as they enter the Concert House between columns dramatically illuminated by flaming torches. Also, Swedes and their guests may hear those laureates who lecture while visiting in Stockholm.

Music, Drama

Stockholm celebrated the seven hundredth anniversary of its founding in 1953 and marked the occasion by staging the first annual Stockholm Festival, which featured indoor performances of opera, ballet, concerts, theater, and films as well as folk dancing by hundreds of dancers in Skansen Park from May through September. Operatic offerings included *The Isle of Rapture,* a modern Swedish opera by Hilding Rosenberg; *Rigoletto,* by Verdi, and *Orlando Furioso,* by Handel. Ballet included *Miss Julie, Suite Classique,* and *Knave and Six Princesses.* Chamber music concerts were presented by the Intimate Music Society in the eighteenth-century Hall of the Stock Exchange where the Swedish Academy gathers. The American Dean Dixon and the Hungarian Antal Dorati conducted concerts by the combined symphony orchestras of the Stockholm Music Association and the Swedish Broadcasting System. *Pastoral,* a drama in three parts by Olaf von Dalin, eighteenth-century Swedish author, originally presented for Her Majesty in the Palace Gardens on August 11, 1752, was produced by the Royal Dramatic Theatre in Drottningholm Court Theatre. The motion-picture portion of the festival featured silent and sound films. A similar cultural conclave to be known as the Stockholm Festival probably will be held annually during the first two weeks in June.

Since 1929 the operatic miracle play *Petrus de Dacia* has been staged in the ruins of St. Nicholas Cathedral at Visby, Gotland, in July and August. It represents scenes from the life of Petrus de Dacía, a Swedish Dominican monk who lived from 1235 to 1289.

Open-air performances of *The Road to Heaven*, an allegorical play of the *Everyman* type, staged in Dalecarlian costume and representing the old Dalecarlian conception of biblical events, are offered in mid-July at Leksand, Dalecarlia. The play was written as recently as 1943 by Rune Lindström, a young student, and has won high critical praise for its representation of Dalecarlian traditions. He has also written and directed a motion picture of the play, and played the leading role himself.

Arnljot, an opera of the Viking era composed in 1910 by Wilhelm Peterson-Berger, is performed on the island of Frösö outside Östersund in Jämtland, the home of the composer, during July.

Intermittently between May and September the curtain goes up on period plays staged in the eighteenth-century style at Sweden's eighteenth-century Drottningholm Court Theatre. The playhouse is unique in that it stands exactly as it was when it was opened in 1765. Typical works presented during the summer season are *Orlando Furioso*, by Handel, *II Matrimonio Segreto*, by Cimarosa, and *Bastien et Bastienne*, by Mozart. The actors and the musicians in the pit wear costumes of the eighteenth century. In fact, some of the costumes worn in the plays are the very ones that were used when the theater was in its heyday almost two hundred years ago. The ingenious machinery for making sound effects for storms on land and at sea is still operating, too. So is a rickety old platform on which actors who are impersonating good or evil spirits descend from above. What's more, the stalls, chairs, and benches in the auditorium bear the titles of persons in the court who were to occupy them, from artistic, pleasure-loving King Gustavus III on down the line to his most humble servant.

Customs

Walpurgis Night celebrations, April 30, probably of heathen origin, celebrate the coming of spring. At that time bonfires are lit all over Sweden, and fireworks are set off, but it is particularly in the old university town of Uppsala that student merrymaking reaches its peak with singing and dancing throughout the night. An old belief is that the bright fires frightened away demons of darkness and gloom.

The first of May is also a day of welcoming spring, but it is likewise the day when labor parades its might.

On June 6 the nation honors its flag, at which time the King of Sweden presents banners to various organizations at ceremonies in the Stockholm Olympic Stadium around 4:00 P.M. There are speeches, a parade, music, and songs. The King and the Royal Family ride in open coaches from the Royal Palace through Stockholm to and from the Stadium. Flag Day, of course, is observed all over Sweden.

The American Independence Day is celebrated in Stockholm on July 4 with speeches by the American ambassador and prominent Swedes. In recent years speeches have been delivered by the late Folke Bernadotte, Prince Wilhelm, and Prince Bertil. There is choral singing, fireworks, and dancing. The annual celebration began in 1948 and is sponsored by the American-Swedish Society, the American Club, and the American Women's Club.

Since 1953 the age-old Midsummer Festival has been celebrated in the week between June 19 and 25, with Midsummer's Eve falling on Friday during that week, and Midsummer Day on the Saturday. This ancient celebration is observed throughout the country with Maypole dances. Particularly colorful celebrations take place in the village of Leksand, where the celebrants wearing their regional costumes arrive by longboat, march to the village green, and dance around the decorated Maypole.

On July 26 all Stockholm celebrates Bellman Day, which salutes the memory of Carl Michael Bellman, eighteenth-century poet and troubadour, whose songs and poems are as popular today as they were 175 years ago. Singers from the Royal Opera and ballet dancers take part in the festivities, which usually include a parade and water carnival.

Swedish American Day is celebrated in September at the famous Skansen Park in Stockholm, as well as in other parts of Sweden, such as Gothenburg, Kalmar, and Mora. The first celebration was staged in 1948, the centenary year of the first large-scale Swedish emigration to the United States.

As the year hastens to a close, Lucia Day is celebrated in Sweden on December 13 with festivities honoring St. Lucia, the Queen of Light. High point of the celebration is a big candlelight parade through Stockholm, with the Stockholm Lucia and her escorts riding in open, decorated coaches. At a big party in the Town Hall the Queen of Light receives the Lucia Jewel, which is usually presented by one of the year's Nobel Prize winners. She is also awarded a trip to the United States to visit Swedish America. Similar celebrations take place all over Sweden. In homes and public places where there are parties the reigning queen wears a crown of lighted candles.

Sports

The big springtime skiing event in Sweden is usually staged at Mora on the first Sunday in March. It is the Vasa Ski Race, a fifty-mile cross-country event linking Salen to Mora inaugurated in 1922 to commemorate a similar feat by King Gustaf Vasa in 1521. In 1952 there were 740 participants, and about 70,000 spectators.

The Stanga Games at Roma, Isle of Gotland, originated centuries ago. Among the unusual games are *park,* a very old game similar to baseball but played with the hands instead of a bat, and a leather-covered stone instead of a ball, and pole tossing, an ancient Viking athletic contest that is believed to have been the forerunner of the currently popular pole-tossing competitions in Scotland.

In the Church Boat Race at Leksand, each village around Lake Siljan has its own longboat or "church boat," so called because they are used to carry people to church. Some of the boats are more than a hundred years old, and the race is part of an all-day Fiddlers' Meet in Dalecarlia usually on the last Sunday in June or the first Sunday in July. Although most of the three hundred musicians who take part play the fiddle, there are also a few who play clarinets, herding pipes, and cow horns.

The International Regatta at Marstrand, Gothenburg, usually in mid-July, is a favorite with Crown Prince Olaf of Norway, who always takes part. That meet and the boat races at Sandhamn, Stockholm, are prime social events.

Fairs

The St. Erik International Trade Fair, usually staged in Stockholm late in August and early in September, has become one of the foremost events of its kind in Europe. Founded in 1943 with about 100 local exhibitors occupying about 38,000 square feet of space, it now has as many as 2,000 exhibitors from about 20 countries who fill approximately 1,300,000 square feet of space. Approximately half a million visitors attend the two-week show.

The Swedish Industries Fair at Gothenburg is divided into two parts. The first part, usually presented in May, is devoted to Swedish heavy industries, and the second part, usually in

September, features heavy industries from many nations.

Other important fairs include the *Skåne* Fair at Malmö in July, the Lapp Midsummer Fair in Lapland during the fourth week in June, and the Lapp Fair at Gallivare, Lapland, during the fourth week in March. The fairs are the two most important gatherings of Lapps from all over northern Sweden, because they afford opportunities for reindeer trading, christenings, weddings, and the sale of Lapp handicrafts.

When the National Craftsmen's Competitions are held in October at the City Hall in Stockholm, or other places such as Falun, Gothenburg, Karlstad, Lulea, Malmö and Soderhamn, spinners and weavers take part, and many contestants wear their folk costumes.

The exact dates on which festivals will take place in Sweden, as well as the latest travel information pertaining to that country, may be obtained by writing to the Swedish National Travel Office, 630 Fifth Avenue, New York 20, New York.

Bank holidays in Sweden: January 1; Twelfth Day or Epiphany, January 6; Good Friday; Easter Eve; Easter Monday; May 1; Ascension Day, forty days after Easter; Whitsun Eve, forty-eight days after Easter; Whitmonday, fifty days after Easter; Midsummer Eve, the Friday during week between June 19 and June 25; Midsummer Day; All Saints' Day, Saturday during the week between October 31 and November 6; Christmas Eve, December 24; Christmas, December 25; December 26; and New Year's Eve.

Chronological list of events in Sweden:

JANUARY. Stockholm: Opening of Parliament; tennis tournament for King Gustaf V Cup.

FEBRUARY. Åre: Swedish skiing tournament. Jokkmokk: Lapp fair, fur sales.

MARCH. Boden: cross-country skiing. Gallivare, Lapland: fair. Mora: Vasa skiing race.

APRIL. Nationwide: Walpurgis Night, April 30, with most interesting celebrations at Lund, Uppsala.

MAY. A different place each year: Swedish motorcycle reliability trial. Drottningholm: Drottningholm Court Theater, near Stockholm, open intermittently to September. Gallivare, Lapland: fair.

Gothenburg: Swedish Industries' Fair. Nationwide: Labor Day, May 1. Jonkoping: small industries' fair. Omberg: folk festival. Stockholm: Djurgarden Pleasure Fair; Grand Prix horse race; trotting races.

JUNE. Falsterbo: one of starting points for Swedish auto rally to the midnight sun. Gothenburg: one of starting points for Swedish auto rally to the midnight sun. Lapland: fair. Leksand, Dalecarlia: Fiddlers' Meet, Church Boat Race, June or July. Malmö: horse show, trotting, horse races. Nationwide: Flag Day, June 6, with most impressive ceremonies in Stockholm; Midsummerfests, week end nearest June 24. Nykoping: historical play. Örebro: fair. Roma, Isle of Gotland: Stanga games. Stockholm: one of starting points for Swedish auto rally to the midnight sun; Stockholm Festival. Sundsvall: one of starting points for Swedish auto rally to the midnight sun.

JULY. Hedemora: motorcycle road race. Kivik: fair, folk festivities. Leksand, Dalecarlia: Fiddlers' Meet, Church Boat Race, June or July; play, *The Road to Heaven,* folk music, dancing. Malmö: Skåne Industries Fair; Swedish Derby, horse race. Marstrand: regatta. Östersund, in Jamtland: fair. Rättvik: folk song, dance festival. Sigtuna: modern Swedish drama. Stockholm: American Independence Day; Bellman Day, July 26. Vilhelmina: folk songs, dancing, chronicle play, peasant wedding. Visby: *Petrus de Dacia,* miracle play with music.

AUGUST. Helsingborg: trade, crafts show. Kalmar: Swedish American Day. Malmö: Swedish Grand Prix motor-cross, for motorcycles. Sigtuna: modern Swedish drama. Stockholm: St. Erik's Fair. Visby: *Petrus de Dacia,* miracle play with music.

SEPTEMBER. Gothenburg: Swedish-American Day; Swedish Industries' Fair; Swedish Oaks, horse race. Helsingborg: tuna fishing tournament. Kristianstad: motorcycle road race. Linköping: agricultural machinery show. Mora: Swedish-American Day. Stockholm: Children's Day; Flax Festival at Skansen; horse races; Scandinavian Grand Prix horse race; Swedish-American Day; trotting races.

SEPTEMBER or OCTOBER. National Craftsmen's Contests: Falun, Gothenburg, Karlstad, Lulea, Malmö, Soderhamn, Stockholm.

OCTOBER. Malmö: Swedish Criterion, horse race. Sodermanland: motor-cross (motorcycle) races. Stockholm: horse, trotting races. Strangnas: motor-cross (motorcycle) races.

NOVEMBER. Gavle: trotting races. Nationwide: anniversary of death of King Gustavus Adolphus, November 6. Stockholm: Christmas fair, spinning, weaving contests, into December; trotting races.

DECEMBER. Nationwide: Lucia Day, dedicated to the Queen of Light, December 13. Stockholm: Christmas fair, spinning, weaving contests; Nobel Prize Awards, December 10.

SWITZERLAND

SWITZERLAND is
probably the most international nation in Europe, not because of its traditional neutrality, or because it is often considered an ideal place for the headquarters of important world
organizations, but because French, German, and Italian in-
fluences strongly flavor separate and distinct areas there and
create charming contrasts that are difficult to find elsewhere.
The distinctions are noticeable in the traditional, cultural,
religious, economic, and sports festivals with which Switzerland is well supplied. But in spite of this the Swiss are fiercely
patriotic. They are proud, too, of their national unity and
the independence that their nation has enjoyed for centuries.

Patriotic, Traditional Festivals

August 1 is to the Swiss what the Fourth of July is to Americans. For it was on August 1, 1291, that the towns of Schwyz,
Unterwalden, and Uri formed a perpetual alliance to help
each other and thus started the Swiss Federation, which now
consists of twenty-two cantons. The anniversary is usually cele-

brated in the evening with bell-ringing, festive assemblies, fireworks, and beacon fires on mountaintops, even above the timber line. The fires are a throwback to the days when fires were used as a means of communication between towns on different mountains in much the same way that American Indians used smoke signals. One of the shrines of independence in Switzerland is the Rütli on the Lake of Lucerne. There, according to legend, beneath the crags of the Seelisberg on the night of November 7, 1307, Walter Fürst, of Attinghausen in Uri; Werner Stauffacher, of Steinen in Schwyz; and Arnold Anderhalden of Melchtal in Unterwalden, each accompanied by ten colleagues, met and vowed to drive out the Austrians. That was a renewal of the pledge made by their people in 1291 at Brunnen on the opposite side of the lake when they sought to oust the Hapsburgs. According to legend three springs of clear water are said to have burst out of the ground where the three patriots stood on the meadow of Rütli. The "springs of the three cantons" may still be seen, for they are part of a national park purchased by Swiss schoolchildren in 1860.

One of the principal patriotic holidays of the Canton of Glarus is the pilgrimage to Näfels on the first Thursday in April. Songs, speeches, and sermons there on that date salute the memory of 600 Glarus men who on April 9, 1388, defeated 6,000 Austrians. A procession visits the 11 memorial stones that mark the 11 unsuccessful attacks by the Austrians.

On the Friday after Ascension, Ascension Day being the fortieth day after Easter, a pilgrimage to William Tell's chapel at Tellsplatte on the southern shore of Lake Lucerne honors the archer of Altdorf who is supposed to have killed Gessler, mythical Austrian bailiff, and incited the forest cantons to independence.

How greatly the Swiss cherish their independence is shown by the communal assemblies called *Landsgemeinde,* in Ap-

penzell, Trogen or Hundwil, Stans, and Sarnen on the last
Sunday in April, and at Glarus on the first Sunday in May.
According to tradition the citizens take great pride in carrying their swords as a token of their right to vote. Women and
children often don their regional costumes, while canton
officials wear long black gowns. Civic matters are discussed,
officials are elected, and the multitude renews the oath of
fidelity to the state, a very solemn and impressive part of every
Landsgemeinde.

Throughout the year there are numerous Swiss folk festivals that have patriotic overtones. Around the third week in
January the *Vogel Gryff,* or festival of the three companies of
honor, the Griffin, Lion, and Wild Man, brings some jollity
to Basel. The celebrants dance through the streets just as their
ancestors did some seven hundred years ago. Early in the day
the "Wild Man," accompanied by drummers and standard-
bearers, sails down the Rhine on a raft as far as the middle
bridge where he is welcomed by *Vogel Gryff,* the Griffin, and
the Lion. There all three perform an ancient dance. The
routine is repeated from time to time as the celebrants parade
through the streets toward their favorite restaurant.

Pre-Lenten carnivals are also popular in Switzerland for
a full week before Ash Wednesday. There is "Dirty Thursday" at Brunnen, a *Fritschi* procession in Lucerne, comic
parades in Coire and in the Valais, and costume parties in
central, northwestern, and eastern Switzerland.

Oddly enough, however, the most impressive carnival celebration of all is the one called *Fastnacht* at Basel on the first
week end in Lent, in February or March. It begins at four
o'clock one morning with noisy processions of various
drumming clubs and continues with satirical parades and
concerts devoted to the diversified performances of star
drummers. The Swiss, it seems, love to beat drums. As
a rule illumination in the evening parades is provided by huge

painted lanterns of original design. Masked balls are given nightly, and local restaurants feature local delicacies, such as the pie called *swiebelwahe, gebrannte mehlsuppe,* and cheese cakes.

Ordinarily there is a lull in festivities between the carnival at Basel and the *Sechseläuten,* ringing of the bells, spring ceremony of the Zurich Guilds to bid good-by to winter, on the Monday following the spring equinox in April. The high point of the two-day celebration is the burning of Böögg, symbolic snowman made of cotton, saturated with petrol, and stuffed with explosives, promptly at 6:00 P.M. on the second day. The execution of this Old Man Winter takes place while fifes and drums are played, and masked merrymakers sing and dance around the fire. There are also a historic parade and pageant by members of the twenty-four guilds still extant, wearing the traditional, elaborate costumes and proudly flying the guild flags overhead. The guilds have figured prominently in this festival since the Middle Ages when, oddly enough, they began to celebrate the return of spring and summer when the working day is one hour longer than it is in winter.

Occasionally, in May, after the plowing is done and the hay is in, about five thousand Swiss peasants in native costumes leave their homes in the mountains and stage the *Trachtentag* Festival. In many instances the costumes go back four or five hundred years and reflect the styles that prevailed during different stages of Switzerland's history. To welcome properly the return of spring at this party the Swiss drink gallons of *dunkel* beer, hop to the jumpy rhythms of *Landler* bands, watch stage shows and folk dances, blow into gigantic alpenhorns, throw flags in flag-tossing contests, and yodel!

At Interlaken from mid-May to mid-September the nights are filled with music because there are concerts or special programs in the casino every evening. The two big evenings of the week, however, are Monday and Wednesday. Monday is the most popular of all because that is when the folklorists take over. Entertainment at these weekly folk fests ranges from alpine horn blowing to yodeling, with dances, flag-throwing, and even Swiss wrestling thrown in for good measure. Most travelers in Switzerland combine a visit to Interlaken with a trip to the Jungfrau, the famous snow-covered mountain whose peak is accessible to tourists the year round. All you have to do to reach the peak is board the Jungfrau cog railway at Interlaken or one of the way stations beyond.

Summer is welcomed to Lucerne with a parade of decorated barges and canoes festooned with lanterns *à la Venice* during the annual *Seenachtfest,* or Night Lake Festival, in June. There are also gymnastics, water sports, and fireworks.

To mark the anniversary of the Battle of 1476 in Murten there are shooting contests and a children's festival during the fourth week of June.

Less than two weeks later, on the Monday after July 4, the people of Lucerne and Sempach join in a celebration commemorating the Battle of Sempach on July 9, 1386. The Swiss victory in that fight shook the power of the Hapsburgs in Central Switzerland, west to the Jura Mountains, and north to the Rhine. Today the Swiss march to Winkelried Monument, a band plays patriotic hymns, there are speeches, an ancient chronicle of the battle is read, and there are thanksgiving services.

The logical time for the annual Rose Week in Geneva is around the middle of June, because that is when the city seems like one immense garden. During that period some favorite walks are along the lakeside, through the parks, and especially through the rosary in the Parc La Grange. Ordinarily at least a hundred thousand roses bloom then. At night the gardens are flood-lighted, and entertainment includes symphonic concerts, performances by the *Comédie Française,* and the corps de ballet of the Opéra de Paris.

During the second week in August at Geneva the *Fêtes de Genève* include a battle of flowers, a fancy-dress parade, open-air balls, confetti fights, water carnivals, and fireworks displays.

Four months later, on December 12, at Geneva, the Escalade commemorates the vain attack on the town by the Savoyards in 1602 with a proclamation and procession. The sneak attack by the Savoyards was frustrated by Mère Rayaume, a housewife, who looked out of her window overlooking the town wall just in time to see one of the invaders climb stealthily up a long-hinged ladder, or escalade. Obeying an impulse, Mme Rayaume grabbed a pot of hot soup, poured the steaming contents on the nearest climber, bounced the iron kettle off his head, and sounded the alarm. Today the trade-mark of the festival is a miniature caldron made of chocolate and sold in candy stores. The festival includes masked balls, parades by the inevitable fife and drum corps, maskers in seventeenth-century costumes, and psalm-singing. The psalm-singing was the idea of one of Calvin's disciples. He persuaded the townsfolk to sing their thankfulness for help in vanquishing the invaders. Now the singing is usually done by a men's choir on the steps of the cathedral.

Drama, Music

The most representative dramatic show in Switzerland is the open-air performance of *William Tell* at Interlaken as a rule in even years from mid-July to the end of August. The afternoon performances are given chiefly on Sundays, and there usually are five evening performances on selected Thursdays and Saturdays. The legendary Tell has become a symbol of freedom and national independence, and the subject of plays by Knowles, Lemierre, and Schiller, and an opera by Rossini. In 1938, when the independence of many European nations was threatened, the people of New Glarus, Wisconsin, heart of the region settled by Americans of Swiss descent, thought it would be a good idea to remind the world of the successful fight the Swiss waged against oppressive Austrian dictators more than 600 years ago, so they began staging Schiller's play every year during the first week end in September. On Sunday the show is in the Swiss dialect, and on Monday in English. As almost everyone knows, Tell is supposed to have refused to salute the cap of Gessler, the imperial governor, and for that disobedience was sentenced to shoot with his bow and arrow an apple from the head of his own son. He succeeded, later shot Gessler in the narrow pass near Kussnacht, and was credited with freeing his country from Austrian rule. The Interlaken Tell Players' Society stages the play with a cast of eighty.

The June Festival, which has become the crowning event of the cultural and artistic season in Zurich, began soon after the end of World War I when the various powers of Europe are said to have tried to win the favor of Switzerland by presenting their finest artists in concerts and recitals. Opera companies were there from Frankfurt, Milan, Paris, and Vienna, and from that start began the present festival of ballet, drama, opera, and symphony concerts.

Lausanne is gaining in popularity as an international ballet center, and the month of June is usually the peak of the summer season for visiting companies. In recent years the schedules have included such well-known groups as the New York City Ballet, the Marquis de Cuevas Ballet, and the Paris Opera Ballet. The Lausanne debut of Boria Kniaseff's International Academy of Dancing has been scheduled for the first two weeks in June, 1954. Long a resident of Paris, M. Kniaseff opened his school in Lausanne in April, 1953.

He is composing a new ballet that will be presented with the collaboration of international ballet stars. During the second half of June the Paris Opera Ballet, with the Orchestre de la Suisse Romande, will give several open-air performances. That is a typical program for the annual festival.

From time to time a Narcissus Festival at Montreux during the third week in June includes flower pageants, confetti throwing, and outdoor evening lakeside fetes, as well as performances by such famous musical organizations as the Italian State Opera.

Braunwald, in the Canton of Glarus, has been entertaining visitors with an international music festival during the third week in July since the mid 1930's. A typical festival program calls for about five public evening concerts and a series of discussions led by persons prominent in the field of music.

It was in July and August, 1938, that Lucerne held its first Music Festival in the park of Villa Tribschen, which once was a happy haunt of Richard Wagner. Today artists of the caliber of Arturo Toscanini take part in a series of symphonic, chamber music, and choral concerts, serenades in the park, and recitals in the cathedral. In 1953 the program included Verdi's *Messa da Requiem*, with Antonino Votto directing the orchestra and choir of La Scala, Milan, and six symphony concerts by the Swiss Festival Orchestra.

Ascona has been entertaining visitors from mid-August to mid-September with a music festival since 1946. The standard repertoire includes at least three symphony concerts under famous conductors, historical concerts in Casa Serodine, ballet, oratorios, and art exhibitions.

The fall musical season is ushered in at Geneva during the last week in September when the annual international competition for musical performers is presented. There usually are contests for harpsichord, oboe, piano, saxophone, and violin, as well as for vocalists.

A different type of festival is Engadine Concert Weeks from mid-July to mid-August at Celerina, Pontresina, St. Moritz, Samedan, Silvaplana, Sils-Baseglia, and Zuoz. At those places a total of about eighteen concerts feature top-flight chamber music groups, quartets, and concert ensembles.

Since Switzerland has long been synonymous with yodeling, a report on musical events would not be complete without a reference to the triennial Swiss National Yodelers' Festival, which attracts about three thousand yodelers for three days of singing in mid-July. The most recent conclave was held at St. Gall in 1952.

At the annual Film Festival inaugurated at Locarno in 1947, and staged regularly during the first two weeks in July, no prizes are awarded, but the judges issue a list of best films. Some 28,000 movie-goers look at the pick of feature films and documentaries from Europe and the United States.

Religion

Good Friday is the holiest day of the entire year among Swiss Catholics and Protestants. It is the one day on which just about everyone goes to church, and is usually the day of confirmation in the Protestant churches. In many Swiss towns the historic events of Passion Week are dramatized. One of the more impressive presentations is at Mendrisio, near Lugano, where the re-enactment of the journey to Golgotha at 8:00 P.M. on Holy Thursday and the torchlight procession on Good Friday evening retain elements of the mystery plays that the clergy staged for their congregations in the Middle Ages.

Corpus Christi, sixty days after Easter, is another great church festival in Switzerland where exceptionally beautiful processions and ceremonies, brightened by regional costumes and soldiers in uniform of various periods, take place at Appenzell, Bulle, Châtel-St. Denis, Dudingen, Einsiedeln, Estavayer-le-lac, Fribourg, Guin, Lucerne, Porrentruy, Romont, Saas-Fee, Sion, Sitten, Vitznau, Wil, and in the Alpine villages of the Valais. The observance at Fribourg, for example, is high-lighted by the ancient vestments and richly decorated chasubles of the clergy, the antique *chassets* of the guilds, and the heady aroma and beauty of the bouquets of wild mountain spring flowers carried by the women and children. Papal guards in their traditional uniforms escort the canopy under which the Bishop of Fribourg, Lausanne, and Geneva carries the Holy Sacrament, surrounded by members of an ancient congregation carrying emblazoned lanterns. Furthermore, a curious and interesting tradition that originated when an area of the town was destroyed by fire requires all the houses in the main street to be adorned with tapestries when the procession passes.

The Aubusson, Flanders, and Gobelin tapestries date from the seventeenth and eighteenth centuries. They form a handsome setting for the long procession of the faithful, which advances slowly to the flourish of trumpets and the music of bands. Temporary altars are set up on the town's principal public squares, and that is where the Bishop, surrounded by the Chapter of St. Nicholas and by the clergy, pronounces benediction. The ceremony concludes with a solemn salute on Place Notre-Dame in the presence of all the groups that have taken part in the parade, while the choir of seminarists and members of the choir schools sing an accompaniment.

On Benediction Sunday, three days after Corpus Christi, one of the most frequently photographed traditional national ceremonies is celebrated at Blatten and Kippel, in the Lachschen Valley. The *Herrgottsgrenadiere*, or Lord God's Grenadiers, who are the center of attraction at this festival, are tall, stalwart men who wear ancient uniforms of red and white, full military equipment, and a shako. Their parade through the beautiful, peaceful Alpine valley is the personification of the church militant.

At least thirty relics of SS. Placidus and Sigisbert are carried by the faithful in the religious procession that honors Placidus in Disentis on the morning of July 11. That is the date on which he was beheaded near the abbey that he and Sigisbert founded. Now the two are the patron saints of the region, and the celebration in July is famous for its showing of old folk costumes, muskets, and flags, and the singing of the Song of St. Placidus, which dates to 1680 and has at least sixty verses.

On September 14 the religious festival of the *Engelweihe*, or Consecration of the Angels, is marked by a great torchlight procession in the Monastery Square at Einsiedeln, perhaps the most important religious center in Switzerland. The huge altar in the square is ablaze with light, and thousands of candles gleam in windows of buildings on the square.

The traditional appearance of St. Nicholas with a body-guard in Küssnacht between December 4 and 6 is one of the more elaborate parades in Swiss religious life, for Santa Claus is followed by about fifty white-robed dancers who wear gigantic six-foot-tall hats resembling stained-glass windows through which the lights of candles shine. Other St. Nicholas celebrations are at Weggis and Zurich.

Fairs

The Swiss Industries Fair in Basel, which lasts for about ten days during April or May, gives visitors a good idea of the productive capacity of Switzerland. As a rule there are over 2,000 exhibitors whose booths cover more than 1,000,000 square feet. Emphasis, of course, is placed on the products of the watchmakers, the electrical and precision tool industries, and textiles. The latest fashions employing Swiss fabrics are featured in the Creation Pavilion. The special exhibit of

Swiss watchmaking is a co-operative enterprise by more than 150 firms in the watchmaking industry, and since this industry exports 95 per cent of its production, the display can be described as the most important one of its kind. The technical side of Swiss production is illustrated by the display of the smallest precision instruments and apparatus up to the largest types of machinery, including the heavy industry covering general engineering and the electrical industry. Textile machinery and machine tools take it in turn to exhibit at Basel, textile machinery being shown in even years, machine tools in odd years.

All important automobile and automobile accessory manufacturers take part in the *Salon de l'Automobile* at Geneva in March. Since Switzerland produces very few cars, import restrictions are not necessary to protect the industry, so the show is made up mainly of foreign products. The 1953 show included exhibits by 73 motor firms, 53 makers of commercial vehicles, 112 makers of motorcycles and bicycles, and 15 body-building firms. Manufacturers of camping materials, miscellaneous accessories, and boats also took part.

At the Watches and Jewelry Exhibition in Geneva during the first three weeks of September all the latest creations of the Montres de Genève and great watchmakers of Switzerland are luxuriously displayed. Geneva's reputation as the center of the watchmaking and jewelry arts is world-wide, and this annual show affords an opportunity to specialists, technicians, and artists to meet and compare knowledge. Each year different arts allied to the watchmaking and jewelry industries are arranged in exhibition while the Watches and Jewelry Show is on. For example, in 1952 well-known clockwork figures, such as the famous chess player, were shown. In 1953 the first international exhibition of contemporary enamels was a big success.

The first annual gastronomic fair in Switzerland has been

planned for Berne, May 14–June 21, 1954. The official title of the show will be the Swiss Tourism and International Cookery Exhibition. Expert chefs from many countries are expected to take part in all sorts of cooking contests designed to launch this new type of festival for Switzerland. Every day special dishes and exhibition pieces will be prepared. Other attractions that are expected to become fixtures at future editions of the gastronomic fair are a typical Swiss military mess, Oriental food served in a Chinese junk moored on an artificial lake, and a pond where visitors can catch the trout they want to have cooked and served to them at a nearby inn.

At Saignelégier in mid-August the National Horse Fair features parades and races, with girls in national costumes riding the famous Jura horses noted for their exceptional strength.

The *Braderie*, a sort of fair combined with an autumn festival at La Chaux-de-Fonds, usually takes place during the second week in September and is noted for the figure of a giant that is guided through the streets by a bevy of young girls.

For two weeks during the middle of September every year in Lausanne the *Comptoir Suisse*, an agricultural, industrial, and trade fair, brings together farmers and merchants from all over Switzerland. Each year the products of one foreign country are also put on display. The fair was inaugurated on a small scale during the time of World War I and now attracts about 300,000 visitors.

The Swiss Agricultural and Dairy Show at St. Gall in October draws visitors from all parts of Europe during the ten days it is in session.

At the beginning of October when the grape harvest is in, there are noteworthy vintage festivals at communes on the banks of the Lake of Bienne, at Neuchâtel, around the Lake of Geneva, in the Valais, and at Lugano. There are parades of floats, confetti fights, and dancing in the streets, seasoned with sampling of grapes and wine.

Sports

Tourism is one of Switzerland's major industries, probably because the highly utilitarian Alps work all year long to provide an attractive background for visitors. From December to April, at least, Switzerland is a paradise for lovers of winter sports, and often the Swiss calendar of events has a number of seasonal meets of international importance. It was at such a stellar event, the 1953 world figure-skating championship at Davos, that Tenley Albright, a seventeen-year-old ice ballerina of Newton, Massachusetts, became the first United States girl ever to win the world figure-skating championship, when she outclassed nineteen competitors from eight countries in the free-skating maneuver and received the unanimous vote of a seven-man panel of judges. Miss Albright's victory was particularly spectacular because it capped a courageous six-year comeback from polio. For her maneuvers at Davos she chose the double *axel,* double loop, double *rittberger,* and double *solchow.* At the same meet Hayes Alan Jenkins, of Akron, Ohio, won the men's competition to give the United States the sweep of the two world individual figure-skating crowns.

Around the second Sunday in January at Flims and St. Moritz there are *schlittedas,* parties in which fifteen or twenty handsomely decorated sleds with twenty-five or thirty-five costumed couples go visiting neighboring villages to bring a little excitement and break the monotony of the long winter with dancing.

One of the well-established skiing events in Switzerland is the Parsenn Derby at Davos the first Sunday in March. It started in the winter of 1922–23 when a discussion arose at the

Parsenn Hut as to the shortest time in which a good skier could run down from the Parsenn Furka to Küblis. Widely different estimates were given, and Mr. F. W. Edlin, an Englishman who was present, offered to give a cup to be competed for in a race to decide the question.

The first Parsenn Derby was held in 1924, time: 22 minutes, 27 seconds. It has been run off annually ever since. At first the course was from the Parsenn Furka to Küblis; then the start was put back to the watershed at the Weissfluhjoch, and for a number of years it has started from the Weissfluh summit, a distance of over six miles with a total fall of 6,600 feet, the longest uninterrupted downhill run in the Alps. The existing record of 13 minutes, 10.4 seconds was set by Ralph Olinger, of Engelberg, in 1948. Mr. Edlin, the founder of the race, was known as "The King of Parsenn" because he did the Parsenn-Küblis run so many times. In his will he left directions that when he died his ashes should be scattered somewhere in Parsenn, and that was done.

While Easter and blossomtime arrive together in Switzerland, up in the highlands the season of spring skiing is at its best. Among skiers, Easter is observed at Villars, in the Vaudois Alps, with a sort of obstacle race. Contestants assemble early in the morning on the Chamossaire, 6,949 feet at the summit, then take off for a downhill race that is packed with curves and thrills. At intervals, mostly at the end of breath-taking turns, red flags are planted in the snow to mark the locations of small baskets containing one hard-boiled egg apiece. During his descent the contestant has to grab a total of five baskets, preferably without stopping. At the finish the eggs are carefully examined. A cracked egg will earn a penalty of ten seconds, and a totally crushed one a loss of thirty seconds. A skier is disqualified if he misses an egg.

One of the best toboggan runs in the world is the St. Moritz Cresta Run, a steep 1,323-yard-long ice channel through which racers flash on a steel sled called a skeleton that measures four inches high, 35–50 inches long, and 20 inches wide. The run is, of course, the scene of important international contests. The record for the Cresta Run was set in 1932 by Jack Heaton, an American, who traveled at the rate of 82.04 miles per hour. The eight hairpin turns are known as Stable Junction, Church Leap, Battle Dore, Shuttlecock, Stream Corner, Bullpetts Corner, Scylla, and Charybdis.

Curling, another winter sport played on ice rinks, is a team game. Each team consists of four players. Each has two stones, forty-pound granite blocks with metal handles, which they push toward the target area known as the "tea" or the "dolly." One important rule forbids players talking to each other, so, on the ice at least, silence reigns at regional, national, and international curling matches during the winter in Switzerland.

Quite different from the poetical spring and summer festivals and rough and tumble games of the season are the cow fights that are staged in the Canton of Valais during the last half of June. The cows bred in the Val d'Hérens are accustomed to grazing on lofty pastures where their instinctive fighting for leadership is not suppressed. Often when a cow has definitely established herself as queen of her herd, her owner enters her in the contest for the cantonal championship at Martigny. The cows are small and black with white markings. They wear great bells, without which they would not fight. The injuries inflicted during the tournaments are said to be negligible.

The Summer Navigation Festival, or *Nana*, which takes place late in June at Ouchy-Lausanne, is organized by the Fraternity of the Ouchy Pirates, a club of fresh-water sailors who claim descent from a guild that, in Roman times, grouped professional navigators of Switzerland's inland sea. The modern festival features regattas, rowing races, a tilting contest, band concerts, a parade, and a procession of automobiles driven by girls in the latest summer styles. There are also a fun fair, fireworks display, and dancing to accordion music.

The Swiss Grand Prix for racing automobiles is usually run in August on the elliptical-shaped circuit that has a lap length of about four and a half miles at Berne. It is one of the ten major events that contribute points to the world championship each year. The others are: Argentina, Belgium, France, Germany, Great Britain, Holland, Indianapolis Speedway, Italy, and Spain.

A plain yellow jersey is a coveted garment during the last week in June when the world's foremost cyclists compete for it in the Tour de Suisse, annual round-Switzerland cycle race that was inaugurated in 1933. It begins and ends in Zurich, the entire race being divided into eight stages over a total course of approximately a thousand miles via a different route every year.

Since 1942 an unusual cross-country running race for four-member teams takes place near Zurich during the first week in October. At the start the competitors are told of the various spots they have to pass, and it is up to them to work out the best route. The race was held for the first time in 1942, and by 1950 some 5,000 runners were taking part.

The Swiss are much interested in gymnastics, so every few years the Federal Gymnastic Festival, which dates at least to 1890, is staged for three days in mid-July. There are team and individual stunts, a procession, and general free exercises.

Marksmanship is another favorite sport in Switzerland. For that reason the traditional *knabenschiessen,* boys' shooting contest, enjoys great popularity in Zurich on a week end in September. As far back as medieval times it was the custom to give small boys and youths supervised training in arms, and to hold a festival in their honor when they contended with one another for the championship in crossbow shooting and later in shooting with the first muskets. The best marksman among them, the *schützenkönig,* was decorated with a Zurich thaler fastened on a silver chain, the so-called *kettelitaler.* That custom is still followed. Toward the end of the sixteenth century the City of Zurich Shooting Society took over the organization of the juvenile championships, and now it makes all arrangements for more than six thousand boys, aged twelve to sixteen, who take part in the contests on the military shooting range at Albisgütli, near the foot of the wooded slopes of the Uetliberg. Watched over by experienced instructors, the boys fire five shots from the kneeling position at a target three hundred yards away. The festival is staged on Saturday, Sunday, and Monday, and the third day becomes a real public festival. Young and old go to the fairground directly behind the shooting range to watch the distribution of prizes that day. The contests are followed by a traditional meal of fried sausage, bread, and tea, then a procession of the young marksmen. The *schützenkönig* receives his prize from a city official of Zurich; there are songs by a boys' choir and general festivities.

The exact dates on which festivals will take place in Switzerland, as well as the latest travel information pertaining to that country, may be obtained by writing to the Swiss National Tourist Office at 10 West 49th Street, New York, New York, or 661 Market Street, San Francisco, California.

Bank holidays in Switzerland: January 1, and sometimes January 2; Good Friday and Easter Monday, March or April; Ascension Day, forty days after Easter; Whitmonday, fifty days after Easter; Independence Day, August 1; Christmas, December 25; and sometimes December 26.

Chronological list of events in Switzerland:

JANUARY. Andermatt: Gotthard Skiing Days. Arosa: horse races on snow track. Basel: *Vogel Gryff,* festival of the three companies of honor of Lesser Basel. Crans: skiing races for Mont-Lachaux Trophy. Davos: Swiss speed-skating championship. Engelberg: Curling Week features contests for International, Shield Cups.

Flims: *Schlittedas,* sled parties. Grindelwald: women's skiing races. St. Moritz: horse races on snow track; *Schlittedas,* sled parties. Wengen: Lauberhorn skiing races; no-fall skiing championship for Sunday Times Cup.

FEBRUARY. Pontresina: no-fall Malicheff skiing race. St. Moritz: White Ribbon skiing races.

FEBRUARY or MARCH. Pre-Lenten carnivals: Coire, Lucerne, the Valais, central, eastern, and northwestern Switzerland. The 4:00 A.M. Procession: Basel.

MARCH. Andermatt: international military skiing patrol race; Swiss Army winter sports championships. Arosa: Three Summits giant *slalom.* Geneva: auto show. Klosters: Parsenn skiing derby. Mendrisio: Passion Play, Good Friday, March or April. Pontresina: Diavolezza Glacier skiing race. Villars: skiing obstacle race. Zermatt: Gornergrat skiing derby.

APRIL. Appenzell: *Landsgemeinde,* people's open-air parliament. Arosa: Oklahoma, David Zogg Cups skiing races. Basel: Swiss Industries' Fair. Hundwil: *Landsgemeinde,* people's open-air parliament. Mendrisio: Passion Play, Good Friday, March or April. Näfels: pilgrimage. Sarnen: *Landsgemeinde,* people's open-air parliament. Stans: *Landsgemeinde,* people's open-air parliament. Trogen: *Landsgemeinde,* people's open-air parliament. Zurich: *Sechselauten,* spring festival.

MAY. A different place each year: round western Switzerland bike race. Aarau: horse races. Altdorf: *Trachtentag,* Swiss National Costumes Festival. Basel: dog show; Swiss Industries' Fair. Berne: gastronomic fair. Burglen: Tell relay race. Champery: lower Valais music festival. Chiasse: motorcycle races. Dornach-Goetheanum: drama, lectures. Erlen: auto, motorcycle races. Geneva: Bach Week; rink-hockey championship. Glarus: *Landsgemeinde,* people's open-air parliament. Interlaken: folkfests, concerts. Lausanne: *Les Grandes Fêtes de Lausanne;* Vaud choral festival, opera singers' contest. Lucerne: Swiss artillery days, military reviews. Montreux: motor-coach rally. Neuchâtel: sports equipment show. Ragaz Spa: The May Bear, old folk custom. Schaffhausen: Bach Festival. Tellsplatte: pilgrimage. Zug: Swiss professional musicians' festival. Zurich: auto tests, gymnastics meeting; bike race, Zurich–Munich; folk festival.

MAY or JUNE. Benediction Sunday: Blatten, Kippel, Lotschental. Corpus Christi: nationwide, with more impressive processions at

Appenzell, Bulle, Chatel-St. Denis, Dudingen, Einsiedeln, Estavayer-le-Lac, Fribourg, Lucerne, Porrentruy, Romont, Saas-Fee,
Vitznau, Wil. Music, theater festival: Lausanne.

JUNE. A different place each year: Swiss golf championship;
Swiss rowing championship. Basel: canoeing regatta. Berne: gastronomic fair. Swiss fencing championships. Burgdorf: "Solemnity," children's festival. Geneva: Rose Week; Western Switzerland Gymnastic Festival. Interlaken: folkfests, concerts, in the
Casino. Klosters: summer skiing race, Silvretta Glacier. Lausanne:
ballet season. Lucerne: *Seenachtfest,* night lake festival; Swiss
workers' choral festival. Montreux: Narcissus festival, every few
years. Murten: battle anniversary. Pontresina: Forest Dell concerts. St. Gall: "Solemnity," children's festival. The Valais: cow
fights. Zurich: festival; Swiss relay championships, light athletic
contests; *Tour de Suisse,* bike race, begins and ends in Zurich.

JULY. A different place each year: Federal gymnastic festival;
Swiss amateur golf championship: Swiss national yodelers' festival;
Swiss tennis championships. Amsteg: shooting the rapids, canoeing
contests. Arbon: swimming festival. Basel: Swiss light athletic
championships. Bienne: festival. Braunwald: music festival. Fribourg: Swiss musicians' band festival. Interlaken: folkfests, concerts in the Casino. Lachen: small-bore shooting contests. Langnau:
Crossbow shooting contests. Locarno: Film Festival. Lucerne:
Central Switzerland choral festival. Neuchâtel: auto mountain-
climbing race. Pontresina: Forest Dell concerts. Ragaz Spa: horsemanship contests. Sempach: Battle of Sempach. Thun: Swiss
canoeing *slalom* championships.

JULY or AUGUST. Engadine Concert Weeks: Celerina, Pontresina,
St. Moritz, Semedan, Silvaplana, Sils-Baseglia, Zuoz. William Tell
Festival, even years: Interlaken.

AUGUST. A different place each year: Swiss road cycling championships. Ascona: music festival. Berne: Swiss Grand Prix auto,
motorcycle races. Champery: *Journée du Champery* (1830). Emen-
tal: Swiss wrestling, Alpine festival. Geneva: *Fêtes de Genève.*
Interlaken: folkfests, concerts in the Casino. Lucerne: music festival. Nationwide: Independence Day, August 1. Pontresina: Forest Dell concerts. Saignelégier: National Horse Fair features parades, races, people in native costume on the Jura horses, famous
for strength.

SEPTEMBER. A different place each year: Swiss golf open championship. Ascona: music festival. Basel: horse races. Bienne: *Quinzaine gastronomique,* a fortnight for epicures. Einsiedeln: Consecration of the Angels Festival. Interlaken: folkfests, concerts. Geneva: watches, jewelry exhibition. Lausanne: *Comptoir Suisse,* agricultural, industrial fair. Montreux: music festival. Zurich: *Knabenschiessen,* boys' shooting contest.

SEPTEMBER or OCTOBER. Vintage Festivals: Lugano, Neuchâtel.

OCTOBER. Geneva: farm, garden show; international contest for musical performers. La Chaux-de-Fonds: *Braderie,* fair. Locarno: golf tournaments. Lugano: fair. Montreux: music festival. St. Gall: Swiss farm, dairy fair. Zurich: cross-country running race.

NOVEMBER. Basel: Bruckner Festival.

DECEMBER. Basel: Bruckner Festival. Davos: Spengler Cup, ice hockey. Geneva: *Escalade,* December 12. Pontresina: *Schlitteda,* folk festival. Zurich: St. Nicholas Day processions, December 4–6.

TURKEY

ALTHOUGH Turkey is proud of her geographical position in relation to the Middle East, she is equally proud of her importance as a European power, and continues to work more and more with the West in a mutual exchange of ideas and security. That tendency gained immediately after World War II when Turkey became closely affiliated with several American-sponsored agencies designed to rehabilitate Europe, and it reached a high point of co-operation when Turkey became a member of the Atlantic Pact in February, 1952, and concluded a five-year treaty of friendship and collaboration among Turkey, Greece, and Yugoslavia. It was signed and exchanged in Ankara, Turkey, on February 28, 1953. Turkey's determination to look forward instead of backward is evident in her celebration of anniversaries connected with the establishment of the Republic in 1923, the emphasis on Children's Day, and the attention the nation pays to its international trade fairs. Her link with Christian nations is strengthened by the fact that the world headquarters of the Eastern Orthodox Church is at Fener, where many important religious festivals are observed.

Patriotic Festivals

Turkey's membership among the republics of the world dates only to the 1920's. Thus far she has had just three Presidents—Mustafa Kemal Atatürk, 1923–38; İsmet İnönü, 1938–50; and Celal Bayar, elected in May, 1950. In the nation's calendar of patriotic festivals the three anniversaries that are celebrated with particular pride fall on May 19, August 30, and October 29. On May 19 young athletes carry a burning torch from Samsun to Ankara and hold games in Ankara to mark the day Mustafa Kemal Atatürk landed at Samsun and began the national struggle for independence. On August 30 tribute is paid to the memory of the warriors who fell in the battle of Dumlupinar in 1922, the final major military engagement in the fight to establish the republic. On that date children distribute commemorative rosettes, and airplanes dominate the military aspects of the observance. Republic Day, October 29, recalls the day of the proclamation of the republic in 1922, and is celebrated with parades, band concerts, torchlight processions and dances.

Children's Day on April 23 is a patriotic holiday that serves two purposes. It commemorates the inauguration of the Grand National Assembly on April 23, 1923, and calls attention to the fact that children symbolize modern, democratic Turkey. It emphasizes Turkey's intention to look to the future and not to the past. There are all manner of modern enjoyments for the youngsters of Turkey that day, too. Movies are free, taxi drivers give them free rides, and quite a few merchants distribute free ice cream and candy. Elected representatives from schools in Ankara visit the President, who receives them in company with his wife and children and presents them with small gifts. Other young people take over the duties of civic officials for the day, and there are dances and parties in public places and private homes throughout the nation.

Fairs

The month-long International Trade Fair at Izmir, held from mid-August to mid-September, features the country's artistic, agricultural, and industrial products. As a rule there are more than 2,000 displays by foreign exhibitors in addition to the thousands arranged by Turkish firms. The Turkish products include hand embroidery, silverware, ceramics, meerschaum pipes, filigree work, rugs, and carpets. Entertainment includes traditional Turkish folk dances in colorful costumes and music that was popular in the days when the Janizaries were all-powerful. A great many visitors make side trips to nearby sites of historical, archaeological, cultural, artistic, and religious interest, such as the Temple of Zeus, and the shrine erected to mark the house where Mary, the mother of Jesus, is said to have spent the last days of her life.

The Istanbul Fair, inaugurated in 1949, puts the spotlight on Turkish products and entertainment during the month of June.

Religious Festivals

Although the vast majority of the Turkish population is Moslem, Christianity is well represented by the Eastern Orthodox Church. The world headquarters of the religion is the patriarchal church at Fener, on the Golden Horn, a short ferryboat ride from Istanbul. During the past 1,600 years 261 patriarchs have sat on the episcopal throne of St. John Chrysostom. The 261st is Athenagoras I, the first American to be elevated to that high office. He was installed in 1949. Typical of the several important, colorful religious services at which the patriarch presides is Easter. In keeping with a decision made by the first Ecumenical Council in 325 Easter is celebrated by Greek Orthodox Churches throughout the world on the Sunday after the full moon that follows the spring equinox. Visitors who plan to attend the services at Fener must reserve seats in advance. The rites are high-lighted by a procession that usually includes small boys dressed in white and gold carrying the sacred ornaments, a choir, the bearded clergy in rich brocaded chasubles, and the Patriarch wearing white satin embroidered with blue, green, and gold, a domed, crownlike miter, and a diamond cross. He is preceded and followed by acolytes carrying candles.

The Feast of the Epiphany in January is celebrated on the shores of the Bosporus with the traditional blessing of the waters and diving for the golden or wooden cross by men in bathing suits.

Since the church at Fener is the Ecumenical See, the first church of the Greek Orthodox Church, Orthodoxy Day is celebrated there with great pomp and ceremony on the first Sunday in Lent. The festival marks the restoration of the icons by the Byzantine Empress Theodora, who was acting as the regent for her son Michael III, on February 18, 843.

The Greek Orthodox Church in Fener also observes St. Andrew's Day, November 30, with special ceremonies, because St. Andrew founded the church at Fener.

Authorities of the Sacred Congregation for the Oriental Church believe that Mary, the mother of Jesus, spent some of the last days of her life in a house at Panaya Kapulu, near Izmir and Ephesus. Devout people in many lands regard the house as a shrine, so every year thousands of them take part in pilgrimages to it. To encourage such visitations the Sacred Congregation for the Oriental Church in a decree issued on August 1, 1953, in the name of the Supreme Pontiff, "has accorded a seven-year Plenary Indulgence applicable to all the Faithful who, having received the Sacraments of Penance and of the Holy Communion, shall visit the Sanctuary at Panaya Kapulu and offer prayer for the intention of the Supreme Pontiff, on any Sunday or Holy Days of Obligation, on days dedicated to the Blessed Mother, or on any day during the whole month of May."

Sports Events

The Turks are fond of their own particular brand of wrestling, which differs from the western or Olympic type of wrestling in that the contestants smear olive oil over their bodies and the leather knee breeches that they wear. Ordinarily it would be difficult to get a grip on such a slippery opponent, but the wrestlers train for it by kneading clay, squeezing out the water until the clay becomes almost too hard to dent and thus strengthening their grips. As a rule the Turkish wrestling championships are held at Kirkpinar, close to Edirne on the Turkish-Greek border, during the last week in May. On the first day of the meet the contestants gather at the village green where preliminary bouts are staged to the tune of base drums and *zurna,* a kind of Turkish oboe.

The exact dates on which festivals will take place in Turkey, as well as the latest travel information pertaining to that country, may be obtained by writing to the Turkish Information Office, 444 East 52nd Street, New York 22, New York.

Bank holidays in Turkey: January 1; Children's Day, April 23, anniversary of inauguration of the Grand Assembly (1923); May 1; Youth Day, May 19, anniversary of inauguration of fight for independence (1919); *Seker Bayram,* ancient Moslem Feast, first day after the Feast of Ramazan in June; *Kurban,* ancient Moslem Feast on day of new moon in August; Memorial Day, August 30, honors soldiers who fell in final big battle to set up the Republic; Republic Day, October 29, anniversary of proclamation of Republic (1923).

Chronological list of events in Turkey:

JANUARY. Bursa: winter sports contests, through March. Fener: Epiphany, Eastern Orthodox patriarchal church. Istanbul: wild-boar hunting trips arranged.

FEBRUARY or MARCH. Fener: Orthodoxy Day, first Sunday in Lent, Eastern Orthodox patriarchal church.

MARCH. Izmir: fair.

MARCH or APRIL. Fener: Easter.

APRIL. Nationwide: Children's Day, April 23; most impressive celebrations in Ankara, Istanbul.

MAY. Bergama: Festival of Pergamum, near Izmir. Edirne: Turkish wrestling championships. Nationwide: Youth Day, May 19; most impressive celebration at Ankara. Panaya Kapulu: pilgrimage to house of Mary, mother of Jesus, throughout May, on Holy Days of Obligation, Sundays.

JUNE. Istanbul: fair.

AUGUST. Izmir: fair, to mid-September. Nationwide: Memorial Day, August 30; most impressive ceremonies at Ankara.

SEPTEMBER. Izmir: fair; Liberation Day, September 9.

OCTOBER. Nationwide: Anniversary of Turkish Republic, October 29 (1923); most impressive ceremonies at Ankara.

NOVEMBER. Fener: St. Andrew's Day, November 30, celebrated at Eastern Orthodox patriarchal church.

YUGOSLAVIA

AS Yugoslavia struggles to maintain its individuality, it seems to be trying to extract the more desirable elements from two conflicting ideologies, Communism and the western type of democracy. Yet while the political battles rage and the leaders try to fathom the future, the people of Yugoslavia, perhaps more than those of any other European country in the western bloc, cling fast to their cultural ties with the past as represented in folk dances that have been part of their way of life for centuries.

Special Days

The first of May is the workers' day throughout Yugoslavia, with the most important observance of all taking place in Belgrade. The big attraction there on that day is the five-hour-long parade reviewed by Marshal Tito in which military units, representatives of the working collectives with models of their products, boys and girls in sports dress, peasants in regional costumes, and others take part. After the parade there is folk dancing in the public squares and parks and athletic contests at all sports arenas. Secondary celebrations take place at Ljubljana, Sarajevo, Skoplje, Titograd, and Zagreb.

Cultural Events

Almost everywhere one wanders in Yugoslavia he comes upon performances of native dances. In fact, musical folklore has been declared the basis of all contemporary Yugoslavian music. The government is taking special pains to preserve every aspect of the nation's folklore customs and dress, and to that end maintains state ensembles of folk dancers in Croatia, Macedonia, and Serbia. The performers make tours of western Europe, and on their excursions abroad they have proved so proficient in their art that one year they danced away with first prize at the international folk music competition in which twenty-nine nations took part in Llangollen, Wales. However, to all loyal Yugoslavians the most important folk festival anywhere is their own national one that usually takes place in September in a different city each year. A typical week-long festival of this type features hundreds of prize-winning dancers, singers, and instrumentalists in costume. They perform the national round dance, the kolo; the regional mountaineer steps of Slovenia, the dramatic, emotion-charged movements of the Macedonians, as well as the lively rhythms of Croatia, Serbia, and the Vojvodinian plains.

The Summer Festival staged at Dubrovnik from mid-June to mid-September always arouses great interest among natives as well as foreigners. It is particularly attractive for vintage plays, which can be staged out of doors in medieval surroundings. A typical program might include theater, music, and sports events. At the Dubrovnik Theater one may see the comedy *Ljubavnici* (The Lovers) by an anonymous Dalmatian author; Shakespeare's *Hamlet,* and *A Midsummer Night's*

Dream; Goldoni's *Fishermen's Quarrels,* Drzic's *Dundo Maroje* and *Mande.* The Dubrovnik Symphony Orchestra provides classical music, and the swimming club *Jug* often sponsors international contests.

During the first ten days in July Ljubljana plays host to tourists with a cultural festival featuring music, dancing, handicrafts, sculpture, and painting.

The festival at Pula, usually staged during the first and second weeks in July, emphasizes opera. One year the program included *Mila Gojsalica, Fidelio, Cavalleria Rusticana, Pagliacci, Othello, The Barber of Seville, The Flying Dutchman, Faust,* and *Aïda.*

On July 27, and again on November 29, 30, Korčula stages the traditional pageant *Moreska* in commemoration of the battle with the Moors on the island of Korčula in the sixteenth century.

At least three other summertime music, song, and dance festivals held regularly in Yugoslavia are the traditional Maribor Week at Maribor, which actually lasts for ten days during the first half of July; the Macedonian folklore festival at Ohrid in August; and the traditional harvest festivities of the Slovak national minorities at Backi Petrovac on the Vojvodinian Plains. These festivities last for at least a week during the beginning of August and feature national dances performed by young people in the brilliant costumes of their native land.

In 1949 the first Yugoslav Musical Contest was held. There were competitions for vocalists and instrumentalists, and the pattern established then has been followed pretty much since during the third week in October in one of the large cities.

Since the end of World War II Yugoslavia has made progress in the professional theater and the field of ballet. Although the best place to see such performances these days is at the Belgrade Dramatic Theater established in 1948, one should not believe that the theater is new to Yugoslavia. Its dramatic tradition goes back at least to the religious dramas of the eleventh century. The first theater was opened on the Adriatic island of Hvar in 1612.

Fairs

The oldest international fair in Yugoslavia is the Zagreb fair, which is said to have had a small beginning as an exhibition place for agricultural products in 1852. At present the Zagreb fall fair during the last two weeks in September is the most important of the semiannual expositions because it is more international in character than the one staged during the second and third weeks in May. In the spring fair machinery, metalware, electrical goods, handicrafts, and toys made in Yugoslavia are on display.

Two other national fairs worthy of note are the *Mariborski teden* at Maribor in July, and the fair at Skopje. The Skopje Fair was inaugurated in August, 1953, at which time the industrious Yugoslavs proudly displayed their industrial products, such as leather goods, textiles, farm machinery, canned goods, wood carvings, and other handicrafts.

Sports

One of the big annual sports events in Yugoslavia each year is a grand relay race staged in honor of Marshal Tito on his birthday, May 25. The race is a sort of marathon from all parts of the nation and converging on Belgrade, where specially selected boys and girls present the batons to Tito with their greetings.

In the little town of Sinj, in Dalmatia, traditional ceremonies and jousting contests known as the *Alka* have been staged late in August since 1715. The parade that opens the show is noted for its display of ancient uniforms worn by the Sinj who drove the Turks out of Dalmatia, the march of the shield and cudgel bearers, and the armor worn by Edek, a horse named after the steed of Sarakhez-Pasha.

International horse races are held at Belgrade in May, and sailing regattas that attract boats from many countries are staged at Istra and Split during July and August.

The exact dates on which festivals will take place in Yugoslavia, as well as the latest travel information pertaining to that country, may be obtained by writing to the Yugoslav State Tourist Office, 816 Fifth Avenue, New York 21, New York.

Bank holidays in Yugoslavia: January 1; May 1 and 2; November 29 and 30; anniversary of the proclamation of the Republic (1943).

Chronological list of events in Yugoslavia:

JANUARY. Planica: skiing contests in Slovenian Alps, to May.

FEBRUARY. Bohinj: Yugoslav winter sports championships.

MARCH. Planica: Yugoslav ski-jumping championships.

MAY. Belgrade: horse races; motor races; relay race, May 25, birthday of Marshal Tito. Jalovec: Yugoslav grand *slalom*. Nationwide: Workers' Day, May 1; most impressive celebration in Belgrade. Pula-Rijeka: Istrian regatta. Zagreb: fair.

JUNE. Dubrovnik: summer festival. Opatija: folklore, flower festival; motor races; summer fashions show.

JULY. Dubrovnik: summer festival. Istra: sailing regattas. Korcula: *Moreska,* pageant, dates to sixteenth century. Kvarner Riviera: tennis championships. Ljubljana: festival. Maribor: festival, fair, Pula: opera festival, Roman theater. Split: regattas.

AUGUST. Backi Petrovac: harvest festival. Dubrovnik: summer festival. Ohrid: Macedonian folk festival. Opatija: Opatija Cup, sailing regatta. Sinj: *Alka,* jousting, dates to 1715. Skopje: fair.

SEPTEMBER. A different place each year: national folk festival. Belgrade: Yugoslav shooting championship. Dubrovnik: summer festival. Opatija: Yugoslav wine fair. Zagreb: fair.

OCTOBER. A different place each year: Yugoslav music contest. Opatija: Yugoslav wine fair.

NOVEMBER. Belgrade: Yugoslav hockey championships. Korcula: pageant.

INDEX